Also by Mark Ribowsky

The Complete History of the Negro Leagues, 1884–1955
Don't Look Back: Satchel Paige in the Shadows of Baseball
Slick: The Silver and Black Life of Al Davis
He's a Rebel: The Truth About Phil Spector

The Power and the Darkness

The Life of Josh Gibson in the Shadows of the Game

Mark Ribowsky

Simon & Schuster

SIMON & SCHUSTER
Rockefeller Center
1230 Avenue of the Americas
New York, NY 10020

Designed by Levavi & Levavi

Manufactured in the United States of America

10 9 8 7 6 5 4 3 2 1

Library of Congress Cataloging-in-Publication Data
Ribowsky, Mark.
    The power and the darkness : the life of Josh Gibson in the
shadows of the game / Mark Ribowsky.
       p.   cm.
    1. Gibson, Josh, 1911–1947.   2. Baseball players—United States—
Biography.   3. Negro leagues—United States—History.   I. Title.
GV865.G53R53   1996
796.357'092—dc20
[B]   96-292
                                                                        CIP

ISBN 0-684-80402-6

PHOTO CREDITS

Josh Gibson Jr.: 1, 2, 3, 9, 14, 15, 17
National Baseball Library & Archive, Cooperstown, NY:
    4, 7, 11, 12, 19
Craig Davidson: 5, 16
James Riley: 6, 8, 10, 18
Negro Leagues Baseball Museum: 13

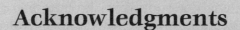

Acknowledgments

Reconstructing the life of Josh Gibson meant pulling together minute details and broad abstractions. Fortunately, the load of research that made this book possible was lightened, and I was certainly enlightened, by the guidance of several people who helped me understand the entire picture.

The pieces concerning Josh Gibson the man spilled from the sharp memory of Josh Gibson Jr., a gust of fresh air whose ingratiating wit, round face, and booming voice make him seem like the reincarnation of his father. By the caprices of heredity, Josh Jr. has endured a near lifetime of physical pain, yet at sixty-four he has lived far longer than his father did, and this is a tribute to his unquenchable spirit. For injecting these pages with that spirit and thoughtful insight, I am deeply thankful to him.

Through Josh Jr. came the delightful bonus of another surviving Gibson family member with a long and vivid memory, Rebecca Mason, who filled in gaps and provided perspective that smoothed out some critical landscapes.

No less vital a contributor to the Gibson profile is Jim Riley, author of *The Biographical Encyclopedia of the Negro Baseball Leagues*. The gatekeeper of Negro league history, Jim aided me in molding the pieces of Gibson the ballplayer into a statistical and biographical record from a mass of archival material long forsaken through time and neglect. The vault-sized argosy of Xeroxes and microfilms in Jim's basement may be as close to a complete Negro league record as exists, and students of baseball can take heart knowing these invaluable Americana rest in his hands.

Invaluable as well are the hours any baseball annalist can spend with the surviving warriors of those storied Negro league seasons. History is always given its flavor by eyewitness testimony, and I was blessed to be able to spice these pages with the vibrant reminiscences of men who watched Josh Gibson from the Hill to Homestead to Havana. My sincere thanks to Harold "Hooks" Tinker, Teenie Harris, Buck Leonard, Josh Johnson, Wilmer Fields, Gene Benson, and Garnett Blair.

I would also like to thank Mulkey McMichael and the other kind folks in Buena Vista, Georgia, for conducting a Gulliver-like expedition through the backwoods of Puttville to try and find Josh Gibson's birthplace.

I am indebted to two people who envisioned this book and helped me see it through, Jay Acton and Inge Hanson; and to Jeff Neuman, my astute and erudite editor at Simon & Schuster, who also oversaw my Satchel Paige book and recognized how interlocking Paige and Gibson are in the wide scope of history, and why each deserved his own book; and to Stuart Gottesman, who provided invaluable service on the final manuscript. Finally, to my wife, Sandi, who never tells me to get a real job, all my love.

For Sandi and Jake, two great clutch hitters

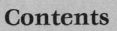

Contents

Introduction

Of all the legends that have sprung from the much fabled Negro leagues, Josh Gibson's life and career most closely echo the history and fate of the doomed ship of black baseball. On the plantation of segregated baseball, where several generations of African American men born too soon labored year after year trying to establish their worth as professional ballplayers, Gibson went about as far and as high as any black player could. Yet his fame would be no greater than the tragedy of his demise, which like black ball's own fall was hastened and, in many ways, made inevitable by self-inflicted wounds.

The hoary men who spent their better days on the same tattered fields as Gibson can be found today scattered in barbershops, billiard halls, and taprooms still shaking their ash gray heads about how Josh up and died at age thirty-five in January 1947. The dramatic irony of his passing—a mere three months before Jackie Robinson shattered the major league color line by emerging from the dugout at Ebbets Field wearing a Brooklyn Dodgers uniform—instantly transformed Gibson's life and death into the stuff of epic tragedy.

By any measure, Gibson's story is indeed a tragic one. The Aristotelian definition of tragedy, that "he who hears the tale told will thrill with horror and melt to pity at what takes place," certainly applies to the tale told in these pages. Gibson, who gained renown as the "black Babe Ruth," actually lived out the final days of his life more like the black Lou Gehrig. Both Gibson and Gehrig were magnificent athletes, each suggesting metaphorical images of brawny, wiry thoroughbreds—"Iron Horses." And both men, alas, withered and died much too young, in the twilight of long and brilliant careers. However, unlike the great Yankee first baseman's, the breakdown of Josh Gibson's powerful body was only part of what ailed him and ultimately killed him. The other parts are more delicate, more saddening, and much more difficult to comprehend.

Certainly, a good many folks who spent long, seamless hours with him in black ball believed they knew Josh, but most knew him not much or not at all. This was partly because Gibson preferred to hide his troubled inner self from others, and partly because most people didn't care to look beyond what appeared to be a bearish man with childish delights who could unleash godly thunder with one swing of his bat. Later, when these same men witnessed Gibson's body and mind in decay, few believed his drunken and deranged behavior was a serious cause for alarm or that they somehow needed to save Gibson from himself.

To these men, memories of Josh having to be restrained and taken to hospitals for a little "boiling out," as they called it, did not add up to a larger crisis. For those who did not see the crisis, or who did and instinctively looked the other way in deference to a fallen comrade, denial was always easy, since the hardest thing to accept about Josh Gibson was that he was not impregnable after all.

That quality—that *perceived* quality—was Gibson's calling card. Arriving on the Negro league scene in the late twenties, about the same time that the flashy Satchel Paige had begun to convince black baseball fans that an African American could throw a fastball as hard as any Caucasian, Gibson brought the tape-measure home run into the black purview. It was at this time, one might argue, that baseball became a truly American game, if not, for another decade and a half, an integrated one. In that interim, when it seemed that liberation would never arrive, Gibson was a black ball constant, standing resolute against Negro league pitching and immune to personal scrutiny.

The truth was that Gibson, like Paige, thought nothing of walking out on signed contracts. Yet his salary holdouts and team-jumping episodes were made almost parenthetical when compared to the fuss people made when the garrulous, self-promoting Paige did the same. While Satch's every move was magnified and covered in large type and overheated prose in the weekly black newspapers—the only available source of information about African Americans—black fans had to comb the small print for news of Josh's latest blasts out of the park, though in later years he certainly won his share of large type, and made the pages of *Time* magazine in 1943.

Indeed, as different as they were in style and function, Josh and Satch both existed within the same mythological realm, as icons perfectly compatible with each other and with black ball's need for varying shades of African American identity. When the two men were teamed to form the battery of the Pittsburgh Crawfords in the thirties, the mad rush of publicity they set off carried the black game through the Depression.

Out on the barnstorming circuit, the marquees promised that Paige would strike out the first nine men who stood in against him and that Gibson would hit three home runs. Whether these vows were met or not could not have mattered less; Paige and Gibson kept the faith just by suiting up, to be seen and venerated. Inevitably, and fittingly, after Satchel Paige was elected to the Hall of Fame in 1971, as the first player to be so honored for his Negro league career, Josh Gibson went in next, in 1972.

When Gibson was in his grave and Paige was an old man trying to hang on with any big league or bush league team that would allow him to suit up, in the years after baseball had become an integrated game, their power did not diminish among those who had come of age doting on their outlaw image. In the 1970s, Count Basie and Oscar Peterson cut an album of jazz piano duets on Peterson's Pablo Records label with the knowing title of *Satch and Josh,* which was meant to contrast Basie's quiescent restraint with the more frenetic bombast of Peterson; more trenchantly, it brought back to life the moody blues that served as the sound track of Paige and Gibson's days on earth. Not for nothing was one of the album tracks titled "Satch and Josh Blues."

As I suggested in my biography of Paige, an even better parallel—one that accounts for the pain they endured in their lives—would have Charlie Parker in the Josh role and Miles Davis as Satch. In a strong sense, Paige and Gibson can be distinguished by the way they coped with that pain. Like Miles, Paige was able to use it to drive him and to erect a protective scab around himself. Josh Gibson, on the other hand, dealt with his agonies about as well as Charlie Parker, which is to say not well at all.

Thus, for all of Gibson's brute power and his fortress of a body, he was a man who was weak, too fragile for his own perpetuation. Accordingly, there is something about Josh Gibson that makes one withhold complete adulation. Unlike in the case of long ball hitters such as Babe Ruth and Hank Aaron, the home run—with its swashbuckling mythology of confident, dashing men winning games with one swing in the bottom of the ninth—is not central to Josh Gibson's legacy. Rather, his legacy remains incomplete, awaiting further review, not because the white baseball establishment screwed him (which it did) but because so much about Gibson remains hidden.

It is the purpose of this book to bring Gibson's demons to light. Rough stuff though it may be, these dark and at times harrowing details are essential to understanding who and what the man was—a riddle that has been left unsolved in previous Gibson volumes, even when some of the gorier details have been mentioned. On the other hand, it is not the business of this book to waste time by revisiting the question of whether Gibson was the best hitter who ever gripped a Louisville Slugger. These speculations have already tainted too many volumes about black ball by speciously elevating Negro league statistics to the major league performance level.

For example, Josh Gibson has long been credited with hitting as many as seventy-five home runs in one season and sixty-eight in another while playing for the Homestead Grays of Pittsburgh, and later Washington, D.C. These numbers, as well as unverified reports that he hit the only fair ball clear out of Yankee Stadium, have been cited as proof that Gibson was in a class of his own among history's most venerated long ball hitters. He may well have been, but the claim loses water fast when it is based on such questionable anecdotal and statistical evidence.

One should bear in mind that Negro league record keeping was hardly on the order of Price Waterhouse, notwithstanding the often overlooked fact that the Negro leagues, for all their deprivations, compulsively maintained big league standards. Even when riding on buses with broken axles and smoking engines, black ball clubs arrived on time for games and met their schedules. They printed tickets, cleaned their uniforms, polished their shoes, and even if they had to sleep on the field overnight because no hotel would put them up, carried themselves as big-leaguers, refusing to let anything break their will. Within this framework, Negro league executives understood the need for competent statistical tabulations as a means to advance the black game's credibility.

In practice, however, the central bureau of black ball information, the league offices, were often manipulated by one or another high commissioner acting in the interest of his own team. While box scores and game reports mottling the sports pages of black newspapers such as the *Chicago Defender,* the *Pittsburgh Courier,* the *Baltimore Afro-American,* and the *New York Amsterdam News* were accurate, they were often incomplete records.

Because they were weeklies, the black papers could report on only so many games, and that coverage was sometimes chaotic and selective. The box scores that appeared rarely included at bats, not always home runs, and never RBIs. Often, two or three games in a four-game series were summarized in a few lines without any hard details. Overall statistical compilations, which were released sporadically throughout the season, didn't necessarily reflect which hitters or pitchers were most proficient, but which teams' flacks were chosen to forward data to the league and which teams carried the most influence. Not by coincidence, players on teams with the greatest influence usually placed high in every category. Gibson, who spent most of his career playing for teams owned by two of the more powerful Negro league owners—Cumberland Posey of the Homestead Grays and Gus Greenlee of the Pittsburgh Crawfords—was a prime beneficiary of these discrepancies.

Another problem with relying on statistical records is that they seldom differentiate between home runs Gibson hit in Negro league play and those that came against semipro and amateur competition. League games made up only a fraction of a black team's schedule. While league solidarity was a dream and a cause, black ball was a business contingent on cramming as many games as possible into six months of warm weather; some teams played as many as three times in one day in three different locations. During the week of August 12–18, 1932, for example, the schedule of Gibson's Pittsburgh Crawfords looked like this: August 12, North Side Civics; August 13, House of David; August 14, Book Shoe; August 15, Glassport, at McKeesport, Pennsylvania;

August 16, Washington Pilots, at Barnesboro, Pennsylvania; August 17, Corry Merchants, at Corry, Pennsylvania; August 18, Altoona Works, at Altoona, Pennsylvania.

All of which is not to say Gibson was *not* a more perfect slugger than Babe Ruth, though the typical Gibson home run was more like a mortar shell still climbing through the sky as it screamed over the fence rather than a parabolic Ruthian moon shot. Gibson's documented 500-plus-foot drives against the best Negro league pitchers, and the similar monsters he clocked against big-leaguers such as Dizzy Dean in exhibition games between Negro-leaguers and touring white major-leaguers, are of inestimable value to Josh Gibson's reputation and to black ball's. But the point here, to be dispensed with quickly, is that we simply do not know where Gibson stands in the ranks of the power pantheon, whether he was better than Ruth or Aaron—or, for that matter, better than less glorified Negro league sluggers such as Mule Suttles and Turkey Stearns, both of whom wore the moniker of "the black Babe Ruth" in the black press before Gibson and are credited with racking up more career homers than Gibson. In the final analysis, the baseball fundamentalists who enforced separatism must also answer for this historical void.

As it was, the credibility that Gibson's home runs and legend brought to the Negro leagues was as short-lived as the man. The melancholy irony of black ball is that the Negro league game—a province operated by men who were both visionary and venal—could exist only until men like Gibson had made the case for their big league inclusion; once the case was proven, no rationale remained for the black game to endure. Knowing this, white baseball men like Branch Rickey skillfully manipulated Negro league teams out of business by looting the best players from their rosters. Those players not young or lucky enough to have been chosen to make the transition simply died with the game that had given them life.

Josh Gibson, who was reaching his mid-thirties just as Jackie Robinson was about to break the integration seal, was

aware that he would be just another face in the crowd left behind, and he was understandably hurt. But his apocalyptic
doom was not, as his coda has been described in affective
Negro league narratives, caused by a heart and spirit crushed
by white disregard. In truth, Josh had kissed off the majors as
a viable future by the mid-1940s.

Rather, Gibson's death had been charted years before by
physical and psychological tortures that had left him scarred
forever. His life, then, can be viewed as a tale of alienation, in
which Gibson distanced himself from what he feared most:
feelings of dependence or neediness, which he had resolved
never to reawaken. The pity was that this lifetime of disaffec-
tion left him with an abscess where a soul should have been
and that it made him far too vulnerable to self-destruction.

Even as a desperately sick man, however, Gibson was still
able to stand erect and pound baseballs as impressively as he
could knock back shots of straight whiskey. The only plausible explanation for this is that baseball, with its promise of
emotional shelter, may have been Josh Gibson's most obses-
sive, most rewarding, and most bedeviling narcotic.

There is a line in the August Wilson play *Fences* that cuts
to the heart of the Gibson riddle. Wilson, a native of Pittsburgh, is said to have based the lead character, Troy Maxson,
on Sam Bankhead, an alcoholic teammate of Gibson's with
the Pittsburgh Crawfords and the Homestead Grays who was
closer to Gibson than any other man and whose life also
ended in tragedy. Maxson, an aging sanitation worker, finds
the bottle his sole comfort, his memories of black ball his
source of wisdom. At one point, when his wife warns him
he's going to kill himself with his drinking, he manages a
weary laugh.

"Death ain't nothing," he says. "I done seen him. Done
wrassled with him. You can't tell me nothing about death.
Death ain't nothing but a fastball on the outside corner."

Maxson/Bankhead may as well have been speaking for
Josh Gibson, because his folk wisdom would have served

perfectly as Gibson's last testament. In his years of self-crucifixion, each home run that Gibson hit saved him only until his next at bat, when he'd have to dodge death again and hit one even farther. If he didn't, he'd run to the bottle or the needle.

So in the end, maybe it was a kind of heartbreak that put him in the ground, though it had little to do with the white big leagues. Perhaps it was the game itself that broke his will. If so, if baseball helped to kill the beast, that is the saddest line in the elegy of Josh Gibson.

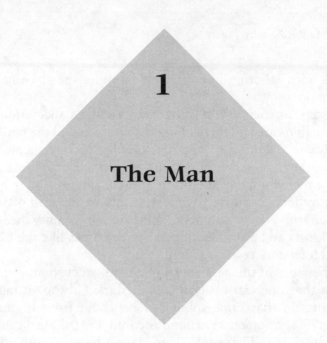

1

The Man

I'll tell you what the problem was with Josh Gibson: he grew up too damn fast, way before he was ready.
—HAROLD "HOOKS" TINKER, MANAGER,
PITTSBURGH CRAWFORDS, 1929

Hard by Highway 41 in rural southwest Georgia and some twenty miles east of the Chattahoochee River, there is a jerry-built bar and grill in Marion County that they call, with no shame, the Po' Folks' Place. Here, gathered on splintered benches, black men of many ages sit shrouded in baggy overalls awaiting the arrival of white farmers in need of migrant sharecroppers to work in the nearby cotton and peanut fields.

This weary ritual is played out almost every day in the retrograde town of Buena Vista, which remains unchanged by time or such abstractions as cultural evolution. Buena Vista is, in fact, a place where monuments like the Po' Folks' Place seem to reconstruct a society epitomized by huddled black men laboring in cotton fields under the stern gaze of white men.

Today, so many years after supposed emancipation, the slave cabins are still there along the rivers and in the flatlands, disguised as homes by the blacks who occupy them. High above them, standing imperiously, are the burgeoning mansions, renovations of the original manor houses built by the slave traders. Exclusively white, the hills are the stuff of Southern charm and wistfulness, splotched by dainty bed-and-breakfasts and roadside lodgings with names like the Cotton Gin Hotel and Yesteryear Inn.

The vibes of the past are so resonant, so current, in Buena Vista that one can easily imagine Mark Gibson sitting and waiting on that same splintered bench in front of the Po' Folks' Place, sometime around the mid-1910s. Mark, the son of slaves, would have taken his place among the other black men who faced a collective future that stretched no further down the road than the next cotton field.

Trapped in the lowlands of Buena Vista, he made his home in the Puttville part of town, in an area that was once known as Tazewell County, but the exact location of Mark Gibson's parcel of land cannot be flagged. The townsfolk old enough to know his name and to remember the family seem to think the house was on Pineville Road, some two miles southwest of the Buena Vista city limits, in what is now—and was then—a dirt basin of wooden shacks without plumbing, built around screen doors, rusting drainpipes, and dirt driveways.

In one such shack lives an old man named Lee Gibson, who is in ill health and is almost never seen outside his house by his neighbors these days.

"The only thing I can tell you about him is that he has a fireplace and a front porch, and that's it," one of the neighbors said recently. "We think he's related [to Mark Gibson], like a second cousin or something. He's a real big guy; he's built like Josh Gibson, but he drinks some and he don't make a whole lotta sense."

Whether or not it occurred in the house on Pineville, Joshua Gibson, named after Mark Gibson's father, was born in or around Buena Vista on or about December 21, 1911. That is the date that has been given through the years by Josh's six-years-younger sister, Annie Gibson Mahaffey. As is often the case with birth dates and other pertinent biographical data about African Americans reared in the Deep South, however, that date cannot be regarded as gospel.

A few years ago, Josh Gibson's son, Josh Jr., who is sixty-four and lives in Pittsburgh, wrote to the Marion County authorities to obtain a copy of his father's birth certificate.

"Well, I tried to, but I couldn't get it," he recalled, "because they told me the state of Georgia wasn't keeping records in nineteen eleven for black people. Plus, they didn't send me my ten dollars back for filing the application."

It occurred to Mark Gibson, living in the vacuum of Buena Vista, that if he had any hope of making a future for his family, he would have to leave the town behind. So, in 1923, Mark joined the great wave of black urban migration that had begun around the turn of the century. He saved up his money and headed north on a segregated railroad car, his final destination Pittsburgh, where sturdy men like him could find good-paying jobs working in the cavernous iron and ore mines of western Pennsylvania.

Mark left his family—his wife, Nancy Woodlock Gibson, as well as Josh, Annie, and his second son, Jerry, who was three years younger than Josh—in Buena Vista and supported them with money he sent from his paycheck at the Carnegie-Illinois Steel Company. It took three years before Mark was secure enough to bring his family to Pittsburgh. But once they were there, the Gibsons finally got to live on high ground, moving into a brick home Mark had purchased on the north side of Pittsburgh, at 2410 Strauss Street in the Pleasant Valley section.

The only thing more obvious than Pleasant Valley's elevation—it was built upon a series of hills—was its dank, sooty air. Decades later, Mark Gibson's grandson laughed about the irony of the Gibson brood's shift in geography. "Buena Vista is Spanish for 'good air,'" Josh Gibson Jr. said, "and they left all that good air to come to Pittsburgh and all that smoke."

Pittsburgh had its own racial boundaries, but the composition of its inner-city ghettos was based primarily upon economic considerations. Most of these ghettos were strewn over other concrete-covered hills throughout the city, which is divided into distinct sections by the Ohio, Monongahela, and Allegheny Rivers. The Ohio severs the north side from downtown Pittsburgh and its bordering area, which is known as the Hill.

In reality, there are several hills, including the Lower Hill, Upper Hill, Squirrel Hill, and Polish Hill. Despite the name of the latter, none of these areas—or Pleasant Valley to the north—were exclusive to any ethnic group. Poverty seemed to be the only common denominator of Pittsburgh's cauldron neighborhoods, although blacks had been living in them since before the Civil War. There were around fifty thousand blacks in Pittsburgh when Mark Gibson arrived. The racial mix of these neighborhoods wasn't diluted until many years later.

"When I grew up, places like Pleasant Valley and the Hill, there was Jewish people, blacks, Italians, Sicilians, the whole thing," said Josh Gibson Jr. "We all lived together, man. There was no prejudice; if there was, I didn't know it. Only in later years did these places become all black, because the Jewish people ran to Squirrel Hill, and the Italians and the Sicilians, they left too. But back then, I remember I hung with the Jew boys. Unlike now, Pittsburgh was all right then."

For Josh Gibson, it was nirvana. He had been strangulated in the good air of Buena Vista, and even the turbid air of Pleasant Valley couldn't choke the freedom he felt now, which was why his main recreation as a young teenager was nothing more than putting on a pair of roller skates and tearing down the steep inclines of the neighborhood. When he'd get to the bottom, coming to a stop at the edge of the Ohio River, he'd run up the hill and go even faster and more recklessly the next time down.

While life in both Buena Vista and Pleasant Valley was hardly as blissful as their names suggest, especially for blacks, Josh could measure the difference between the two places by the quality of education available to him. In Buena Vista, he had gone from the first through fifth grades in a state of catatonia, in schools that were little more than converted barns, deprived of state funds by Jim Crow laws, which sanctioned segregation in all public institutions. In Pittsburgh, cash and textbooks were almost as scarce, but not community commitment. Josh began the sixth grade at the Allegheny Pre-Vocational School and was placed by choice in the electrical studies program. At thirteen, he entered a similar program at Conroy Pre-Vocational, a high school in Pleasant Valley.

As soon as he reached fifteen, though, he was primed to help support the family by joining Mark Gibson in the steel mines. Josh was built for such backbreaking work; at six-foot-two and two hundred pounds with broad shoulders, he was nearly as big and wide as his father. He had a neck like thick piping, a torso like a slab of bullock, and squabby legs that kept him upright even after hours of slogging metal up a shaft. Though he was underage, his heaping bulk left the bosses at Carnegie-Illinois with no qualms about hiring him for after-school work. Josh was a dutiful and effective worker. And soon this labor made his big body even stronger.

By seventeen, Josh Gibson, who had been meek and soft in Buena Vista, commanded respect. If you saw him coming closer, you made way for him, and this rule applied to the multiracial street gangs that fought for asphalt turf in Pleasant Valley. Josh was untouchable, a hard egg, a *man*. In fact, he was so imposing that he could avoid the gangs and the pressure to prove himself on those tough streets. The gangs were cool, as far as he was concerned; he even hung out with some of the bad guys. But mostly he kept to himself and kept on going his own way, shoring up his self-respect by finding avenues through which he could excel. Increasingly, the main avenue was baseball.

The ball field offered Josh comforting sanctuary from the difficulties he found at home. As physically strong as Mark Gibson was, he had begun to feel tired all the time and to miss workdays. Although he didn't have a name for what was happening, he was suffering from hypertension. In time, Mark receded into the umbra of his wife, Nancy, a large and domineering woman who was known to throw a lot of noisy parties for her friends and to drink heavily.

Often, when Josh awoke for school, he would find his father out cold after another bruising day in the mines and his mother in the same condition after another party that had stretched into the wee hours. He would then fix breakfast for Jerry and Annie and head out, not eager to come back home.

Clearly, Josh Gibson saw in his mother and father a vision of his own future, and it must have scared him. Without understanding what genetics meant, he didn't have to look far to see what could happen to him if his gaze was unfocused, if he was lazy, if he lacked ambition; that would only put him on the same treadmill. So, having taken to sports and found out how gifted he was at them, he made it a top priority to dive into competition—sometimes literally. During the hot summer, if he wasn't called to work a shift in the blistering mines, and if there was no ball game in the sandlots, he would spend his days at the public swimming pools and burn off his energy there. When swimming and diving contests were held, he would routinely win medals.

The first organized baseball team he played on was a black amateur unit sponsored by the Gimbel's department store, when he was sixteen. Because of his size, he was immediately put behind the plate, but he wasn't a terribly effective backstop and was moved all around the diamond. Eventually he settled in at third base, though at first he stopped more hot grounders with his barrel chest than with his mitt. It was his bat, though, that kept him in the lineup. Even then, Josh Gibson could put a charge into a baseball—and into the crowd—just by stepping into the batter's box.

At this time, Josh still cared a great deal about his schooling. Warming to his trade, he was given a job as an apprentice electrician at Westinghouse Airbrake. He was under no delusion that he could actually make a living playing baseball, something very few blacks were able to do, either with semipro teams or in the unstable Negro leagues. Money wasn't the driving force in Gibson's baseball reveries as much as being able to prove himself at what he did. The ideal situation for him was to have the stability of playing with a company team where he worked, as he did at Westinghouse Airbrake and at Carnegie-Illinois. Gimbel's thought enough of his ability that the store gave him a job as an elevator operator so it could keep him in its uniform.

All of these black amateur teams, which were organized to offer recreation to black employees, belonged to the all-Negro Greater Pittsburgh Industrial League, which also included such lunch-bucket entries as Garfield Steel, Homestead Steel, Pittsburgh Railways, and Pittsburgh Screw and Bolt. The games between these teams often drew as many fans as those played by the Homestead Grays, an independent black professional team. The Grays, who had no home field, barnstormed throughout western Pennsylvania for up to eight months a year. Indeed, Pittsburgh's sandlot scene was attracting attention not just from baseball fans of all colors but from well-heeled gamblers. A player like Josh Gibson could not only draw a crowd; he could make a lot of people heavier in the wallet—though Gibson himself never made a cent.

With all of this money floating around the game, professionalism began to attract young black ballplayers by the mid-twenties, even though the rewards were still meager. The hot team in and around the Hill at the time was the increasingly professional Crawford Giants, which had originally represented the Crawford Bath House, a community center on Bedford Avenue. Reflecting the Hill's racial mix, the Crawford Giants—or the Crawfords, as they soon came to be known—were initially composed of thirty-two blacks, three Jews, and two Italians. And in keeping with the bathhouse's theme, its mostly teenaged players did community work, such as distributing Christmas baskets around the Hill.

Without the benefaction of a steel company or department store, the Crawfords relied on the alms of black businessmen in the area to carry on. One such merchant, the Pittsburgh Pirates' standout shortstop Honus Wagner, who was running a sporting goods store in Carnegie, Pennsylvania, in his retirement, donated uniforms to the team. But when the Crawfords were about to fold for lack of money, the donation that rescued them came from William Augustus "Gus" Greenlee, a vainglorious black mobster and boss of the Hill's numbers rackets, who also owned a thriving nightclub, the Crawford Grille, on Wylie Avenue.

For Greenlee, this charitable act was typical of his showy and charming sense of self-aggrandizement. His numbers game drained much hard-earned cash out of the pockets of indigent blacks trying to strike it rich, yet he fancied himself—and the Hill fancied him—as nothing if not a gentleman of means, distinction, and benevolence, a man who had an overriding concern for their plights.

Greenlee's rescue of the Crawfords certainly added to his aura of goodwill. Thus reinvigorated, they entered and then ripped through both the city's recreation league and the Negro Industrial League in 1926. By this time, they were an all-black unit, were no longer attached to the bathhouse, and had few of the sandlot boys who formed the team. The Crawfords, in fact, were nearly a transplanted version of the Watt High School team that won the city's schoolboy championship in 1925.

As a further mark of their ascendance as pros, the Crawfords were managed by Charles "Teenie" Harris, a sawed-off street hustler, who also booked the team's games. Teenie then left the club in 1927 to work as a numbers runner in Gus Greenlee's operation, joining his brother, William A. "Woogie" Harris, a professional gambler, who in addition to owning the Crystal Barbershop on Wylie Avenue, was Greenlee's right-hand man and neighbor in an adjoining town house on the avenue.

The team's new manager was Harold Tinker, the Crawfords' center fielder, who was called Hooks because he was so bowlegged that he looked like a pair of walking pliers. Tinker, along with third baseman Bill Harris, whose brother Vic played center field for the Homestead Grays, was responsible for transforming the Crawfords by actively recruiting talented players from industrial and sandlot teams in 1927. This crop included the third Harris brother, Neal, an outfielder, and shortstop–second baseman Charlie Hughes, who Tinker maintains to this day was "the greatest ground ball man I've ever seen."

The eighty-five-year-old Tinker recalled that at the Crawfords ball field, Ammon Field on Bedford Avenue, "there would be a gutter that ran across second base every time it rained. And Hughes would be digging it out and scratching it. Balls would get to that gutter and jump right up in his face. [But] he'd come up with it on his ear and throw the man out. This boy was marvelous."

But Hooks Tinker's most prized catch was Josh Gibson. Hooks had heard the building word of mouth about the burly kid but hadn't seen him play until he was checking out an industrial league all-star game at Ammon Field in the early spring of 1928.

"I had two of my Crawford players on that all-star team, Jimmy Stills and Neal Harris," Tinker said, "otherwise I wouldn't have been there. And that's when I saw Josh. He was playin' third base, and he was very mature in his actions; you wouldn't think he was only sixteen years old. He played a terrific third base, and he was a power hitter even then. His last time at bat he hit one over the top of the mountain in back of center field. I'll never forget that, because that's when I knew we had to have him with our Crawford team.

"So after this game, I told Neal we gotta have this kid with us. He said he thought so too. So I went up to Josh and said, 'Josh, how would you like to play with a real baseball team?' And he gave me that big smile of his and said, 'Yes sir.' I said, 'You come up here next Tuesday and you'll have a position with the Pittsburgh Crawfords,' and the next Tuesday he was there."

For Josh, this was an easy decision. Not only were the Crawfords a step up; they were a step into a larger world. Although the players were paid only what could be collected by passing a hat through the crowd during games, there were rumors that Gus Greenlee was going to turn the club into a full-blown professional operation to rival the Homestead Grays.

And so Josh went to Ammon Field to claim his next job, though he must have arrived with bells clanging in his ears. Days before, while taking some batting practice cuts with his Gimbel's teammates, he had turned toward the dugout and stepped right into the path of another player taking a practice swing. Although the crack on the head knocked him to his knees, he bounced back up and said he was okay. Beyond a headache and a bump on the head, he seemed fine.

Besides, the rush of joining the Crawfords more than soothed the pain.

2

Prelude to Professionalism

The Crawford Giants defeated W.O.W., the Greater Pittsburgh champions, 9–8 Saturday at Ammon Field before 5,000 fans. . . . Leading the attack against the Woodmen was Bucky Williams and "Josh" Gipson [sic] with four hits each.
— *PITTSBURGH COURIER, JUNE 21, 1930*

Josh arrived at the Crawfords camp as advised by Hooks Tinker. Without pause, he began losing baseballs over the Ammon Field fence in batting practice. The only thing that seemed wrong to some of the Crawford players who had seen Gibson play was that Tinker sent him to play at third base.

"They had seen him catch for the Gimbel's team, and they told me, 'What's he doin' at third? He's a catcher,'" Tinker recalled. "And Josh told me that himself, so I said, 'You got a job [at catcher] right now.' And it was a good thing, too, because Bill Harris was playin' third and he was a very good third baseman."

The man Josh displaced behind the plate, Wyatt Turner, was

a popular Crawford and an adequate catcher. At first, Turner was hurt by the demotion, but he soon realized the correctness of the move. By the middle of the season, Turner said years later, "If he put his bat down, I'd be ashamed to pick it up."

That is, if he *could* pick it up. As soon as Josh arrived, he flipped through all the bats in the Crawfords dugout until he found one that suited him. The one that did had never been taken to the plate before.

"He used the longest bat I think I ever saw any player use," said Tinker. "Hey, his arms weren't only big; they were long. He could handle the heavy bat, the forty-ounce one. Man, he could whip it like it weighed nothin'. We needed more of those for him so we had a load of 'em made up special for him, and I don't think any of the other guys ever used 'em."

Some black ball hands through the years have denigrated Josh's catching skills, at least in the beginning—a "boxer," they called him, a guy whose mitt seemed more suited to hand-to-hand combat than nestling pitched balls. Hooks Tinker had a different memory. "He came in as if he had been catchin' all his life," Tinker insisted. "Good arm, good head. And he was just startin' up the ladder then."

Still, nobody came to Ammon Field to appreciate the finer points of Gibson's defensive game—then or fifteen years from then. With Josh's bat providing the bang, Crawfords games became a top attraction on the Hill during that 1928 season, and though not yet worthy of game-by-game coverage in the *Pittsburgh Courier*, the team had come to the attention of John L. Clark, a Hill gadfly who wrote a column in the paper called "Wylie Avenue."

Noting the emerging link between the Crawfords and life on the Hill, Clark waxed eloquent in one column that "Avenue patrons want to see their boys active on the diamond under able direction. [The] games played by [these] youngsters furnish a thrill to parents that is absent in the professional exhibitions. The participants are closer to us. We are interested in their every movement—they are ours."

Although there is little printed evidence of Gibson's early achievements, his exploits live on in the vibrant anecdotal testament of the last living Crawford, Hooks Tinker.

"There were a lotta games, but one I'll never forget. The Crawfords were defeating all the teams we played. I think we had a streak goin', like eighteen wins in a row. Anyway, we were playing a team in McKeesport [Pennsylvania]. And this team jumped out in front of us in the third inning, three-to-two. They had heard about Josh already, because I got on base and the next guy walked and first base wasn't even open, but they were gonna intentionally pass Josh and load the bases rather than pitch to him.

"So they made two of these outside pitches and Josh called time, and he came down toward second base and met me halfway. He whispered to me, 'Hooks, I can hit the pitch he's throwin'.' I said, 'Josh, what are you doin'? We only need a run to catch 'em and they're gonna load the bases. They wanna give you a free ticket.' He said, 'But I can hit that ball he's throwin'.'

"So now I finally said, 'Well, Josh, if you think you can hit it where he's throwin' it, go ahead and hit it.'

"I went back to second base and the guy threw the pitch to the same place, outside, but not that far outside. And you know what? Josh didn't hit the ball to right field, which would have been the normal thing for a right-handed hitter teein' off on an outside pitch. He pulled it over the center field fence! Damn. It was one of the most tremendous home runs I ever saw him hit, and the people there almost fainted. I couldn't believe it myself. But, like I'm tellin' you, he used the longest bat you ever saw."

Gibson's raw power didn't require much analysis; as Tinker said, "He was built like sheet metal. If you ran into him, it was like you ran into a wall." Even so, there were some subtleties to the mechanics of his swing that cut to the core of the science of hitting.

"His power was in his wrists," Tinker noted. "He had

quick wrists. He could hold that bat down on the end, with his pinky over the handle, and wait on the pitch. Then he'd just meet the ball right; he wouldn't need to try and kill it 'cause if he met it his muscle would do the rest. That was the key for him, makin' the contact. He knew his wrists could do the job that most guys' legs and arms had to do.

"That's why his stride was short, like Joe DiMaggio's was. He spread out real wide, which made him even more balanced and his vision on an even line, no bouncin', no twistin'. He was like a ramrod. He didn't move a muscle 'til the ball was almost in on him. That's why you couldn't fool him with a curveball, and you couldn't get a fastball by him. He was like a reflex, a nerve jumpin' all at once. I'm tellin' you, the Lord made that boy to hit a baseball."

As far as Josh's hours away from the field were concerned, Hooks Tinker knew much less, though more than Josh apparently would allow his other teammates to know. "He was a fine boy," Tinker said, "and that was unexpected, because the neighborhood he came from wasn't so hot. I know because I had to pick him up on the north side a few times. With Josh, if you gave him an ice cream cone he was tickled to death. He never thought about drinking or nothing like that then, because we didn't have drinkers on the Crawfords.

"Listen, at that time, he was still in a good, clean environment. He could still be a kid. I couldn't imagine him ending up with some of the stuff that happened to him later on."

The big thing in Josh's off-field life in 1928, Tinker noticed, was that he was spending a lot of time with a young woman a year younger than he who lived just around the corner from Ammon Field, on the 2200 block of Bedford Avenue. Josh didn't socialize with his teammates, so few of the Crawfords knew he was hung up on Helen Mason, a very pretty and chirpy girl whom he had spotted in the stands.

While displaying his adolescent alter ego for his teammates, in reality he was accelerating his rigorous drive toward manhood. By early 1929, he and Helen were sexual partners and hopelessly lovesick. When Helen became pregnant in February, they were married by a pastor named Reverend Robertson at the Macedonia Baptist Church on March 7, before their families but without friends or teammates in attendance.

The only woman to ever capture Josh Gibson's heart was born and raised in Pittsburgh. She was the second of three daughters born to James and Margaret Mason, who had met after they had emigrated from the South. James, who came from Virginia, worked as a repairman for the city's water department, driving a horse and buggy to the scene of water main leaks. His daughters, Dolly, Helen, and Rebecca, went to Schenley High School. The only surviving member of that family, Rebecca Mason, recalled how giddy they all felt when Helen brought Josh home to meet them.

"He came down to the house like all our fellas did, and he was so respectful that my dad thought a million dollars of him," she said. "He was nice and manly, and he seemed to want to be with our family more than his own."

In fact, distancing himself from Mark and Nancy Gibson even further, Josh moved in with the Masons on his wedding night and squeezed in honeymoon time in Helen's room between Crawfords games. At the same time, he continued at his job running the elevator at Gimbel's on his days off, since he had reluctantly conceded that there wasn't time enough to earn his electrician's license now that baseball had become a possibility as a profession.

This career direction became clear to him early in the 1930 season. The Crawfords were now taking on the look of a pro operation, though salaries were still not being paid to the players. That winter, spurred by Gus Greenlee's encouragement, several other big shots on the Hill contributed vital money to the team. One was J. W. "Iceman" King, a policeman and ice delivery company owner who had contacts with both Greenlee and the Democratic Party clubhouse in the Soho district of the Hill. King bought the players new uniforms and let them travel to games in one of his ice trucks.

Greenlee also prevailed on another of his friends, Steve Cox, who owned a sporting goods store, to contribute balls and bats—including Josh Gibson's exclusive forty-inch, forty-ounce model—and book Crawfords games. He broadened their competition to include white semipro teams. By the spring, the club had a set schedule of Tuesday, Friday, and Saturday games at Ammon Field.

While Greenlee bided his time before transforming the team into a professional organization, the Crawfords built their popularity by playing 5 P.M. twilight games. The crowds, which often stretched the stands beyond the ballpark's capacity of five thousand, were able to see the likes of Josh Gibson, Hooks Tinker, Charlie Hughes, and Neal Harris without paying a cent. By city law, amateur teams could not charge for admission, and this created the weird paradox of the Crawfords playing before packed houses yet coming away with nothing in their pockets. Tinker recalled that the most he ever took home after the hat was passed was $10. If the crowd was especially cheap, Tinker couldn't even pay the umpires, much less a visiting semipro team.

On Memorial Day 1930, a reported crowd of six thousand—which seems improbable given the stadium's size, even allowing for standing room—attended the Crawfords game. When the hat was passed, Tinker reached in and pulled out exactly $80. The umps got $24 and the visiting team $50, leaving the Crawfords to divide all of $6. This intolerable stinginess of the crowd rather than the team's victory became the story in the *Courier* that week, as the paper's ace sportswriter, Wendell Smith, blistered the Hill's baseball fans.

"One of the most disgusting things this writer has ever witnessed has been the 'poor sportsmanship' of some of our own people at Ammon Field," Smith wrote.

Here is a young team with all the earmarks of future greatness. They play the game for all that it is worth. Playing for

love of the sport, they give their following thrills that one seldom sees in this age of "machine baseball." They're popular
and that's a fact. . . . And right now, they're playing to larger
crowds daily than ANY team in this section.

A nickel a person would get the youngsters on top. But, no!
Out of every ten people who pass through, nine of them have
"iron-clad" alibis. We say "iron-clad" because very seldom
does one hear the clink of silver copper pennies rattle in the
box from the fingers of "dressed-up" sheiks, who cleverly
hide their contributions. . . .

We feel that "cheapsports," the greatest dredge mankind
has ever known, should take heed. Be a real sport. Pay for
what you see. Surely to see these games is worth at least a
dime a head. Let's vindicate our inherent faith in humanity.
It'll be appreciated.

While the money situation did not improve, still the opposition came, passing up more lucrative games in order to
share in the Crawfords' communal font of popularity. Some
of western Pennsylvania's finest white semipro teams were
on the 1930 schedule, including Book Shoe, J. L. Thomas,
Dormont, and W.O.W., the last a team sponsored by a wood-
working store. Some of these teams used major league players, who used pseudonyms when playing on their off days.
When the W.O.W. team, fresh off its win in the Greater Pittsburgh Semipro Tournament, came to Ammon Field on June
15, the *Courier* sent a reporter to cover the game, guarantee-
ing that the Crawfords would appear in the consecrated
space generally reserved for the Homestead Grays and other
pro black ball teams.

As it turned out, the coverage of this Saturday game was
well deserved. Attended by five thousand fans, it was a
thriller that exhilarated and exhausted the Crawford faithful,
though it appeared for six innings to be a Crawford cakewalk. They broke on top, 3–0, after two innings and 4–0

after five. Josh, hitting cleanup, had four singles in his first four at bats, and shortstop Bucky Williams hit two doubles and two singles in his first four.

But in the top of the sixth, W.O.W.—with a roster of decidedly ethnic names such as Slavinsky, Jedinak, Cholk, Gerlosky, and Atalski—began a comeback with three runs off Crawford pitcher Roy Williams. They then got one run in the seventh, two in the eighth, and two more in the ninth. With the score now 9–8, Crawfords, they had the bases loaded when the last out was made.

The *Courier,* in big block letters, headlined its game story CHAMPS BOW IN 9–8 DEFEAT TO CRAWFORDS. That the black press still had a lot to learn about the Crawfords' big gun, however, was underscored by the *Courier* story's paragraph identifying the Crawfords' catcher as Josh *Gipson;* that was also how it was spelled in the accompanying box score.

The chugging express train that the Crawfords had become was now at breakneck speed. The team that only a few years ago was synonymous with a bathhouse was, through Hooks Tinker and coach Harry Beale, boldly issuing challenges in the papers to the Homestead Grays. And the Grays had certainly been watching the rise of the amateur team that was nipping at its heels. As things stood, though, the haughty Grays could afford to be arrogant in their dealings with the scruffy Crawfords, since the team across the Monongahela River southeast of Pittsburgh could call the shots.

Although the Grays' protocol normally forbade games with amateur clubs—who were prohibited from charging admission, and therefore could not assure the Grays a profitable enough payday—the Grays' owner, Cumberland "Cum" Posey, very much wanted to cut in on the Crawfords' turf. Accordingly, in 1928, he began to tantalize Tinker and Beale with vague promises to play the Crawfords at the fortythousand-seat Forbes Field, which the Grays rented for their marquee games when the major league Pirates were out of town.

Posey's plan was to be friendly to the Crawfords while working to undermine their appeal by taking their best players. And simply by having Posey deign to talk shop with him, Tinker found himself starry eyed enough to unwittingly fall for Posey's deceits.

As one of the most famous black sports entrepreneurs in the country, Posey was able to paralyze Tinker with his aura long enough to strike a sweetheart arrangement that made the Crawfords a kind of minor league feeder for the Grays. For hearing Posey's hazy promises and having the privilege of gaining his attentions, the Crawfords agreed to deliver to Posey any players he wanted. The first to move up was Bill Harris, followed by infielder Johnny Moore.

In 1929, Posey had further slighted the Crawfords by insisting that Tinker take on Cum's younger brother, Seward "See" Posey, as a part-time assistant manager and cobooker. Through See's eyes, Cum could now study the Crawford players up close, as well as their dealings with the white semi-pro teams Posey also scheduled to play the Grays. Of course, Cum's explanation to Tinker was that See would teach him the ins and outs of a professional organization. And the Poseys, who knew all the angles, had a lot to teach.

During one tournament the Crawfords entered in 1930, See closed every gate at Ammon Field but one. While admission was still technically free, Posey required that every fan had to pay a "contribution." The Poseys' influence was such that See stationed two cops at the gate to enforce this brazen way of getting around the law. At the end of the day, See brought a burlap bag into the locker room and dumped its contents on the floor—$2,000 in small bills.

Even with this priceless education, it occurred to Hooks Tinker that Cum Posey's aim was to cripple the Crawfords, not serve them. He saw the light when, midway through the 1930 season, Cum still had not agreed to a Grays-Crawfords game. To Hooks, it was obvious Cum wanted to put off the game—which would be the biggest sporting event to ever go

down on the Hill, but also a potential source of embarrassment to the Grays, who almost never lost—until he could get
Josh Gibson away from the Crawfords.

While such an opportunity would be beneficial for Josh, it
put Tinker in an uncomfortable position. For one thing, Tinker knew that despite the attractiveness of a regular paycheck, playing pro ball was not on the minds of most of the
Crawfords. "These boys played for the love of the game and
because, for many of them, it gave them a family they didn't
have at home," he said.

"Even Josh wasn't that set on it, because it was so rewarding that he had a family with us. These boys loved each other.
In their minds, we were the best team. You couldn't dispute
it, didn't need no salary to prove it. That's why Bill Harris left
the Grays and came back to the Crawfords. We had something money couldn't buy."

In trying to draw the line between creating opportunities
for his players and avoiding the disruption of his team's
chemistry, Tinker realized that line ran under Josh's spikes.
Thus, as the inevitable came closer, the day when Cum Posey
deemed Gibson ready for the Grays, Tinker went through
war with himself over what his response should be. Finally,
the day arrived when circumstances led Posey to look for a
catcher to sign.

Tinker got wind of Posey's intentions during a Crawfords
game against a white semipro team in Ingomar, Pennsylvania.

"What happened was, it was the fifth inning and we already had a fifteen-oh lead and Josh had already hit a couple
of triples and a home run. And I noticed him going down to
the end of the stands, and he was talking to See Posey. See
usually didn't travel with us, so I knew he was out there for
one purpose: to sign Josh.

"After they talked awhile, Josh came down and sat beside
me. He said, 'Hooks, they want me to play with the Grays in
Forbes Field tonight.' And you know, that was the greatest
decision I ever had to make. I didn't want to say yes and I

didn't want to say no. But in the end, I knew it was a great opportunity for Josh and that this was what he was working for. And hell, he was such a great hitter, black baseball needed a guy like him. So in that split second I said, 'Josh, if they want you, you go.'"

In the years to come, a myth would be told about Josh's pro debut. As the Grays player-manager, third baseman Judy Johnson, a future Hall of Famer, spun the tale that Gibson happened to be in the stands during a Grays game against the great Kansas City Monarchs in late July. To add to the fable, the Monarchs had brought their new portable lighting system to Forbes Field.

Mounted on trucks for transit, the light towers were put on the stadium roof, attached to thick cables running down to gasoline-burning generators that ground out a cacophony along with beams of light. The year before, when the Depression battered the Midwest hard, the Monarchs owner, J. L. Wilkinson, a white man, had sunk his life savings of $100,000 into having this contraption built as a way to draw working people to games after their jobs let out for the day.

The move, which opened black ball to the aesthetic of night baseball five years before the majors caught on to it, was an instant hit. Yet for all the system's intricacies, the light it shed on the field was barely enough to enable one to see the ball in flight, and then only with a squint. For the players, every batted ball was an adventure—and a peril.

Thus, as legend has it, the Grays pitcher that July night at Forbes Field, Smokey Joe Williams, threw a pitch that could not be seen by catcher Buck Ewing and split Ewing's finger when it reached the plate. Ewing was unable to continue. According to Judy Johnson, as quoted in Robert Peterson's *Only the Ball Was White*, this is what happened next:

> So Josh was sitting in the grandstand, and I asked the Grays' owner, Cum Posey, to get him to finish the game. So Cum asked Josh would he catch, and Josh said, "Yeah, oh yeah!"

We had to hold the game up until he went into the clubhouse and got a uniform. And that's what started him out with the Homestead Grays.

Of course, Josh was in Ingomar, Pennsylvania, when Buck Ewing hurt his finger. And in that game—which was played on a Thursday *afternoon*—Ewing stayed in, catching in pain, because the Grays backup catcher was also hurt. It was the next day, before the second and last game of the Monarchs series, played under the lights at Forbes Field on Friday, July 31, that Josh Gibson became a pro, signed by See Posey in Ingomar.

Hooks Tinker didn't give in meekly to the heist of his best player. His infatuation with Cum Posey's flattering advances having receded into cynicism, he asked for a commitment from See Posey for a Crawfords-Grays game, to be played in late August. With Josh free of the Crawfords, the Poseys made the game. "Obviously, they wanted Josh away from us," Tinker said. "They figured they took our big gun away and we wouldn't be too much trouble."

Before the game in Ingomar was over, Josh was gone. See Posey took him by car to Forbes Field. But Tinker tells a story about Josh's pro debut that sounds appropriately mythical as well and is similar in part to Judy Johnson's tale.

"They told me Josh was sittin' in the stands there, still wearin' his Crawfords uniform, when they called him into the game. They had to call time and wait 'til he changed into a Grays uniform."

For all of the mythmaking surrounding the event, Gibson's presence had almost no bearing on the actual game, which at the time swallowed him up in its importance, given the two teams and the novelty of the lights. The game, which drew ten thousand fans, turned out to be a beauty. Facing the Monarchs veteran pitcher Chet Brewer, the Grays fell behind, 1–0, in the second before scoring five runs in the bottom of the inning. Then, as Grays pitcher Bill Ross weakened, the Monarchs chipped away, getting even at 6–6 after seven.

Josh, who indeed replaced Buck Ewing in the fifth inning and batted in Ewing's seventh slot in the batting order, went hitless in two times at bat but came up a winner when Vic Harris stepped in with two outs in the last of the ninth and cranked Brewer's first pitch over the wall.

While the Josh Gibson era in black ball began with little fanfare, it presaged events back on the Hill that would affect black ball's future in Pittsburgh and beyond. But more than these repercussions, what concerned Hooks Tinker was how Josh would fare in Homestead.

To the outside world, the Grays were a coldly efficient team, its players arrow straight and the picture of professional conduct. Cum Posey cultivated this image meticulously on and off the field. Posey, an outstanding athlete in his younger days, banned card games from the clubhouse and made the Grays wear suits and ties when they came to the park. But those familiar with the team, among them Tinker and Vic Harris's two brothers, knew of the hidden truths, such as Posey's flagrant adulterous affairs, and the antisocial habits—which Tinker believed bordered on the psychotic—they bred in Posey's players.

"I knew most of the Grays and they were pretty rough guys," he said. "Hard drinkers, nasty drinkers. They'd rough you up on the field, cut you up, spit in your face, call you everything under the sun. Cum knew how to handle those guys. He kept 'em under control, but he wanted them to be mean, and they were mean guys, really the nastiest guys I ever knew.

"Vic Harris was a great ballplayer, but the first time I saw his brothers, Bill and Neal, we were playing on a vacant lot, and Vic came down and he didn't want his kid brothers to play, so he chased 'em home and threw rocks at 'em. He wanted to be the only one of the brothers to be the big man.

And Neal Harris was one of the best hitters around, a great line drive hitter. But Vic wouldn't let him play with the Grays. And Bill Harris felt he was run off the club by his brother. Vic just had to be the best in the family. He had to prove it all the time.

"The whole environment over there . . . I worried if Josh would be able to stay the same person I knew him to be."

Barely a month later, fate would make that all but impossible.

3

Gray and Blue

He never talked to me about my mother. All I knew was, my mother died, period. That's all I knew.
— JOSH GIBSON JR.

I don't know what made him go bad. We heard he had a wife who died a long time ago. Maybe that was it.
— JOSH JOHNSON, CATCHER, HOMESTEAD GRAYS, 1934–42

Still only eighteen, Josh Gibson seemed to have more in common with the Grays batboy than the team's superb roster. The 1930 edition of the Grays, which has come to be regarded as possibly black ball's best team of all time, had a thousand or so years of combined experience and—besides Gibson—two future Hall of Famers, third baseman–manager Judy Johnson and first baseman Oscar Charleston.

Charleston, at thirty-four, was by now a black ball institution, a great big snarling bear of a man with glaring eyes and a temper that periodically drove him beyond the edge of sanity. During his career, which began in 1915, he compiled a long record of achievement on the field and a police record almost as long. Arguably the most versatile of players in his prime, the left-handed Charleston—who played first base, the outfield, and even some second base—could hit, run, field, and make mayhem with equal ability.

Charleston was so barbaric on the base paths that he was known to cut the glove off infielders' hands. In his rookie year, playing with the Indianapolis ABCs, he struck an umpire and was arrested and charged with assault. Charleston jumped bail and was never tried, and his own manager branded his behavior "ugly" and "cowardly."

But his thuggish reputation only added to Charleston's value. By the time he got to the Grays in 1930—a move that came after he punched the owner of his last team, the Hilldale Club, of Darby, Pennsylvania—he had worn the uniform of half a dozen teams in the Negro National League, the circuit that dominated the black game in the 1920s but did little to invoke a sense of loyalty among its players, who jumped between teams for better offers all the time.

Now, with the NNL facing bankruptcy and extinction, Grays owner Cum Posey was cherry-picking superstars off league rosters. That same year, he also signed Judy Johnson from Hilldale, where he had played nine distinguished seasons. The mild-mannered Johnson—whose given name was William but who was dubbed Judy because an old teammate named Jude Gans had been his mentor—was not a member of the Grays' drinking and carousing set, but his compulsion to get on base seemed like an addiction. Willfully trying to get hit by pitched balls, he let out the seams of his uniform shirt to make himself a larger target.

Posey also reeled in another nine-year veteran from Hilldale, diminutive shortstop Jake Stephens; the Grays also featured pitcher George Scales, yet another nine-year man, and catcher Chippy Britt, a ten-year man. But Posey's biggest weapons—pitchers Smokey Joe Williams, Oscar Owens, and Charles "Lefty" Williams—had each been going to the mound for the Grays since 1925, and Owens and Lefty Williams went back to 1923, when the Grays first became a pro team.

The Williams boys in particular were leaving fans and hitters openmouthed with wonderment in 1930—for Smokey Joe, it was his *thirty-third* season on black ball mounds. This six-foot-six Texan, whose hawklike beak and dark eyes emphasized his part–Native American ancestry, was after Gibson and Satchel Paige the most storied black ballplayer in history, and his dominance was unparalleled in 1930.

Though no one could prove any of it, people talked about Smokey Joe's 1914 season, when he allegedly went 41–3 for the Chicago American Giants, or his twenty-five-strikeout game in 1924 while pitching for the Brooklyn Royal Giants. Better documented, but of questionable significance, were his victories over big league pitchers like Grover Cleveland Alexander and Rube Marquand in black-versus-white exhibition games.

In 1930, when Smokey Joe was something like fifty—nobody seemed to know what his exact age was, and he got a lot of publicity mileage out of it—the two Williamses peaked. On the night of August 7, Smokey Joe hooked up with Chet Brewer in an astonishing pitching duel when the Grays traveled to Kansas City for a return-match two-game series against the Monarchs in Muehlebach Stadium.

Since both Smokey Joe and Brewer were known to apply just about any substance or use any utensil on a baseball, when both of them came out with their best stuff that day, hitters on both sides—staring into the Monarchs' dim lights to begin with—had to know it was going to be a very long night. That the pitchers were shamelessly loading up and defacing the ball was hardly a secret—or illegal in black ball but the *Courier* still made a pointed reference to it.

"The opposing pitchers were cheating without the question of a doubt [and] Smokey Joe had everything except a blacksmith file," read the paper's game story. "An emery ball in daylight is very deceptive but at night it is about as easy to hit as an insect in the sky."

Williams and Brewer matched zeroes for eleven innings and seemed to get less hittable as the game went on. Striking out hitters at a mad pace, Smokey Joe no-hit the Monarchs until the eighth, when he gave up a two-out double to third baseman Newt Joseph. First baseman John Turner then lofted a pop fly behind the infield that looked as if it would fall for a hit until Jake Stephens leaped headlong and snared it just off the ground to end the inning.

Brewer, meanwhile, gave up three hits through six. He then struck out ten straight, whiffing the side in the seventh, eighth, and ninth innings. Finally, in the twelfth, Oscar Charleston walked and center fielder Chaney White hit what the *Courier* called a "fluke" double to drive home the first run. Smokey Joe made it stand up, retiring the Monarchs in the bottom of the frame.

In all, Williams fanned *twenty-seven,* a number regarded as a black ball record. Brewer, not far off, struck out nineteen in the loss, the fourth straight suffered by the Monarchs to the Grays over the season.

If this game, like the 1–0 thriller in Forbes Field, wasn't enough to relegate Josh's rookie season into a footnote, Lefty Williams's incredible season—he was said to have gone 27–0 in 1930—and Cum Posey's caution about bringing Gibson along did. Hitting eighth, Josh, who went 0-for-3 against Brewer with two walks, was stuck in low gear for those first few weeks before collecting two hits of an unspecified nature recorded in the box score of an 11–0 Grays win over Homewood in early August.

Actually, rather than concentrating on hitting, it was all Josh could do to hang on to the unfathomable array of baffling stuff served up by the Grays' rotation. For an eighteen-year-old kid thrown onto that hot plate, he did well enough, though some opponents ragged him about his tendency to block balls rather than catch them. Even so, Josh's arm was not subject to jokes; he threw to bases straight and true. On the whole, you could take one look at him and know Josh Gibson would be around for a while.

On August 11, while in Homewood, Josh got the hardest jolt of his life. That afternoon Dolly Mason, his sister-in-law, telephoned the ballpark clubhouse, pleading to speak to Josh. When he was called in from the field, Dolly told him that Helen Gibson, now eight months pregnant with twins, had gone into premature labor and become deathly ill.

As Rebecca Mason, the only surviving sister, recalled of that horrible day, "She was small, and with the pressure of the children on her body, it all came on at once. Helen said she wasn't feeling good, and when she went unconscious we called the doctor—his name was Dr. Boose, he was our family physician—and he said to take her to the hospital."

As Josh hurried to get to his wife, an excruciating drama played out in the maternity ward at Magee Hospital. Helen, drifting in and out of consciousness and delirium, was clearly in much worse health than anyone knew. As Dr. Boose explained it to the family after examining her, Helen's pregnancy had aggravated an undiagnosed kidney condition. By the time she reached the hospital, one of her kidneys had ruptured.

"He said poison had come up in her body, and she was dying from it," Rebecca Mason said. "The doctor looked at my mother and said, 'Well, Mrs. Mason, we can't save your daughter but we can save the children if we act quickly.'

"We were just so shocked. My mother got real angry with him, because Helen had been going to the doctor all along and he didn't say nothing about a kidney problem. And you know, these doctors always got some kind of excuse why they didn't do right, but the truth was, if he knew about it he didn't tell us. Helen never showed any signs of a problem, and this doctor said everything was all right right up until she took sick."

Beyond the anger and recriminations, the dreadful decision had to be made whether, in effect, to terminate Helen's life by putting her through the torture of childbirth, or to terminate the unborn children's lives and hope that Helen could somehow survive. The decision fell to Margaret Mason, Helen's mother, who deferred to the doctor, whom she would never allow to tend to her family again.

Just before Helen Gibson was taken into the delivery room, Josh got to the hospital in time to share her last few minutes of life.

"He was at her bedside, but she was half gone," said Rebecca Mason. "She didn't know him or nobody else. She was just in terrible agony. They wouldn't give her painkillers or anything.

"Josh was totally broken up, and he was yellin' that he would rather have his wife than the children, but they said she couldn't live. And then they took her away."

In the early evening of August 11, 1930, a twin son and daughter were born as Helen Gibson died. One of those children, Josh Gibson Jr., has heard the story of his birth told by family members often through the years and has drawn his own conclusions about this ineffable tragedy.

"I know that my father resented it that we lived and my mother died," he said. "He had to; that was his wife they were takin' away from him. But I don't think he ever held it against me and my sister in later years. It just showed how much he loved my mother."

When the tears stopped, Josh was left to face the sobering matter of attending to the twins' welfare and their immediate future. While he simply could not take on the role of a full-time father, given the Grays' seamless playing schedule, his commitment to the children down the road remained unclear. He did specify, however, that he did not want them cared for by his mother and father.

"He said he didn't want his mother to have the children; he made that known right away," Rebecca Mason remembered.

"His mother said she didn't want them anyway. She didn't want to take care of them."

Rebecca thought it was probably a good idea to keep the kids away from Nancy Gibson, whom she recalled as an overbearing presence. "She wasn't no little woman. She was pretty; she'd dress up and she liked to have a good time. And in doing so, she would drink, and I think Josh was disgusted by that."

So Josh prevailed on Margaret and James Mason to open their home to their grandchildren. But that didn't happen for a month—during which time Josh, who went right back to playing ball, did not give the newborn infants names as they were kept in Magee Hospital for observation.

"As a matter of fact," Josh Gibson Jr. noted, "when I sent for my birth certificate years later, it came back with no first name. In time, we were named after my parents [his sister was christened Helen], and I guess my father named us, but it could've been my grandmother—Mrs. Mason, that is. She was really my mother. She was the only mother I ever knew, she and my aunts."

For now, Josh resolved to deliver support money to the Masons on a regular basis but made no promises about his active participation in the children's lives. If it seemed as if he was altogether too blithe about his fatherhood, perhaps it was because those babies reminded him of Helen and the unspeakable tragedy of her death.

In any case, he went back to the Grays, saying nothing of the whole episode. But even though he went back with fire in his bat, there was something cold in his soul.

"I just thought that when Helen died, it looked like it took some of the energy out of him," said Rebecca Mason. "That enthusiasm he had for life was gone. I don't think he was ever the same."

If so, the tip-off was his eyes. Through the years, Josh's face would remain unchanged. His full cheeks and round, unstriated jowls were an effective camouflage for his decaying soul, a dependable mask that Josh Gibson fixed into the pose of the eternal phenom. But the eyes would refuse to cooperate with the impersonation. They would look weary, almost lifeless, as if that was where Gibson's pain was being stored.

In the end, while Josh told himself he was moving on, part of him moved not an inch beyond August 11, 1930.

Still, if Josh desperately needed a refuge, he had it with the Grays. Within this phalanx of big names and big-time pursuits, he was properly amazed at the insulating diversions of his new life. As with nearly all professional black ballplayers, it was immaterial to Josh that the black game was separate from the white big league game. The prohibitions of race were not a fighting matter, not when the amenities of reaching the top rung of black ball were so upraising to the children of dead-end deprivation.

To a Josh Gibson, it meant far more that as a Gray his name appeared in the *Courier* and other black papers than that the Grays—who could pick and choose from among a bevy of eager white opponents—had to stay in segregated hotels and rooming houses in the suburbs of Pittsburgh.

Within the realm of the Grays and of black ball, in fact, important moves were being made by Cum Posey that August. The success of his team having fed his ego, Posey was eager to become black ball's messiah. Casually disregarding the empty shell of the Midwest-based Negro National League, he was planning to set the black game spinning on a new axis, one located east of the Mississippi River.

The key to Posey's strategy was to establish a partnership with the Lincoln Giants of New York, a team that had been around since 1912 and had originally been made famous by a young Smokey Joe Williams and the team's awesome shortstop, the quicksilver John Henry Lloyd, another future Hall of Famer. At forty-six years old, Pop Lloyd, as he had become known, was the Lincoln Giants player-manager, though his play in the field was limited to occasional stints at first base.

Not only were the Lincoln Giants good; Posey knew they

provided subliminal and sentimental evidence of black ball's continuity as an institution, much like the Kansas City Monarchs and the Chicago American Giants. Pop Lloyd, in fact, had been part of the last sea change in the black game, when he was among a flock of players led by Napoleonic pitcher Andrew "Rube" Foster to jump from the Philadelphia Giants to the Chicago Leland Giants in 1910. That team, which metamorphosed into the Chicago American Giants, with Foster as its owner-manager, gave black ball its first nationally known attraction and gave Foster the impetus to form the Negro National League in 1920.

Pop Lloyd, however, broke with Foster and returned east, first to play with the Brooklyn Royal Giants in 1918, then with the Lincoln Giants in 1926. With Lloyd at the helm, the Lincoln Giants lured talented veterans to New York, like shortstop John Beckwith, catcher Larry Brown, second baseman Rev Cannady, and long ball hitters George "Mule" Suttles and Norman "Turkey" Stearns, whose reputations were such that each, at one time or another, had been dubbed "the black Babe Ruth" in the black papers.

Building up impressive, if unverified, won-lost records, the Lincoln Giants soon found themselves mired in what had become black ball's apocalyptic issue—white booking agents, who through their ownership of the ballparks where black teams played, could exact up to a 10 percent cut of the gate. The discordant image of these men involved in a game and a business that represented black self-sufficiency was responsible for more tension and division within the black game than anything else for years, so much so that each team had to line up on either side of the issue and live with the consequences.

For the Lincoln Giants, that meant having to fight a turf war with the most influential white agent, Nathaniel Colvin Strong, who was also the one most reviled by black ball purists. Strong controlled the New York baseball scene beneath the major league level by dint of his ownership of Dexter Park in Brooklyn and Dyckman Oval in Manhattan, the sites where most black ball games were played. In the twenties, Strong was able to cut into Rube Foster's Negro National League profits through his alliance with Ed Bolden, the black owner of the Hilldale Club of Darby, Pennsylvania. Bolden challenged Foster's reign as black ball czar by raiding the NNL's teams and creating his own Negro circuit, the Eastern Colored League. When this resulted in a potentially suicidal war within the black game, Foster called a truce by recognizing Bolden's league in 1923, paving the way for the first official championship games in black baseball, the Negro World Series, which began in 1924.

By 1930, however, Foster had literally gone mad from the self-induced pressures of keeping peace across the breadth of black ball; committed by a judge to a mental hospital in 1928, he would die there on December 9, 1930. Without Foster's inspiration and steady hand, the NNL could not hope to survive the Depression.

With the league drowning in debt and the Negro World Series suspended since 1928 for lack of interest, Cum Posey, who had wisely kept the Grays out of both the NNL and the badly mismanaged ECL, which folded in 1928, turned to the Lincoln Giants to help bring about a new order. Having complained about Nat Strong's sway over black ball himself, Posey clearly saw the value of joining forces with a team that had successfully resisted Strong's tentacles.

Not that the Lincoln Giants' ownership deserved to be covered with the laurels of black pride. Owned by white businessman James Keenan, the Giants' operating expenses were footed by one Baron Wilkins, a Harlem nightclub proprietor and numbers racketeer. With this kind of muscle behind the team, Keenan wasn't scared off when Nat Strong threatened to deprive the Giants of their home grounds unless Keenan dealt with him. Wilkins's influence was heavy around town, and the team established a long history playing at the Catholic Protectory Oval, on the site of an orphanage in the South Bronx. The Giants also were given membership in the ECL.

Clearly, Cum Posey wasn't half as interested in black ball's racial purity as he was in its seat of power. In early August, he began to pitch a Grays–Lincoln Giants series for a putative, if not official, championship match. Posey wrote the *Courier* that

> we will play against them for 45 percent of the gross admission in New York [with] admission at 50 cents and we will play them in Pittsburgh the same way. . . . As these games will be for the recognized championship of 1930, let the series run to eleven games on consecutive days, including doubleheaders on Saturdays and Sundays. . . .
>
> Many writers . . . consider the Lincoln Giants the best in colored baseball and some say they are the best ever in colored baseball. Personally, I think the Homestead Grays of 1930 the greatest club the Grays have ever had and the finest bunch of gentlemen ever assembled under any management in any sport.

By offering to take less of a cut than the Giants, Posey was baiting the trap. When James Keenan sat on the proposal for two weeks, the *Courier,* eager to promote the series, ran a headline reading "BRING ON THE LINCOLN GIANTS" CRY OF COLORED FANS AS CRUCIAL SERIES HANGS IN BALANCE. But before the series was made, Posey had to sweat out a different challenge to his club. Having had to deliver on his promise to play Hooks Tinker's Pittsburgh Crawfords, he scheduled the game he dreaded on Saturday, August 27, at Forbes Field.

As it turned out, Tinker had figured right when he sensed Posey's angst about this game, especially while Josh Gibson was a Crawford. The Grays, who reportedly came into the game with thirty-three wins in a row, had to fight for their lives. Even though Oscar Owens no-hit the Crawfords for six innings, Homestead could do little against Harry Kincannon, whom the *Courier,* calling him "Tincannon," described as "young but with the phlegmatic disposition which is the heritage of all great pitchers."

The Grays, having scratched out a run without a hit in the first inning, put up two more in the fourth on a Chaney White double. But the Crawfords broke through against Owens in the seventh, scoring two on four straight singles, to make it 3–2. Then, in the eighth, with night closing in, the Crawfords had two men on and two out when Charlie Hughes cracked a liner to left center that Vic Harris stabbed with a diving catch. Cum Posey's honor was saved when the game was now called because of darkness.

For the ten thousand fans at Forbes Field that day, however, the loss for the Crawfords was purely technical, and even Grays fans would not have argued with Hooks Tinker's assessment that "We shoulda won that game." The *Courier*'s coverage practically ignored the victors. Its skewed headline was CRAWFORDS BEATEN BY GRAYS 3–2 IN CLASSIC, and the panting lead paragraphs read:

> An inspired Crawfords nine, playing heads-up baseball . . . and turning in some fielding feats which rivaled anything ever seen on the turf of spike-scuffed Forbes Field, played to the very last ditch before they admitted the superiority of the Homestead Grays. . . .
> The losers clearly demonstrated the fact that they are dangerous contenders in the ranks of big-time colored baseball.

A relieved Cum Posey could now turn to his hoped-for classic with the Lincoln Giants. But on the Hill, Gus Greenlee, seeing all the fuss surrounding the Grays-Crawfords contest, decided he was ready to enter the black ball scene himself. As was his wont, Greenlee dove in headfirst, and the splash would be so big that just about everybody in Pittsburgh—Josh Gibson included—would feel the ripples.

4

Home Run: Gibson

With Rector pitching, on Saturday Gibson hit a home run that went into the leftfield bleachers, a distance of 460 feet. It was the longest home run that was hit at the Yankee Stadium by any player, white or colored, all season.

—NEW YORK AMSTERDAM NEWS,
OCTOBER 4, 1930

As if to express his contempt for Negro National League teams, Cum Posey prefaced his proposed championship match with the Lincoln Giants with a two-week swing through the Midwest, to play, and presumably blow away, three of the NNL's best-known clubs on their home turf. Although the tour was less than a complete success for the Grays, it was during this time that Josh emerged as a real threat.

The opening stage of the trip went according to Posey's script, as the Grays stomped on the Detroit Stars in two games played in late August in Akron, Ohio, by the scores of 11–3 and 16–5. With an almost audible chuckle, the *Courier* declared that "all opposition seems to look alike to the Homestead Grays" and reckoned that, over the season, "the Grays have played 136 games, won 127, lost seven and played two ties so far." And buried deep in the story was the notation that "Gibson, a young catcher with the Grays, collected four singles [in the two games]."

The Grays' merry jaunt continued in Missouri in the opener of a three-game set against the St. Louis Stars, who had won the first-half title of the NNL's split-season format. The first Gray to come up, little Jake Stephens, hit a home run. Later on, pitcher Chippy Britt hit one out and George Scales hit two in the Grays 10–6 win.

But then the Grays ran aground. The Stars were loaded with talent, led by lithe shortstop Willie Wells and a future Hall of Famer with the signature nickname of black ball's elite: center fielder James Thomas "Cool Papa" Bell. (Bell had earned his moniker as an unflappable pitcher prior to being switched to the outfield, which, with his burning speed, he seemed to cover from end to end.)

In the second game of the series, Bell, said the *Courier*, "turned in some sensational fielding," and Alec Radcliff, normally a catcher, showed remarkable prowess by taking the mound and hurling a seven-hit 9–1 victory.

In the deciding game, Posey, who had sat Josh in the first two contests in favor of the recovered Buck Ewing, inserted him in the seventh slot in the batting order. The Grays again fell, 6–5, with Smokey Joe Williams bested by Ted Trent. In retrospect, however, the real meaning of the game, which was overlooked in the *Courier* story, could be found in the simple line in the box score—HOME RUN: GIBSON—the first such notation recorded in baseball agate type. Indeed, Cool Papa Bell would find himself dredging his memory bank for years afterward, describing that home run.

Bell pointed out that, unlike many homers hit in Stars Park, Gibson's was no cheapie. While the left field foul pole was only 250 feet away, so that it wouldn't encroach on the two trolley garages behind the wall, Bell said that Josh's blast went "way over the second shed, four hundred and some feet." Cool Papa recalled the astonishment among the Stars players that a kid had hit the ball so far. "We said, 'Bring him up close so we can look at him,'" to make sure he was really that young.

Still, back then, the St. Louis series was a stumble for the Grays, one they soon rectified. They came into Chicago in early September and whipped the once mighty American Giants, taking five out of six games in a whirlwind series that included Saturday and Sunday day-night doubleheaders at Schorling Park, with its new lighting system. That Josh was still a fresh face was indicated by the *Chicago Defender*'s list of the two teams' lineups, which made no mention of him.

But while Buck Ewing caught the first game, on Friday, when Lefty Williams won, 11–5, Josh played on Saturday afternoon and went 1-for-5, singling in two runs in a 10–4 win. He then played Saturday night and in both Sunday games, the first of which saw the Grays drop their only game, to pitcher-manager Willie Foster, Rube Foster's younger brother. When Ewing got back in on Monday, Josh didn't go to the bench but to right field, batting seventh.

This would continue to be the pattern of Josh's advancement. While Posey wasn't yet ready to yank Ewing, he was gradually making room for Josh around the field and inching him higher in the order. By September 15, when the Grays swept a doubleheader from the Baltimore Black Sox, Josh had made it up to the sixth slot and caught both games, getting three hits in one.

Though no one knew it at the time, the ripening of Josh Gibson was also the quiet prologue to the Grays–Lincoln Giants championship series, which was finally made in mid-September. Growing bigger in importance by the minute, the series, which was to run to ten games, was slated to begin on Saturday, September 20, with a doubleheader in Forbes Field.

Then, in a tremendous coup, Posey and Jim Keenan were

able to rent Yankee Stadium for a Sunday doubleheader, an undertaking that in 1930 meant white baseball people couldn't miss the fact that there was financial gain to be made from exploiting the black game. But seen through the long periscope of history, it was a substantial step forward for the bastard world of black ball. In its urban ascendancy, the black game could now set down in the holy land of Yankee Stadium and make the case that it belonged there if ability alone was the price to get on the field.

Indeed, Posey and Keenan made sure to pound the point home by scheduling all but two series games in big league parks. Those two games were made for Bigler Field in Darby, Pennsylvania, on September 25 and 26, before the series would conclude back at Yankee Stadium with two doubleheaders on the weekend of September 27–28.

By chance, another portent greeted the series. In the September 27 *Courier,* which because of the paper's lead time covered only the opening two games, sportswriter W. Rollo Wilson devoted two-thirds of his column, called "Sports Shots," to the rising nova of Josh Gibson. In this, Josh's first major exposure in the black press, Wilson spun a marvelous parable of a folk hero that Josh might have had trouble recognizing as himself. After relating Judy Johnson's fable about Gibson's accidental debut, Wilson went on:

Well, the kid could catch and did catch and is still catching. He's green but the ripening process is moving apace. He has not mastered the technique in throwing to second base but he kills off all the fast boys who try to steal. His stance at the plate is worse than Pimp Young's [another Gray player] but he gets his basehits. His motto is—"a homer a day will boost my pay."

[He is] strong! . . . And [can he] eat! That boy has a keener zest for food than does your fat correspondent. He spends more money for "snacks" than any of the other players lavish on three meals. It takes a tremendous amount of fodder to sat-

isfy his growing body and nourish his 194 pounds of bones
and muscle.

They should have named him Josher instead of Joshua, for
he sure can kid with the kidders. For confirmation of this
you may communicate with the renowned [catcher] Raleigh
Mackey, now laboring for the Baltimore Black Sox. On a recent Sunday in [Baltimore] the kid worked on the perspiring
Biz [Mackey's nickname] each time he came to bat that he was
fit to be tied, as the expression goes.

"Aha!" sneered Gibson, when Mackey clumped out to the
plate. "So this is Mr. Mackey, the famous catcher and batter.
I've been readin' a lot about you in the papers. I believe you
were in the games in Pittsburgh Friday and yesterday. You
didn't do so well, did you? Well, you're gonna do worse today.

"Oh, you missed that one! Too bad. Now, sir, here is one
right down the alley. What? Only a foul? My fault, sir, I forgot that I had called for one on the inside. Don't hit at this
one, it's an off ball. So sorry! The darn fool pitcher crossed
you up. His control was bad and he cut the corner. Yes, Mr.
Mackey, that was three strikes. You are excused for the time
being. Perhaps you will do better the next time; you may hit it
to the infield."

Most of this was just so much eyewash. Actually, Josh's lip
pretty much stayed buttoned in the presence of old pros like
Biz Mackey, to whom he paid the absolute respect of silence.
But relaxing more and more, he had begun applying alliftera-
tive pet names to teammates, even those who already had
one; Judy Johnson, for example, he dubbed Jing. Josh probably did utter the nifty "a homer a day will boost my pay"
one-liner, because in the future he often exercised a playful
sense of braggadocio with similar lines.

In any case, Rollo Wilson's printed massage was of inestimable value to Josh. As highly visible as it was, and as
timely, he found himself now with a reputation few seasoned
black stars could hope for.

.   .   .

When the ballyhooed Grays–Lincoln Giants series got under way—not by coincidence at the same time that the Detroit Stars and St. Louis Stars played for the NNL title—the unbeatable Lefty Williams won the opener of the Forbes Field doubleheader, 9–1. Then, in the second game, Josh Gibson had his coming-out party.

This was one more routinely nutty black ball affair. Josh, who had tripled against pitcher Luther Farrell earlier in a game that had turned into a hitters' feast, drove Farrell from the hill in the fourth inning with a monster drive, a 460-foot shot that was over the center field wall in an eye blink. That put the Grays up, 13–8, but the Giants fought back and went ahead, 16–13, in the seventh. The Grays tied it in the ninth, then Chaney White singled home the gamer in the tenth.

Less than sixteen hours later, Smokey Joe Williams was facing the Giants veteran junkballer Billy Holland before ten thousand fans in the hollow of Yankee Stadium. But in the *Courier,* the man of the hour was Josh Gibson. On page one of the sports section a photo of Gibson, bat in hand, ran over a caption reading: "19-year-old Homestead Grays catch [*sic*], whose terrific hitting and fine receiving was one of the sensations of the opening colored world series battles at Forbes Field Saturday. Gibson was formerly receiver on the Pittsburgh Crawfords team."

Rollo Wilson, in his column, also weighed in with the observation that "Samson Gibson is green but a terrific threat when crouching over the plate with a bat. . . . His homer and triple in Pittsburgh were mighty wallops."

By now, Buck Ewing was all but a memory. Catching every game in the series and hitting sixth, Josh continued to get timely, if quieter, hits as the Grays established superiority. After Holland beat Smokey Joe, 6–2, the teams went to the tenth inning of the Yankee Stadium nightcap tied 2–2. Jake Stephens then singled, stole second, and scored on an error by poor Luther Farrell to save the split.

Now, with the Grays up in the series three games to one, the Grays took a commanding edge in Philadelphia when Smokey Joe beat Holland, 11–3—with Josh supplying a large exclamation point by taking one deep in the third ballpark of the series, a meteor over the Bigler Field roof and onto the street outside.

While the Giants did win the sixth game, 6–4, the attention was now squarely on the kid from Pleasant Valley, whose performance was matching all the hype about him. When "Samson" Gibson came back to Yankee Stadium for the two concluding doubleheaders, the crowds rose to nearly twenty thousand. And on September 27, he hit two more homers—numbers four and five in the series. It was the second one that became metaphoric, the one that baptized his myth.

What invests this one at bat with its mythic virtues is its mystery. Like so many of his other homers, it was documented only in passing and almost diffidently in the black press. It is fact that Josh hammered one, with two men on, off curveball pitcher Connie Rector in the first inning of game two (his four-bagger in the first game, which was overshadowed by a four-run ninth-inning Lincoln rally to pull out the game 9–8, was apparently run-of-the-mill) and that the ball rose and rose into a darkening sky, then came to rest somewhere far over the left field fence.

By the time the weekly black papers hit the stands, however, the next day's doubleheader had been played. Thus, the angle in the game stories was that the Grays, in splitting the two twin bills, had copped the series six games to four. The next-biggest angle was that Billy Holland, having won the opener on Sunday, had tried to make the series a draw by pitching the second game as well, and had held the Grays to one run over seven innings before shoddy fielding cost him the game. Given runners on base to deliver, Josh, who would wind up hitting .368 in the series, then put the game out of reach by doubling home two runs in the eighth and the Grays won, 5–2.

As well, Pop Lloyd wrote a touching last hurrah to his black ball career by collecting three hits in that game, and the *New York Amsterdam News* went heavy on this theme, reporting that "Lloyd . . . went down fighting. Oldtimers who have watched [Lloyd] play for years, say they never saw him play better than in this series."

It took the *Amsterdam News* seven paragraphs to get around to Gibson's titanic shot of the day before, with its brief mention of Gibson's home run flying 460 feet into the left field bleachers and the addendum that the blast outdistanced any other hit at Yankee Stadium "by any player, white or colored, all season."

According to the *Courier*'s rather sedate coverage, in which the blow wasn't mentioned until paragraph seventeen, "Josh Gibson made the longest home run wallop of the year in Yankee Stadium when he hit into the leftfield bleachers, a distance of over four hundred thirty feet, with two on the bases, in the first inning."

These are the only printed accounts of what would in years to come become the black ball shot heard round the world, though by then it would be heard only as an echo, mainly in the vaporous recollections of those who were at Yankee Stadium that day. Some, like Judy Johnson, obviously a practiced fabulist, swore that the ball cleared the roof and never was seen again.

A clear consensus of witnesses, however, has jelled around the rendering that the ball's trajectory did not take it into the bleachers at all. Rather, it was hit so hard it curled as it rose and veered sharply around the edge of the third tier, and came down against the back of the visitor's bull pen behind the left field fence. That would have made it a 500-foot concussion.

As for Josh, he apparently preferred to let the myth of the blow grow without stroking it himself. "I hit the ball on a line into the bull pen in deep left field," he confirmed succinctly in a 1938 interview. At other times, as the distance of the homer would stretch to 600 feet and beyond in other people's conversations, he would smile and tell them that if that's what they believed, he would not argue the point. This was one riff that would play well by itself.

Cum Posey, who of course had gained much by Josh's two-week rampage, now owned a plausible championship and an ego as large as Forbes Field. And while the *Courier* had aggrandized him for years, now it anointed him. The paper's sports editor, Chester Washington, penned an end-of-season epilogue in the October 11 edition that practically cooed in Posey's ear.

"Never before in the history of the popular local club has it operated on such a 'national frequency' as this season," Washington wrote.

> And probably never before [has] Cum Posey been able to gather together in Gray uniforms a greater galaxy of brilliant stars. . . .
> By their achievement, the Homesteaders have reflected credit not only upon themselves but upon the entire city. . . . The 1930 Grays were without a doubt . . . the most brilliant Negro team ever to cavort around a diamond-shaped arena.

Now courtiers were popping up all around Posey. The sandlot league that had spawned Josh Gibson, the Greater Pittsburgh Industrial League, made Posey its commissioner, and for Posey this was an even greater tap into the local talent pool for the Grays.

In his broadening vision, Posey likely saw himself in the emperor's tunic once worn by Rube Foster. Just as Foster had not satisfied his lust for power by making the local Chicago turf his private kingdom, booking and taking a cut of semi-pro games played in that city, Posey was now looking beyond the sandlots and concrete hills of Pittsburgh. With the Grays as his instrument, he gazed across the expanse of black ball and wanted all of it to come to him for guidance.

The problem for Posey was that, in certain black ball circles, he was considered a pariah, having earned a reputation as an arrogant and ruthless man and as one not to be trusted. And while that description also suited many of his peers, Posey's independent course was seen by other owners as a stubborn refusal to try and reach an accommodation that would benefit the entire black game. That utopian ideal had been Foster's aim in creating the Negro National League, the by-laws of which forbade league owners from raiding other teams.

But Posey, who had a long memory and a thirst for retribution, never got over the raids on his team in the 1910s. He spent the twenties seemingly in a looting frenzy, all but debilitating the Hilldale Club in the process. Posey even offered a public endorsement of such larceny in the *Courier* in 1926, coyly writing that any Grays player "who desires a change to another club is free at all times to change, and any good player . . . in either league will be offered a contract when the Grays' management feels they need this player."

Posey's actions sparked bitter verbiage in the black papers that reflected black ball's regional chauvinism. In 1926, sportswriter Romeo Dougherty pilloried Posey in the *Amsterdam News*. "They say he spends half of his time copping or trying to cop players from other teams to help strengthen the Grays," Dougherty wrote. "Posey has been a menace to sport ever since the day the bug of being a big promoter entered his brain."

The *Courier*'s William G. Nunn issued a blunt riposte threatening more Posey raids: "Watch yourselves, you Easterners. 'Tis a long alley that doesn't have an ashcan in it somewhere, and if Posey comes East, he'll not return empty-handed."

Posey had other reasons for navigating in the free waters between the two Negro leagues. Prime among them was his loathing for the influence of white promoter Nat Strong. Posey also wanted to assume the role of power broker himself, though he refused to play league teams anywhere but on his own turf, at Forbes Field, a proposition rejected by both leagues.

Still, seeing that he would need allies in the game, Posey

tried to mend fences in 1929. He put the Grays into the American Negro League, which had been reconstituted from the remains of the Eastern Colored League. Posey may have foreseen that the ANL would not last long, and the Grays' undistinguished record against league teams hardly vouched for his commitment to the circuit.

In any case, when the league died after the season, Posey felt he had paid his dues to black ball; the Grays, back on their own, then creamed those same teams all through the 1930 season as Posey continued to formulate plans for his own league.

In early March 1931, Posey presumed to advise the black game on its future course. Given his own *Courier* column called "The Sportive Realm," he wrote that "the 1931 base-ball season among the colored clubs of the nation has never had a more dreary outlook" and he called for black ball men to "desert the smallness which has stood out so prominently in past years."

In Posey's vision, a new unified structure would have to be big league in all respects. It must outlaw age-old Negro league bugaboos such as white umpires, hooliganism by players and fans, unbalanced schedules, and white booking agents. Posey proposed that such a new order be headed by men "with much knowledge of all things concerned with the operation of big-time baseball." Nobody who read these words had to guess whom Posey had in mind.

In the meantime, Posey let the matter percolate until the Negro National League petered out in midseason, leaving black ball with no "big league" for the first time in a dozen years. But 1931 saw another black ball development, one that Cum Posey couldn't have figured would have an effect on his power games or on his players. This was the entrance of Gus Greenlee.

After lurking in the shadows for three years, Greenlee had now learned enough black professional baseball that he felt ready to get more involved; up 'til now his primary use for a ball team was as a trough to hide his numbers-running profits (said to be around $25,000 a day) from the government and to scratch the back of one of his political cronies on the Hill, Republican state senator James Coyne.

The first time the Pittsburgh Crawfords took the field in 1931 under the aegis of Greenlee, Coyne was running for county commissioner and the back of the Crawfords uniforms were stitched with the lettering COYNE FOR COMMISSIONER.

But by now, Greenlee had become enamored of the example of Cum Posey's Grays and how that kind of fame could feed his own ego and power, not just on the Hill but in the growing domain of black ball. In fact, even though they appeared to come from different sides of the tracks, when Greenlee looked at Posey he recognized many of his own qualities.

Clearly, he had to look below the surface. Where Greenlee bootlegged beer, Posey banned it from his clubhouse. Where Greenlee dressed his immense frame in snazzy silk suits and spats and seemed to have a Havana cigar surgically implanted in his mouth, the gaunt Posey, for all his hidden vices, maintained a facade of prim, understated dignity. Photos taken of Posey show a craggy-faced, unsmiling man pondering the weight of the world, whereas a beaming Greenlee lit up his black-and-white glossies with an unmistakable urge to show off.

But as Greenlee perceived, they were kinsmen under the skin, with strikingly similar family trees. Each had Caucasian blood in his lineage and had light enough skin to conceivably pass for white; Gus's bright orange hair won him the nickname "Big Red" early on.

Each man had a father of distinction. Posey's ran coal and shipbuilding companies in Homestead and had once been president of the *Courier*. Greenlee's was a contractor in Marion, North Carolina, and his firm had built the county courthouse. All of their sons attended college, and Cum Posey was an outstanding athlete at Holy Ghost College (now Duquesne University) and Penn State before playing with the Grays. He eventually took over as the team's manager and co-owner in the early twenties and soon began to overshadow the Grays' titular owner, black businessman Charles Walker, a randy, hard-drinking playboy who was generally too hung over to make club decisions.

The difference between the young Posey and Greenlee was that Gus was too itchy for the staid conventions of academia. He dropped out of a black college in North Carolina in 1916 and came to Pittsburgh, where he juggled jobs as a fireman, undertaker, and cabdriver. When he returned from a hitch in the army in World War I, during which he was wounded in St.-Mihiel in France, he used his cab in service to the local gin runners. Making the right friends within the Hill's mob families and earning a reputation for making enemies disappear from sight, he later opened his own speakeasies, which attracted the elite among crooked politicians, judges, ward heelers, and cops, as well as top showbiz acts like Duke Ellington's big band.

Sometime around the mid-1920s, Greenlee began to notice that the black ballplayers, who regularly came to his nightclub, the Crawford Grille on Wylie Avenue, were being treated as regally by the crowds as many of the jazzmen and blues singers the club staged. This was Gus's first hint that sports could be a useful tool. Craving association with the scene, he edged into the affairs of the Crawfords, but it wasn't until Cum Posey became man of the year in black Pittsburgh that Gus realized the potential glory attached to baseball.

In the winter of 1931, Greenlee filed ownership papers that officially put him in charge of the Crawfords. By this move, as Hooks Tinker and the other players learned, the Crawfords were transformed into a mercenary enterprise.

"We came in and Gus told us, 'I'm gonna make you professional ballplayers; I'm gonna put you under contract,'"

Tinker recalled. "It was gonna be eighty dollars a month, which was really nothing; over on the Grays they were makin' a hundred and twenty. But we found out why. Gus was savin' his pennies to buy up all the best ballplayers."

By opening day, in fact, the transformation of the old bath-house gang into a rising black ball contender was done. Though Tinker was a pro, he was out as manager, replaced by a Greenlee import, veteran second baseman Bobby Williams—who had begun his career with Rube Foster's Chicago American Giants in 1918—from the Bacharach Giants of Atlantic City.

Other new Crawford hands included Sam "Lefty" Streeter, a squat spitball pitcher who had once been in the Birmingham Black Barons' rotation with Satchel Paige; St. Louis Stars infielder John Henry "Pistol" Russell; Memphis Red Sox shortstop Chester Williams; and outfielder Jimmie Crutchfield and catcher Bill Perkins, both by way of Birmingham. Greenlee also went out and got a Smokey Joe Williams of his own, forty-year-old pitcher Dick "Cannonball" Redding, who began his career with the Lincoln Giants in 1911.

The Crawfords, playing the same schedule of mostly semi-pro opponents, began the season on a high, as Lefty Streeter hurled a no-hitter against the Book Shoe team. But Greenlee was antsy to move the team up in class and contacted Cum Posey about a second Crawfords-Grays game. Posey, dealing as imperiously with Greenlee as he had with Hooks Tinker, struck up the same bargain. The game would be made provided that Seward Posey would again be permitted to step into the team's affairs as business manager. Greenlee, just as eager to learn the ropes of the black ball money game as Tinker was, readily agreed, and two games were set between the teams.

When the first game was played in early June at Forbes Field, the Grays spanked Streeter as Posey's newest pickup, Willie Foster, whom he had stolen from the American Giants, blanked the Crawfords on five hits and won, 9–0.

Now Greenlee's plans were at a crossroads. Another Grays-Crawfords match had already been scheduled for July 18, and another blowout would expose the Crawfords as a team of odds and ends, led by a prima donna reaching for too much too soon.

This fear of not being taken seriously may have been the impetus that created, in Gus Greenlee, baseball's most ravenous appetite. And what Gus felt he needed to be a player on the black ball scene was grade-A sirloin on his plate, in two courses: both of black ball's fastest-rising stars.

5

The Revenge
of Big Red

Gus Greenlee used to carry hundred-dollar bills in his pockets. He had so much money he didn't know how much he had. But he sure knew what to do with it.
—JUDY JOHNSON

Josh Gibson, who by some reports had hit .367 with six homers in thirty-two games against pro black teams in his rookie season, kept his word to financially support his children. But beyond the periodic visit to James and Margaret Mason's home to drop off the cash, he maintained his distance, even during the off season of 1931. In lieu of affordable living quarters, he reluctantly lived at home, with Mark and Nancy Gibson and his brother and sister, although he saw little of them when he worked the late shift in the mines after running the elevator at Gimbel's all day.

For Josh, idle time was the enemy, not only because of his overwound inner spring but because of his aversion to thinking about family, or families, either the one in Pleasant Valley or the one on the Hill, where his two children had grown into toddlers. Still grieving for Helen, he was apparently unable to see the children without also seeing her before his eyes. Even years later, when Josh Jr. thought back as far as he could, he could not remember an instant when he had been cradled in his father's arms or had sat on his knee.

This off season would be the last one Josh would allow to disrupt a life he intended to be defined and dominated by baseball; in the future, he would make the seasons endless by extending them in the seductive winter baseball markets in California and in the Caribbean. That way, there would be less time to confront the open wounds of his private life.

Never did he feel that kind of pain on the ball field. When the Grays opened the new season, he was a fixture, a man who could send a swell of anticipatory excitement through the stands as he stepped into the batter's box. That Josh was still batting sixth, and even seventh at times, indicates just how anomalous it was that a nineteen-year-old was even in this lineup at all, much less becoming its hub, though Buck Ewing certainly recognized the omens. He retired in 1931, leaving the catching exclusively to Josh.

Cum Posey, still refusing to keep his hands off other black ball rosters, had fortified the Grays by bringing outfielder Ted Page and third baseman Jud "Boojum" Wilson to Homestead from the Baltimore Black Sox. Two of the best hitters around, these men also had two of the more volatile tempers, especially Wilson. Reminiscent of the young Oscar Charleston's melee in Indianapolis, Wilson once punched an umpire in Baltimore and was arrested and thrown into a paddy wagon, where cops had to bludgeon him with billy clubs to subdue him.

Wilson was liable to snap at anything and anyone, even those who wore the same uniform. When he arrived in Homestead, he got into an argument with the Grays tiny shortstop Jake Stephens in a hotel room. Wilson ended it by picking Stephens up by his heels and dangling him out the window. Page, who was almost as thin skinned, picked a fight with his new teammate that year, George Scales, while the two were in the shower after a game. Scales, fitting right into the Grays' motif of mayhem, ran to his locker and pulled out a knife before the battle was broken up—by, of all people, a peacemaking Boojum Wilson.

Like most of the Grays, these men could turn their near-psychotic rages into productive deeds on the field. And if the Grays were superb in 1930, they may have been even better in 1931. As for Josh, he wasted no time in reprising his rookie fireworks. In an early-season three-game sweep of the St. Louis Stars, the last Negro National League champs, Josh owned the final game, going 4-for-5, including a double. A week later, he got three hits as the Grays laid waste to the semipro Pennsylvania Railroad team from Cleveland, 24–3. Then came a 3-for-3 game, with a double and triple, in a 15–4 win against the Viscose team of Parkersburg, West Virginia.

In May, when the Grays again journeyed to the Midwest, they routed the pro Cincinnati Tigers, winning three straight by scores of 10–4, 8–1, and 8–0. In those games, box scores showed Josh with three doubles, a triple, and a homer. In two wins in late June against the Hilldale team, he had a double and homer.

These games can be taken as a barometer of the Grays' season, in performance and in the spectrum of the competition. And yet Gibson's raw power and growing status—by the Hilldale series he had been installed in the cleanup spot in the order—had become such a routine story now that it nearly ceased being a story. Seldom did his name creep into the headlines; more often, toward the end of its game stories, the *Courier* would tack on vague, seemingly obligatory references stating that Gibson's slugging had been the highlight of the game. In July, for example, the paper ran the rather tepid blurb that "Gibson, the hustling young catcher of the Grays, showed the fans that he has plenty of stuff behind the plate and at bat as well."

This apparent downsizing applied not only to Josh but to the Grays in general, to the dismay of Cum Posey, who regularly flooded the *Courier* sports department with updates of his team's alleged won-lost record and Gibson's home run totals. Yet now, the paper his father had once served as president and that had blown kisses to Posey only months before seemed to lose interest in the Grays' appropriately colorless, machinelike perfection. By early July, with the second Crawfords-Grays tilt days away, the *Courier* began pumping the other baseball story in town, Gus Greenlee's intriguing Crawfords.

Which is just what Greenlee craved. Despite the 9–0 loss to the Grays earlier in the season, Greenlee had been working hard to establish the Crawfords as a spunky alternative to Posey's team. Faced with the city's midnight curfew law, which stopped some long, exciting slugfests and pitching duels dead in their tracks, Greenlee began some ball games at 12:01 A.M., which, because they technically took place in a brand-new day, got around the curfew. This cute and perfectly legal ploy drew packed houses at Ammon Field.

Pondering those crowds, Gus yearned for more seats and a ballpark befitting a top gate attraction. And so, in 1931, construction began on new home grounds with a permanent lighting system for the Crawfords, to be called Greenlee Field, on Bedford Avenue. This project, which would cost Greenlee $100,000, was a tribute to his broad view of black ball and his imprimatur on the Hill.

As exalted as Cum Posey was, for Greenlee there was a lesson, several lessons, to be learned from the Grays' lack of a ball field. Despite its pretensions of self-dependence, black ball was lagging in the area of property ownership; no black team owned the title to a stadium, and even Rube Foster had done no better in Chicago than to make a deal allowing him to retain rights to the grandstand of Schorling Park, not the entire grounds, which were controlled by Chicago White Sox owner Charles Comiskey.

Greenlee, seeing himself at the epicenter of a historic first, could also see why it was worth the financial risk to build his own ballpark. While the Grays drew fairly well at Forbes Field, which was in the Oakdale section east of the Hill, Posey's team had a tenuous local flavor and relationship with the black community. Posey, who had political connections in Homestead and could have easily gotten a permit to build a field there, seemed unwilling to put any money he made back into the community. Thus, while the Grays' popularity was miles wide, it was no more than ankle deep on its own turf.

Greenlee, who could make living things move on the Hill, moved a few unliving things to make his ballpark a reality. He secured a tract of land being used as a graveyard, had the bodies dug up and relocated, and accepted no delays in the project. Greenlee Field, it was announced, would be ready early in the 1932 season.

In the meantime, Gus worked to undercut Posey's influence in the black press, while at the same time buffing his own image. That spring, John L. Clark, who had written glowingly of the bathhouse Crawfords in the *Courier,* had moved to the black *Pittsburgh American* and was preparing a series of articles about the city's numbers rackets, which of course would include Greenlee's involvement. When Greenlee's snoops informed him of the impending articles, he moved in, not with goons but greenbacks. Abruptly, Clark moved again, to the West Penn News Service, a black news syndicate, the offices of which happened to be in a building owned by Greenlee. The articles never ran, and an appreciative Gus struck up what would become a long and useful relationship with Clark.

Whether by Greenlee's influence or because the Crawfords were, as always, a good story, by the time of the second Grays-Crawfords game of 1931, which had been rescheduled to be played on August 6 because of a rainout, the *Courier* seemed to be siding with Greenlee's boys. The Crawfords, reported the July 18 edition, have not forgotten the drubbing the Grays gave them. Instead of being downcast over their setback, the Crawfords are as cocky as ever and still hold the impression that they are capable of beating the Poseymen.

The Crawfords immediately dismissed all thoughts of the setback at the Grays' hands and plunged into another winning streak which has assumed gigantic proportions, so that their followers are looking for them to make a much better showing in the second game than they did in the first.

The rivalry between the clubs is as intense as ever, so that the game on Saturday evening is going to be just as hot as the clubs can make it. One thing the Crawfords can be depended upon to do, is to present a scrappy brand of baseball. The players and the management alike believe they are equally as good as the Grays.

Another helpful item, billboarding a charity game, touted "Gus Greenlee's fast-stepping Crawfords, managed by Bobby Williams, who, in the days immediately after the war, ranked as the greatest colored fielding shortstop in the business. . . . [The Crawfords] are going to give their patrons a real treat and at the same time help sweet charity."

The charity case the *Courier* seemed to be trying to help was Greenlee, since ticket sales for the game lagged. Indeed, Gus now realized a victory wasn't the only thing necessary to make the Crawfords profitable enough to cover that $100,000 tab for Greenlee Field. Almost right up until game time, he was pursuing his prime show dog: Satchel Paige.

Gus had homed in on Paige from the start, and his other player pickups were meant to pave the way for the great pitcher to come to Pittsburgh, since Paige had played with Lefty Streeter, Jimmie Crutchfield, and Bill Perkins in Birmingham. As Gus found out, though, getting him was no easy matter.

Paige was something of an outlaw, and proud of it. Notorious for playing fast and loose with signed contracts and for making decisions on a whim, he was also out of the loop most of the time; he'd play weekday games for semipro teams in the sticks on a one-shot basis for a cut of the gate and come back to his Negro league team for the more heavily attended weekend games.

Born in Mobile, Alabama, the lanky Paige had rarely pitched north of the Mason-Dixon Line, and his reputation seemed to be based more on word of mouth than documented achievement. He began his career in 1926 for the semipro Chattanooga Black Lookouts before moving to the Negro National League's Birmingham Black Barons for the next four years, and then the Nashville Elite Giants in 1931. While in Nashville, he carried on a secretive affair of the heart, incredibly, with the wife of the team's owner, Tom Wilson, a black numbers racketeer who would become one of black ball's most respected leaders. Rumors had it that Wilson knew of the liaison and put up with it in order to keep Paige on his team.

When dwindling crowds forced the team to attempt a soon aborted relocation in Cleveland in 1932, however, Greenlee's agents came after Paige. They offered him $300 a month, which for Paige was double his salary, though he made his real money from his outside gigs. Finally, in early August, the deal was done. Paige drove his overburdened roadster to Pittsburgh, arriving on August 6, the day of the Grays-Crawfords game, but too late for Bobby Williams to be able to start him or for the papers to report his signing.

This made for a strange, expectant atmosphere at Forbes Field that overshadowed the game. Only about five thousand people showed up for another act of the rivalry that had lost its novelty, and as word filtered through the stands that Satchel Paige was a Crawford, necks craned as fans tried to spot him on the field. Paige, however, remained out of sight in the shade of the dugout, while Harry Kincannon faced the Grays' Ted Radcliffe on the mound.

Even without Paige, the Crawfords were indeed a different team. They roughed up Radcliffe and led 8–2 going into the fourth. Stunned, the Grays woke up and charged back with five runs in that inning, cutting the lead to 8–7 and chasing Kincannon. With no one out, Kincannon walked off the mound and the long, lean figure of Satchel Paige ambled onto the field to an eruption of noise when his name was announced on the loudspeaker.

From this moment, and for the next half decade, Paige owned black ball in Pittsburgh, even when he wasn't there, which was often. With his unearthly fastball melting the edges of the plate and never straying over its heart, he dispatched one Gray hitter after another. "I've often said that Satchel threw aspirin tablets that day, because he threw 'em small, man," Hooks Tinker said, smiling. "That's what his pitches looked like. He didn't have no change-up or anything. He didn't need it. He used an underhanded fastball as a change-up."

Whiffing six in five innings—Josh, in his first look at Paige, went 0-for-2—and getting credit for the win when the Craws put up three in the sixth, Paige prevailed, 11–7. The *Courier,* grateful to have the hip icon in town, hailed his Steel City debut as "magnificent and sensational." Similar hyperbole in the black press would greet just about every move he would make in and out of Pittsburgh over the next decade and a half.

For Hooks Tinker, the victory over the Grays was a rush that could not be equaled. But it would be short lived. As soon as Gus Greenlee got a taste of success, he wasted little time freeing the Crawfords of their lunch-pail legacy. After the game, Gus told his players he wanted only full-timers on board.

"Let me say that Gus Greenlee was a fine man, a gentleman," Tinker said. "He was a generous guy, and he didn't force me out. But when he gave us an ultimatum to quit our jobs or give up baseball, well, I was workin' as a head shipper for the RKO motion picture company, making eighty dollars a month there, just like with the Crawfords. But I couldn't chance giving up that job, because with baseball you never knew what would happen. So I had to quit. But I felt I went out on top of the world."

For Cum Posey, the unexpected loss to the Crawfords was the only setback in an otherwise charmed season. A day after the game, it was business as usual, as the Grays beat the semi-pro Dormont club, 8–1, and Josh collected two doubles. A day after that, he had five hits, including a triple and a homer, in a 16–2 laugher against Oakhurst.

At no time did Posey stop to reconsider his position in regard to Gus Greenlee and the Crawfords. But soon enough, Cum Posey was going to pay up for underestimating Big Red.

For now, Posey pushed ahead with his plans for a first-class Negro league. In early 1932, he had enlisted seven teams to join the Grays in the East-West League: the Hilldale Club, the Baltimore Black Sox, the Newark Browns, the Washington Pilots, the Cleveland Stars, the Midwest Cuban Stars, and the Detroit Wolves (which Posey also owned).

One team that wanted in was Greenlee's Crawfords. Having proven that it belonged on the same field with the Grays, Gus eagerly petitioned for entry into the league. This gave Posey a chance to pull rank once again with the Craws. Although his league could have used an attraction that had Satchel Paige on its roster, Posey may have been scared that such an attraction might eclipse his own. Thus, Posey laid out terms for the Crawfords' entry that all but ensured that they would stay away.

According to these terms, Posey would have had the right not only to set the Crawfords' league schedule but *all* their games, against pros and semipros, and to place a $2,400 salary cap on Greenlee's spending. Posey would also move players off the Crawford roster as he saw fit in order to bolster other league teams. Finally, See Posey would have to be promoted to field manager.

Attempting to preempt any flak that he was acting in a heavy-handed fashion, Posey said the terms were warranted because See Posey, not Gus Greenlee, had made the Crawfords viable. "The real truth," Posey claimed in his *Courier* column, "is that in 1931, when the Crawfords were floundering around looking for games, I lent them the services of my brother Seward to book games for them."

Greenlee, though, was having none of it and, probably as Posey knew he would, dropped his bid. The Crawfords remained an independent, which bought Posey's team exclusivity in Pittsburgh and a serenity that he hoped would not be disturbed by Greenlee. As the driving force behind the new league, Posey presumed to set himself up as a one-man high council. He announced in the *Courier* the members of the Cum Posey All-Star Team, and his choices in what would become an annual black ball liturgy were given much weight.

The inaugural team looked like this: first base, Oscar Charleston (Pittsburgh); second base, Newt Allen (Kansas City); shortstop, Dick Lundy (Baltimore); third base, Boojum Wilson (Homestead); outfield, Cool Papa Bell (Pittsburgh), Mule Suttles (St. Louis), Martin Dihigo (Hilldale), Deke Mothel (Kansas City); pitchers, Satchel Paige (Pittsburgh), Willie Foster (Chicago), Lefty Streeter (Pittsburgh), Smokey Joe Williams (Homestead), Ted Radcliffe (Homestead), Pud Flournoy (Baltimore), Charles Beverly (Kansas City). And at catcher there was Josh Gibson, who Posey told his readers and all of black ball had hit seventy-five home runs and batted over .600 in 1931.

All the groundwork of his self-coronation in place, Posey approached the East-West League's first season with every base covered, or so he believed. He drew up a balanced schedule, put umpires on monthly salary, hired an outside statistics bureau to keep records, and even arranged for a network of black radio stations to broadcast some games.

But for all of Posey's attention to detail, his broad view of black ball was myopic, and his league was as doomed as the Negro National League and the Eastern Colored League. The ravages of the Depression, of course, put the league in a hole right off. But Posey also woefully misjudged the ability of this lineup of teams to afford even minimal operating expenses. Posey was so eager to get off the ground that he ignored the terminal condition of the Hilldale Club—which he had helped to bankrupt—as well as the nonexistent track record of every team save his own, Baltimore, and the Cuban Stars.

Worse, if Posey hoped to make a statement of purpose about racial purity, he fell into the same snare that Rube Foster and Ed Bolden had tripped with their leagues' relationships with white booking agents. While Posey despised the New York booker Nat Strong—a man who openly stated that no black ballplayer was worth paying more than $75 a month—he soon discovered that, with the Lincoln Giants now out of business, writing off Strong meant his league would have no presence northeast of Darby, Pennsylvania.

Looking around the black ball map, Posey was aghast to find that most of the successful teams had even more direct connections to white men and white money than the New York teams had to Strong. Needing thriving teams, Posey suddenly modified his vigilance about race and embraced white owners such as the Baltimore Black Sox' George Rossiter and Charles Spedden.

These men had drawn ire in the black press for some astonishing statements and business practices. They refused to hire blacks to work in the front office or in the stands at the team's ballpark because, as Rossiter said, he had "not found them satisfactory in the rapid handling of change," and because of them the team was "most always short when the count-up is made." Incredibly, Rossiter and Spedden kept a section of the stands open to special reservations for white fans.

To some black ball observers, worse crimes were being committed by the white owner of the Cuban Stars, Syd Pollock, a New York promoter. The Cubans players were actually black men instructed not to admit it—a method of operation common in black ball in the 1800s but antithetical to the cause of black nationalism with which Posey was identified. The Cubans would chirp and babble and generally act like jungle creatures when they took the field—the *Courier* called them "monkeys" and "a collection of chattering jackasses." Indeed, this team displayed the sort of stereotypical behavior Posey would not have been able to stomach but for the personal prestige he had staked in his league.

In time Posey was forced to make room for Nat Strong after all, though not openly. Strong's booking agency had taken in a Philadelphia promoter named Eddie Gottlieb, who owned property rights to that city's bush league ball yards, as a partner. Gottlieb, whose major claim to fame was an ethnic semipro basketball team, the South Philadelphia Hebrew Stars, or Sphas, refused to employ blacks in the city's basketball leagues that he served as commissioner. He also charged a 10 percent commission on all-black baseball games at his stadiums, double his fee for white semipro contests. But Posey could not give up the Philadelphia market and risk losing the Hilldale team.

Furthermore, a new black ball team in New York, the Black Yankees, had been formed by the great black tap dancer Bill "Bojangles" Robinson in 1932, and many of their Sunday games were to be played at Yankee Stadium. Posey, craving games against the Black Yankees on nonleague dates, was now prepared to kick back some of the Grays' gate receipts to Nat Strong, who booked the Black Yankees games. So, while Strong was not allowed official entree to the EWL high council, he was present and accounted for anyway in Posey's new world.

Caught in these maddening incongruities, Posey's legendary acumen was nearly ruined among black ball people. In fact, by the time the East West League was up and ready to run, Posey had already lost a good bit of altitude, dragged down by Gus Greenlee, who struck right at Posey's heart. His weapon of choice: money. His main target: Josh Gibson.

• • •

Just after New Year's Day 1932, Greenlee struck like a bar-
racuda. He began by lifting Oscar Charleston, who became
the Crawfords player-manager, and Ted Page, each of whom
he offered $100 a month more than Posey had paid them.
This wasn't small change, since they had been making around
$500 a month. At that rate, which was more than any other
black ball owner could afford, Gus was able to secure a who's
who of the black game; next came Judy Johnson, Cool Papa
Bell, Pistol Russell, Ted Radcliffe, and Rev Cannady. All this,
though, simply set the table for the main course.

In early February, Cum Posey called twenty-one-year-old
Josh Gibson into his office to sign a contract for 1932. This
was routine business and Josh signed for $150 a month, a
$25 increase from the year before. However, the very next
day, Greenlee rang up Josh and offered him $250 a month.
His head in a spin, Josh, either out of naivete or deceit, ne-
glected to tell Gus about his Grays contract, on which the ink
was still not dry. It was loony even by Negro league standards, but Gibson took pen in hand and endorsed his second
contract in two days.

Posey was justifiably livid but had to know his case was se-
verely crimped by the anarchy he had helped foster in black
ball when it came to the heavy traffic between teams. Because
of arrogant men like Posey, the black game could never have
instituted a major league–like reserve clause in their contracts,
binding players to their teams for life or until traded, with a
straight face. In effect, all the players were free agents, by
order of their owners.

Posey could have chosen to take Gibson to court, but his
dilemma was plain: if Gibson didn't want to be a Gray, he
couldn't be compelled to be one. Posey also didn't want to
alienate Gibson, nor did he need the cost of a court battle.
Thus, Posey tried to tactfully shame Josh into changing his
mind, preferring to believe he had been misled.

Posey's forum was his *Courier* column, which was now

being syndicated to many black newspapers. Gibson, he wrote, choosing his words with care, was "induced" to sign with the Crawfords, likely by pitcher Roy Williams, who had recently done so. "As Gibson is very young, he is easily advised [and had been] poorly advised."

If Posey intended to come across to Josh as a gently rebuking father figure, he evidently failed to realize that that role had already been taken by both Oscar Charleston and Judy Johnson, whose defections were crucial to Greenlee's Gibson strategy.

When Gibson failed to respond, Posey talked tougher, threatening that if Josh didn't honor his Grays contract, "he will not play in Pittsburgh [in 1932]. Today, baseball is a business. It is time an example was made of a few players who have no respect for their signed obligations but will jump to any club for a few dollars more."

Posey, who must have felt sheepish writing those words, knew how empty this threat was. He also had to know he could only come out a loser in his town if he somehow exiled Josh Gibson. Instead of making good on his threat, when Josh left for the Crawfords spring training camp in Hot Springs, Arkansas, in mid-February—accompanied by a large *Courier* headline reading CRAWFORD VANGUARD OFF FOR HOT SPRINGS; JOSH GIBSON, RADCLIFFE DEPART—Posey changed tactics and trained his column's fire on Gibson's new boss.

Posey had until now trod lightly on the matter of Gus Greenlee, either out of respect for, or fear of, Gus's gangland reputation or out of disdain for him as a baseball man. But now he went on the record with his outrage that a "numbers man" had edged into the black ball picture. Posey also revealed the story of John L. Clark's remarkable conversion from investigative reporter hard on Greenlee's tail to a Greenlee employee at West Penn News Service. "Clark had to be put someplace to keep his mouth shut," Posey bluntly wrote.

Greenlee, suddenly feeling very smug, brushed off Posey's attacks. He wrote to the *Courier* defending his signings on the grounds that, given his expansive new stadium, "it was obvious that we must have the best attractions which Negro club owners could produce. . . . I sincerely believe that you or any person with a $100,000 investment on his hands would make the very same decisions which I made." Greenlee also detailed the onerous conditions Posey had placed on the Crawfords' entry into the EWL. Posey, he said, "forced me to believe that I was about to enter a trap from which there would be no escape."

With these mortar shots, Greenlee declared war on Cum Posey. Gus had purchased a $10,000 Mack bus, a six-cylinder, seventy-nine-horsepower twenty-two-seater with vacuum booster brakes and a top cruising speed of sixty miles per hour. Painted black-and-white, it had on its side the words PITTSBURGH CRAWFORD BASEBALL TEAM . . . FROM GREEN-LEE FIELD. More accurately, they were from a hole in the ground, since Greenlee Field was not yet built and wouldn't be for many months. Thus, Gus intended these wheels to carry the team on a two-month sabbatical through the hamlets and jerkwater trails of the South, to commence in March 1932. For a baseball novice, this was inspired thinking and a page out of Rube Foster's primer on turning black ball into a nativist tradition. As with the American Giants in the 1910s, the Crawfords would both spread and be the beneficiary of the gospel of baseball and race pride.

A two-column-wide photo of the Mack ran in the February 28 Courier, under the headline CRAWFORDS TO 'CARRY ON' IN THIS BUS, followed a week later by news that the Crawfords would compete in a league after all, the Negro Southern League, an eight-team combine based in the South. Though they were inferior to the good Northern teams, Greenlee, in his first hours as a black ball power broker, arranged for the NSL's members to play games not only in Pittsburgh in 1932 but in Chicago, Indianapolis, and New York.

Leader of men that he was, Gus boarded the bus in early March, sometimes taking the wheel himself, bound for Hot

Springs and points beyond, leaving his numbers business in the hands of his adjutant Woogie Harris until mid-April.

Cum Posey's big ideas turned to dust in 1932, crushed under the weight of mundane realities when the East-West League stumbled out of the blocks. The first bitter pang of reality came when Hilldale—to which Posey had allowed Judy Johnson to return, in the hope that he would lift the fortunes of the club, only to see Judy sign with the Crawfords—drew 910 fans on opening day. Two months later, they were drawing around 200 for Sunday games, 50 for weekday games. Worse, the new Hilldale owner, John Drew, had to tithe 10 percent of the meager income to Eddie Gottlieb. Soon, Drew took the team off salary, rendering the league's pro status a joke. Then, in mid-June, the Hilldale Club went to its grave.

That same month, Posey's Detroit Wolves were also on the ropes. But rather than swallow the loss and funnel their players to other teams to shore them up, a stubborn Posey poured funds and even some Grays players into the Wolves' floundering ship. As a result, with expenses stretched so thin, the losses spread into a leaguewide hemorrhage.

In early July, when the Wolves went under, Posey ordered all players' salaries cut, fired his full-time umpires, and cut a month from the league schedule. Even that was optimistic. In mid-July, Posey had to suspend league play, his experiment in black ball fellowship a dismal failure, and a most expensive one. The Grays, exfoliated by Greenlee's lightning raids, had lost much of their luster and drawing power, and Posey had to squirm as the team trailed the Baltimore Black Sox in the EWL standings all season long. Now, with his assets nearly depleted, Posey had to worry about how he would manage to pay the players he still had.

More humiliating still, when Cum Posey turned his attention back to the local black ball scene in Pittsburgh, he found that Gus Greenlee was running the show.

6

Satch and Josh

Putting them two boys together wasn't only great for black baseball. It was the greatest show on earth.
— HOOKS TINKER

Just as he had planned it, Gus Greenlee lit bonfires in the Crawfords' path during their march through the South— though the flames were held down somewhat by the sudden loss of Josh. Stricken with appendicitis in training camp, he was hospitalized and had to remain in Hot Springs for three weeks while the Craws hit the long road through the heart-land of black America.

And yet the difference between being a Gray and a Craw-ford was highlighted by the press coverage Josh received just lying in his hospital bed. Whereas Gibson's picture had not been seen in the *Courier* since that magical "world series" with the Lincoln Giants in 1930, his likeness appeared—iron-ically, he was still wearing a Grays shirt—in the March 17 edition under a headline reading CONVALESCING and a caption revealing his appendicitis attack.

On the same page, a full schedule for the Negro Southern League was printed, the kind of coverage Cum Posey couldn't buy for his doomed East-West League. And on March 31, a team picture ran, which included Greenlee and his wife, under the heading CRAWFORDS BASKING IN SPA'S SUNLIGHT.

What this showed was that for all of Cum Posey's influence at the *Courier,* Greenlee had primed the pump for the Crawfords on the sports desk. Picking up the tab for the travel expenses of several of the paper's ethically unconcerned sportswriters on the tour, he was guaranteed a ton of favorable notices for even the most obscure of games down South. And just to be sure the coverage would be favorable, Gus arranged for the *Courier* to run a special column by his top press toady, John L. Clark, who ostensibly made the trip for West Penn News Service; Clark, though, had been on Gus's payroll for a year.

Clark would send back reams of vibrant copy about the team, as well as gleanings of the black South that were like a walk through the past for the South's expatriates back home. Clark's first dispatch, on March 31, provided a folksy glimpse into the team's personal side, passing along tidbits like "Sad news breaks into our release this week. [Outfielder] Clyde Spearman's mother was called by the Grim Reaper on March 21," and "Not a few of the visitors wonder how Mrs. McClinton can serve chicken dinner twice each week [to the players at their lodging]. . . . It should be remembered that farm eggs can be bought here for ten cents a dozen." Clark also had an item about the Crawford catcher: "Josh Gibson is being closely watched. He has convalesced to the point where he visits every practice session. While there he busies himself fumbling with the bats, balls and gloves. Just rarin' to go—that's all!"

But Clark's best work was sent from telegraph stations between stops of the Crawford bus excursion. These pieces generally surveyed outposts in the black South, not unlike Buena Vista, Georgia, where the hands of time had refused to budge. In one such homily from Monroe, Louisiana, Clark wrote:

> We observed that the Negro sections in the South can easily be distinguished by railroad sidings and cemeteries. Even the Negro High [School] is on a lot adjacent to a white cemetery. Yet, with all these disadvantages the best equipped drug store we have ever seen is operated by a Negro at the corner of Tenth and Desiard.
>
> Although a visitor to Monroe might say that no compliment should be passed on the way Negroes are huddled together, they seem to get along alright, and enjoy themselves. The cultured stock draw their lines and the people of the "life" operate regularly but not openly. Police make raids only on complaint and the fines are graduated for each offense. Incidentally, the policemen all seem to be over 6 feet high and weigh over 225 pounds.

The long Crawford trip featured games against not only the Negro Southern League but independent pro units like the Texas Wildcats and Houston Black Buffaloes, and nines from Wylie, Bishop, and Texas Colleges. Sometimes the road was rough—against the Black Buffaloes, both Satchel Paige and Lefty Streeter were defeated on successive days, a real rarity. But for the most part, Greenlee's road strategy went perfectly, both on the field and in the newspapers.

As it happened, Greenlee quickly tired of his doings with the Negro Southern League and downshifted the Crawfords' participation in the league to that of an associate member. This meant the Craws could drop from the NSL ranks and play only selected games with the circuit's teams. Relieved of having to prop up the league, and its small-time trappings, the Craws made their way back home in mid-April, capping a journey that covered seventeen thousand miles and ninety-three games.

When they arrived, the *Courier* heralded their return with three Crawfords-related stories on sports page one. As Greenlee had orchestrated it, the absence of the team created more of a thirst to see them, if not yet at the now avidly awaited opening of Greenlee Field, then at the many social functions that included them. One such shindig on the eve of the park's dedication was a black-tie welcome-home dance in the grand ballroom of Princess Hall at Center and Miller Streets on the Hill, which was attended by over one thousand people.

The next day, with Cum Posey's East-West League no more than a rumor in Pittsburgh, not to mention the rest of the league's towns, the party for the Crawfords moved to the club's new digs. Before a full house at Greenlee Field, amid the churning of mortar-mixing machines and bricklayers still putting the place together, nearly five thousand fans saw the Craws defeat the white semipro Vandergrift team.

The real party, though, was reserved for April 30, the date of the park's official opening. The opposition would be Bojangles Robinson's New York Black Yankees, who had beefed themselves up by taking Ted Page away from the Crawfords before the season. Already out $100,000 for the construction and another $6,000 to install a permanent lighting system atop the grandstand roof, Greenlee spared no expense or drama in honoring the stadium and its benefactor.

Clad in a white silk suit, shirt, tie, and buck shoes, Gus entered the park standing inside a red Packard convertible, to the cheers of five thousand people and much of the political establishment of Pittsburgh. There was, of course, Greenlee's patron, James Coyne, along with the other county commissioners. But also paying homage to Big Red were the mayor and the city council. Given the plum of handling the dedication oratory was *Courier* editor Robert Vann, who afterward strode to the mound and tossed the ceremonial first pitch. When the Crawfords took the field, the next person on that mound was Satchel Paige, looking in for the signals from Josh Gibson.

This lavish celebration of civic pride and black entrepreneurial spirit was like a dream for Gus Greenlee and a salve for black ball fans all around the land who had only recently wondered if the black game could survive the Depression and its own missteps. Indeed, this one game—or rather the event that surrounded it—was pivotal to the black game's redemption. If it was boffo as sport and as spectacle, it was even better as a statement of purpose. It was raw, unrepentant capitalism, in which color was incidental.

Gus's example, in fact, would demonstrate the viability of property ownership to all of black ball. The *Courier*'s coverage of Crawfords games from that day forward abounded with reminders that Greenlee Field was the first self-owned black sporting facility in America. And though the ballpark faced an uncertain road, Gus was altogether confident that wherever the black game went, he was going to be its liege.

The game that took place at Greenlee Field that momentous day lived up to the hype of the occasion. For eight crisp innings, Paige and the Black Yankees' Jesse "Mountain" Hubbard kept the hitters quiet, Satch by blowing the ball past the hitters, Mountain by defacing it with the sandpaper he was known to keep in his pocket. Then, in the ninth, Ted Page, knowing that Paige was slow to get into fielding position after uncoiling from his massive windup and delivery, laid down and beat out a bunt. He stole second, and when he kicked the ball out of Chester Williams's glove, went to third; he scored on a scratch hit.

The Craws' last shot at Hubbard came with two outs in the ninth, when Josh stepped in. On a one-and-two count, he crushed a sandpaper pitch to dead center. Clint Thomas, on the run at the crack of the bat, got to the wall just as the ball came down and put it away to seal the 1–0 win, a three-hitter for Hubbard.

Greenlee, drinking in the cascade of publicity despite the loss, kept the momentum going. Now every game at Greenlee

Field would strike the same vibe of self-conscious felicitation. Gus prevailed on his VIP friends to make the scene at the park, and those lucky enough to get a seat were treated to sights on the order of Lena Horne throwing out the first pitch and then singing with the Duke Ellington band in an impromptu gig on the field after the game.

Media coverage of these games stretched beyond the sports pages to the society page and the gossip columns. Who was seen with whom and who was wearing what was common sport at Greenlee Field. And while there was still a hard core of scruffy fans, gamblers, and boozers—and the games themselves were played under no rules of conduct and could degenerate into gang wars on the field at any time—a ticket to the park now required of most fans a shared sense of fashion and social correctness. This was in sharp contrast to the clothes-hamper style of the crowds at many other parks around black ball.

Greenlee could take immense pride that while high society was beating a path to his turnstiles, the black papers were tearing into the managers of Schorling Park in Chicago, which Rube Foster had envisioned as the mecca of a black ball–centered society but which was now a concrete sewer dressed up as a ballpark. The *Chicago Defender* was particularly incensed by "the condition of the women's toilet" there and by fans removing their shirts on hot days. "Men naked to the waist have no place at our baseball games," the paper said. At Greenlee Field, this practice had no place literally and was cause for ejection from the grounds.

Perhaps more than he knew, Greenlee was soldering black culture and sport in ways Foster had only dreamed about, and in ways that certainly boded well for that culture and that sport. Accordingly, Gus could not afford to let his guard down, not while smarter baseball men roamed the black ball earth. Seeing how much the loss of Ted Page had hurt his team, Gus immediately moved to get him back. Only days

after the Black Yankees game, Page returned to the Crawfords and was given a Satchel Paige–like salary of $300 a
month and—contrary to Gus's decree that he wanted only
full-time ballplayers—a supplemental job in Greenlee's numbers racket. For $15 a week, Page had only to keep his eyes
focused.

"They had an old vacant house . . . in Hazlewood . . . a
long space up there [with] tables where they turned in all the
numbers [cash]," Page once told author John Holway. "They
give me a chair [and] my job was to sit right downstairs on
the sidewalk and ring a bell. Anybody who wasn't supposed
to be there, I would just push a button and alert them upstairs
to get rid of all that money."

Since Gus's spies in the police department usually tipped
him off well in advance if a raid was coming, and because
Gus himself scared off possible enemies in the underworld,
Page never had to ring that buzzer. In fact, Gus was far more
concerned about his baseball spoils and losing his players to
raids launched by other black teams. It stood to reason, then,
that he was adamant about keeping Satchel Paige and Josh
Gibson.

In Paige's case, that meant complying with the pitcher's
beyond-arrogant practice of skipping out on his Negro league
club during weekdays and being available on a regular basis
only for weekend games. The first owner forced to accede to
this stipulation had been Birmingham's R. T. Jackson, who
was willing to let Paige stray rather than lose him altogether,
provided Paige shared his cut of the gate from those games in
the sticks. This arrangement, the only one of its kind in the
Negro leagues, was now perpetuated by Greenlee. Indeed,
that Gus could be big about this moonlighting was shown in
September 1931, when he permitted Paige to toss a game
even for Cum Posey's Grays, against the Baltimore Black Sox.

The 1932 edition of the Paige solo tour had a new wrinkle.
During his selected sojourns into the countryside, Satch
would sometimes take Josh with him, thus driving up the

profit percentages all around. The placards that touted these jaunts promised that Paige would strike out the first nine batters and that Gibson would hit three dingers, and are evidence enough that Satch and Josh must have shared a few laughs about the ways of man and hype marketing. For Gibson, in fact, studying at the knee of the great self-promoter was an invaluable education in the art of getting over on the fans.

Clearly, Josh was not in Paige's league when it came to the game of racial merchandising. In retrospect, Paige's slow-motion, bug-eyed performances, complete with double- and triple-whammy windups and his front leg kicking so high that, by his description, "it blocked out the sky," may be interpreted by modern sensibilities as a permutation of Uncle Tomming. Paige's self-named repertoire of pitches was virtually a catalogue of concepts whites could freely associate with blacks; among them were his Trouble Ball, Midnight Creeper, and Hesitation Pitch.

It is also possible that Paige was self-aware enough that he intended his act to be a subliminal send-up of American racial sensibilities, black and white, of the day. This was an era, to be sure, when only the most dim-witted Hollywood movie roles were available to blacks and no one in either the white or the black press had the faintest idea how to portray gifted black athletes with the dignity they deserved. To Paige, the notion of being a showman first and a great athlete second was one he could easily exploit for his own good.

The main thing for Josh was that, even if prodded, he wouldn't have known how to clown it up, nor would he have wasted a moment in thought about what was funny about baseball. He likely would have preferred to return to the suffocating steel mines than be forced into imitating Paige's antic behavior the way too many black teams did in pursuit of Paige's visibility. Luckily for Josh, he was never forced to, since Satch had no intention of making room in his virtuoso routines for another harlequin—his main riff, after all, was having all his fielders, save the essential catcher, leave the field so he could face the hitters *mano a mano*.

For Paige, the riff was really an extension of his life's experiences; from his earliest days, which were spent in unspeakable poverty in Mobile, Alabama, Leroy Paige's mission was to fend for himself in any way he could. As a child he did it by stealing satchels from unsuspecting travelers arriving at the Mobile railroad station, only to earn himself an enduring nickname and a four-year term in a reformatory. While he learned how to behave within the law, he would never escape the conceit that he would get where he wanted to go by making his own rules and guidelines of morality.

In his alienation, of course, Paige was similar to Josh. But there were certain differences. Josh was nowhere as embittered. He also had a greater sense of loyalty to and affinity with his teams. Satch, in fact, had already begun to cause some static in the Crawford clubhouse, though some of it wasn't his fault. As a Southerner among a claque of mostly Northern-bred black men, Paige was the victim of some stereotyping by black teammates because of his geographical roots.

Jake Stephens, the thorny little shortstop for the Crawfords and Grays, who was from York, Pennsylvania, would in time recall Paige as a cloddish man with pedestrian tastes. Decades later, Stephens ripped Paige and others of "those Southern boys" as "clowns." Said Stephens: "They didn't dress the way we dressed, they didn't have the same mannerisms, the same speech. . . . Paige was a big mouth, didn't have any education."

All evidence to the contrary, Stephens insisted, "Satchel Paige is the most overrated ballplayer ever God put breath into." That Paige made the big bucks and men like Jake Stephens didn't made the rift larger, though all Negro-leaguers envied and none begrudged Satch for elevating the black game to a higher level of consciousness among blacks and whites.

Josh was no such cause célèbre. Plainly, he had no misan-
thropic tendencies, and not for a minute was he crude or self-
pitying, which is why no one seemed to know of his personal
heartache. While he was self-absorbed, his outer shell was
pliable, at least when the topic of conversation was kept light.
And so, willingly reduced to Satchel Paige's junior partner on
the caravan, he just played ball and gazed in wonder as Satch
rewrote rules that seemed immutable to black players. When
they were out on the road, Paige would demand and get ac-
commodations in whites-only hotels. Satch seemed unfazed
by the grave hazards of bringing white women into the room
he shared with Josh, though at those times Josh likely was
grateful Satch also brought along his hunting rifles, should
they need protection from the town folk.

Yet it would be a stretch to call Josh and Satch running
mates. Paige, a habitual night crawler, loved the attention he
amassed among strangers in the recesses of dark taverns. But
on those treks with Josh, he crawled alone, as Josh was still
afraid to imbibe, his fear of Nancy Gibson's example still
fresh in his mind. The irony was that Josh probably enjoyed
the company of people, on a human level, more than Paige
but chose to remain aloof, sheltering his painful secrets.

Through the years, these two remarkable men developed a
relationship of sorts out of mutual respect and gain; periodically, they would merrily rag each other, each one boasting he
had the other's number if and when they ever faced each
other in a game. But there was also distance between them,
and Paige even seemed to claim proprietary rights during
some Crawford games, when Satch preferred that his old
crony Bill Perkins catch him, rather than Josh. Gibson would
then play left field or sit out altogether. The explanation for
this has always been that Paige felt more comfortable and
wired in to Perkins, and that may have been. But another
plausible theory is that Paige preferred a caddy giving him
signals, not an equal in terms of crowd appeal. Thus, he
could claim to have drawn the big houses.

"Even though [Gus Greenlee] advertised both Josh and me, Gus knew I was pulling the big crowds," a truculent Paige still insisted in 1961, when he wrote his autobiography. "When I was out there, there'd be a park full watching. But when Josh was there and somebody else was pitching, there'd be only about half or two-thirds as many."

Whatever the level of their relationship, if Josh Gibson learned anything from Satchel Paige it was that rugged, even amoral individualism could pave a path to great reward in baseball. The problem for the kid from Pleasant Valley was that he had neither the street sense nor the toughness in his gut to go down that road alone and know he was headed the right way.

Rounding into shape after his appendicitis attack, Josh gradually regained the twenty pounds he had lost and was ready for Mountain Hubbard in the Greenlee Field opener. Though he went hitless in that game, in the ensuing game against the Black Yankees he had three hits, including a triple, in the Crawfords' 2–1 win.

That he was back in form and more feared than ever was demonstrated in another Black Yankee game. He had already gotten two hits when he came up in the top of the ninth, the Craws trailing 1–0. Connie Rector had held the Craws to five hits. But Rector—who probably still had nightmares of Josh's titanic shot at Yankee Stadium two years earlier when he had pitched for the Lincoln Giants—played it safe and walked him. After moving to third on a Harry Williams hit, Josh scored the tying run on a single by Henry Spearman. In the tenth, with Williams on second and one out, Rector again faced Josh—and again walked him. Rev Cannady then singled to get Williams home to win it.

At this stage, it had become a given that Gibson's name would come up in any discussion of black ball's best hitters. The pitcher Willie Foster, who had returned to the Chicago American Giants, told the *Courier* in 1932, "I like to pitch to such men as Charleston, Cannady and Gibson better than to second-class men, because I know that I've got a real job on my hands." Still, Foster believed he had found the only area where he could pitch to Josh and not allow him to extend his arms. This, he said, was a six-inch slip that could be marked by Gibson's belt buckle. Anything that strayed beyond this zone allowed Josh to uncoil his swing cobralike and get his weight behind. Even if he couldn't extend, of course, this was a man who could muscle a ball into the next state. Thus, pitching him down the middle might have the added compensation of making him hit to the canyon of center field.

This was an especially seductive strategy when pitchers encountered Gibson in spacious ballparks like Forbes Field and Yankee Stadium. And though these two parks had been shrunk to size by some of Josh's more awesome shots, Negro league pitchers—who had to have felt condemned pretty much whatever they tried with Gibson—generally stuck with the book Willie Foster had described. Taking a large gulp, they aimed for that belt buckle and threw the ball at great peril down the alley, knowing that any lazy serve would be pounded.

Buck Leonard, the great Hall of Fame first baseman of the Homestead Grays, who joined that team in 1934, recalled how the Grays aligned their fielders when Gibson came to bat as a Crawford; in tune with the pitchers' down-the-middle strategy, they would play him straightaway, not to pull as they would a typical slugger. "Actually," Leonard said, "we woulda put the center fielder in the bleachers if we could've. Josh could hit a ball five hundred feet to center just going with the pitch. In fact, I never saw Josh try to pull a ball, not a fastball anyway. He wasn't only a great hitter. He was a damn smart hitter."

This was what separated him from most others, in any league. The Kansas City Monarchs second baseman Newt Allen once made this point by comparing Gibson with another Negro league power hitter of the day, third baseman

John Beckwith, who played for twenty years with ten different black ball teams and was reputed to have amassed the kind of bloated home run totals against all levels of competition that Josh did.

"Beckwith never learned to step into [an outside] ball," Allen said. "He'd hit a couple fouls; a smart pitcher would throw one on the outside, he can't reach it, and it's an easy bounce out. That's the reason he was a much easier out than Josh was."

Negro league old-timers talk about Gibson's remarkable discipline at the plate, his accurate batting eye, and his quick wrists as much as his brutish power. Unlike most long ball hitters, he struck out rarely and seemed not to care if the pitchers threw a ball slimed with bodily fluids or worked over with sandpaper. Nor did he have to worry about one being aimed at his ear. "Nobody threw at Josh," said Hooks Tinker, who became a regular in the grandstand at Greenlee Field. "It didn't do no good anyway, and you didn't want to rile him up any." Tinker laughed. "Josh always held his temper, but you didn't want to be the one he was lookin' at if he lost it."

Having had a crash course in the techniques of Negro league public relations, Gus Greenlee attempted to quantify his team's success with the requisite eye-popping won-lost records—which of course meant little in light of the overall competition. Spurious records, however, don't quantify the Pittsburgh Crawfords as much as the presence of five future Hall of Famers: Oscar Charleston, Judy Johnson, Satchel Paige, Cool Papa Bell, and Josh Gibson.

Still, the team had some trying moments in 1932. Greenlee, aping Cum Posey's method of toddling to Chicago to fatten up on the American Giants, saw the Craws go down in three of five games, though Gus had to be pleased that Willie Foster—who won two of those games with shutouts—had left the Grays to jump back to the Giants. What's more, even Greenlee's leapfrogging over Posey in the new black ball order did not bring corresponding success on the field against the Grays, although the fact that the two teams met at all in 1932 was a testament to Greenlee's newfound power and the ebbing of Posey's.

This match occurred in late May, when Posey could see his East-West League was a lost cause. Even though the league was still technically alive, shriveling crowds at EWL games forced Posey to swallow his pride—which took an enormous gulp—and placate the man he had condescended to only months before. Posey, who had placed unconscionable restrictions on the Crawfords' bid to join the EWL, now came to Gus on bended knee and asked to join the East-West League, as a way of reviving the intracity rivalry. Gus, who wanted no part of the dying league now, still held Posey and his team in awe and knew what these games meant in Pittsburgh. Consequently, he readily agreed to a five-game series, with games in Sharon, Pennsylvania, Greenlee Field, and Forbes Field.

For a while, it looked as if the Grays would reestablish their dominance. They drove Paige from the mound with a six-run first inning and won the first game, 10–3, then led, 5–4, in the ninth of the second game. But the series turned when Josh stroked a triple off Joe Strong and came home on a Rev Cannady hit to tie it. Chester Williams then won it with a hit that scored Cannady. The Craws' Charles Beverly beat Ted Trent, 4–1, in game three, and Paige clinched the series with a 10–0 wipeout the next day, rendering the Grays' 9–2 win in the final game meaningless.

An ecstatic Greenlee, grabbing the *Courier*'s sports page, must have found himself flush faced reading Chester Washington's prose describing his team's triumph in "the Steel City's classic battle of bats and pitchers" and Washington's observation that "thrills, spills, brilliant fielding, fence-splitting hitting and sensational pitching made the series one of the most colorful sports events ever staged in this district."

Greenlee could also turn to the pages of the out-of-town

papers and become intoxicated. In the June 11 *Baltimore Afro-American,* for example, writer Bill Gibson concluded that the series

> proved conclusively that the fans preferred to see their games at Greenlee Field, home of the Craws. . . . Only 971 fans turned out for a game at Forbes Field . . . while 8,156 turned out for the two games at Greenlee Field. . . .
>
> Will Pittsburgh support two teams? It does not seem probable, and it appears that the move to have the Crawfords affiliate themselves with the league was not done out of altruism, but largely in an attempt to save embarrassment, financial and otherwise, to the Grays. It has been whispered around the Atlantic seaboard for some days now that the Grays would probably go on the rocks.

Though such dire predictions about Posey's team were premature, Greenlee, as boss man of the victors in this charged-up series, savored every word and wanted more of the same. And so another five games were scheduled between the teams, one in late June and four more in September. But now the Grays at least partly saved Posey's honor by rising up and taking four of the five.

By then, though, Greenlee could be forgiven if he believed Posey and the Grays were irrelevant. With Gus having broadened his team's schedule to include more big league black ball teams, the Craws barely had time to pause for the Grays games. When the *Defender,* picking up on the Craws as a good story, reported on the club around the time of the first game of the Homestead rematch series—a 6–5 Gray win—the Craws had also played the Cleveland Stars, another EWL team that made room for Gus's boys, with a doubleheader at Greenlee Field on June 24.

This twin bill was another rousing affair. After Josh's three-run homer drove the Craws to a 10–1 win in the opener, the Stars staged a two-run rally in the ninth inning to take the nightcap, 6–5, in the process banging out twelve hits off Satchel Paige, Harry Kincannon, and Lefty Streeter. In covering the two Crawfords series, the *Defender* nearly brushed off the Grays' victory to report CRAWFORDS LOSE TO GRAYS, BUT SPLIT PAIR WITH CLEVELAND NINE.

Indeed, Posey seemingly couldn't catch a break in the black papers for anything good his team did. Continuing his jeremiad against Posey, the *Afro*'s Bill Gibson ignored the latest Grays-Crawfords contest and composed a scalding obituary for the East-West League, with a thinly veiled slap at Posey's leadership abilities and business sense. "I was of the opinion that the league would at least be able to play through its first-half schedule, but the league moguls disappointed me sorely," he wrote.

> There are many factors entering into [the league's decline] and while there are those who are wont to dismiss the matter by blaming it on the depression, there are others who are more analytical and who are not willing to let the matter drop so quickly. . . .
>
> Bert Gholston, one of the league umpires who was summarily fired a few weeks ago, has some ideas regarding the failure of the league to function. . . . Says Bert: "The failure of the East-West League to click was due to the inability of the owners to cooperate. I am very sorry to say that very few business men engaged in [the league] understand the fundamental principles of the game as a business asset."

While Posey's troubles continued, Greenlee's dreams got bigger and bolder. As Gus saw it in those moments of reverie, Cum Posey had had his shot at erecting a Negro league kingdom. Now it would be Big Red's turn, in 1933. But the 1932 season would not end before Josh, aiding Greenlee as he had Posey, made some more long ball mythology.

7

Seasons End-to-End

We didn't have many lay-offs. Sometimes we would play three games a day—that was common. When we'd play a double header, we'd think it was a holiday.

We played in Chicago one Sunday, a double header. We put all our clothes and things on top of the bus. We left Chicago six o'clock Sunday night and rode to Philly without stopping. We got in Philly Tuesday morning and played a double header that afternoon. No interstates either. We played after two nights without rest. You see the travel we put up with?

We used to play two games every Thursday, two on Saturday, and three on Sunday. After we played that double header and had to go for that third game at night, boy, you heard some bad words! We'd fuss like a bunch of chickens. But when we put those uniforms on and got to the ball park, we'd forget the games we'd just played. As soon as we hit the field, it was all forgotten.

—JUDY JOHNSON, IN *BLACKBALL STARS*

The second of Josh Gibson's pantheon of legendary home runs came in York, Pennsylvania, only a few days before the four-game September series between the Crawfords and the Grays. This was providential for Gus Greenlee since the exhausted Craws hit the final stages of the 1932 season stumbling and sucking air after a brutally long eight months on the go.

As if driving his boys with a lash, Gus kept the Craws bouncing from one tough opponent to another, and they were only able to split six games with the Baltimore Black Sox and two with the Black Yankees in late August. Then, in a doubleheader with the Black Yankees in York, Josh went cosmic again, dimming for future generations of baseball fans trivialities like won-lost records and the preening of egomaniacal owners.

For the record, the Craws and Black Yankees again split, the Craws taking the opener, 5–1, behind Ted Radcliffe, and the Black Yankees the closer, 2–1, when Luther Farrell beat Satchel Paige in a seven-inning game called for darkness. But little of this would be remembered in York decades later. Instead, those old enough to recall the day would hand down tales of Josh's fourth-inning home run in the nightcap.

Again, history would only partially be aided by coverage in the black press about the scope of this homer. Only the *Afro-American* found space and deadline lag time to cover the game in York, and the lead paragraph in the paper's story focused on the "record-breaking crowd of 4,300" at the ballpark that day, though it was unspecified what record this was. The second paragraph told of "great catches in the outfield in which Rap Dixon and [Fats] Jenkins were featured." In the sixth and last paragraph came the citation that "Gibson, Crawfords catcher, tied the score in the fourth with a home run that cleared the left field fence and the pike."

Once again, this informational void would be filled by the

imagination of eyewitness embellishments. This time, the main mythmaker was not Judy Johnson but Cool Papa Bell. According to Cool Papa, the ball did indeed carry out to the Pennsylvania Turnpike behind the ballpark—right into the back of a large truck that kept on going until the end of its route. How he knew that he never explained, but this perfect example of why black ball blarney is so lovable and so unreliable made Josh Gibson the owner of baseball's only 500-*mile* home run.

Like Satchel Paige, Josh never seemed to tire, but both of them were off their games in the ill-fated but now meaningless Grays series. Josh got two hits in the opener, but the tone was set when the Grays fell behind early, 4–1 after two innings, then wore down Ted Radcliffe and won, 6–4. The pattern was repeated in the second game when the Craws staked Paige to a 9–3 lead against Lefty Williams after three innings and the Grays battled back—helped by two errors by Gibson and two by Judy Johnson—to win, 13–10. Chippy Britt won game three for the Grays, 6–4, and after an 8–1 Craws win the Grays clinched the series with a 5–1 victory.

Finally, the season came to an end with another Gus Greenlee look past the Grays and reach for the sky. Gus, understanding the compulsive black ball need to claim victory over some semblance of white big league competition, arranged a seven-game series against the so-called National League All-Stars. This barnstorming unit of players from that major league, managed by Dodger coach Casey Stengel, could only charitably be called an all-star team, but it did feature a big name in Brooklyn's Hack Wilson, who racked up a big league record of 190 RBIs as a Chicago Cub in 1930 before alcoholism softened his bat. Wilson still hit .297 with twenty-three homers and 123 RBIs in 1932, which was celestial compared to the other all-stars, among whom only Dodger outfielder Johnny Fredericks and Pirate pitchers Larry French and Bill Swift stood out.

When the Crawfords hit the field at Cleveland's League
Park for a doubleheader that began the series, they found the
field occupied by big-leaguers with names like Chuck Fullis,
Gill English, and Tom Pidden. There was a minor-leaguer at
shortstop, and first base was being played by pitcher Larry
French. Though big league touring teams in black-white
games generally were composed of odds and ends like these,
Negro-leaguers knew they couldn't have gotten away with
putting a similar ragtag team of their own on the field for interracial contests. To a man, they figured they had to be better just to be able to get on the same field with big-leaguers.

Thus, it never surprised anyone in black ball that their
fully assembled teams usually won these play-for-pay exhibitions, which had little to do with bringing down baseball's
color barrier but had a tremendous effect on the black players'
sense of manhood. Stacked up against athletes who in many
cases had half their talent, the Crawfords nonetheless found
themselves trailing, 4–3, as they hit in the top of the ninth in
the first game. They tied it in that inning, then won it with a
score in the tenth. The pressure off, the Craws would win five
of the seven games, Paige winning two and Gibson pounding
three hits in one victory, four in another.

Actually, the season had no ending for Josh, who headed
for Puerto Rico to play winter ball in mid-October. This was
more salve for his ego since he was paid a top salary of $250
a month by the Puerto Rican League's Santurce Cangrejeros
and was idolized by baseball fans he hadn't even known existed. With the warm tropical breezes and the adulation he received on the island, Josh couldn't believe there was any
greater reward back home in the winter tundra of Pittsburgh.

In fact, so lost was he in this paradise that, back on the
Hill, Margaret Mason—whom Josh told he was going to
Puerto Rico the day before he left—heard nothing from him
over the next three months. Josh had done little to involve
himself in the lives of Josh Jr. and Helen, and while he
promised that the extra money he made playing winter ball

would benefit his children, there would be no change in his sporadic pattern of contributing child support. Indeed, Margaret had a terrible sense of foreboding that as Josh got bigger and saw more of the world, his role as a father would waste away altogether.

As promulgated by Gus Greenlee, Gibson's hitting numbers were certainly getting bigger and bigger. After the 1932 season Gus came out with a set of figures that showed Josh had a .380 average and thirty-four homers in 190 at bats over 123 games against all competition. By other measurements, done decades later by piecing together box scores and game reports, his numbers against black pro teams that year were quite good, albeit more modest: seven homers, five triples, and a .286 average in forty-six games and 147 at bats.

The fantasy of Negro league numbers aside, the run of Crawford fever in 1932 couldn't help but swell the head of the team's cleanup man. Suddenly, little ego affectations began to show up when Gibson came out for the 1933 season. Sometimes Josh's uniform sleeves would be rolled up toward the shoulder, the better to show off his blacksmith arms. Or the bill of his cap would be turned up when he hit, a jaunty demonstration of a brash, new style among athletes, who played in a universe in which individuality was buried under flannel baggies.

But Josh was not alone in strutting his stuff. Other players had also gotten into the act. Ted Radcliffe was even flaunting a new identity because of the attentions of a famous white newspaperman. When the Craws had played a doubleheader against the Black Yankees in Yankee Stadium in the summer of 1932, Radcliffe caught Satchel Paige's 5–0 shutout in the first game, then went out and pitched a 4–0 shutout of his own in the nightcap. Watching this feat—which was actually fairly routine in the Negro leagues—was Damon Runyon, the nicknaming caricaturist of quirky, street-savvy *Guys and Dolls*. In the next day's paper, Runyon's column touted the marvel of "Double Duty" Radcliffe, opening doors of self-promotion for Radcliffe, who at once adopted the moniker.

Bearing the Crawford banner, Paige was becoming the proudest peacock around. His reputation now bolstered by displays of his Trouble Ball in big league ballparks and in front of huge crowds, Satch's front leg seemed to kick higher and with more flourish every game, and requests for his weekday exhibitions in the sticks were coming in so fast that he could have used an adding machine to keep track of the cash he pocketed. Even Josh got winded going out on gigs with Paige and by 1933 he had pulled out of his role in the two-man caravan in order to concentrate fully on Crawford games.

Then, of course, there was Gus Greenlee. Although Gus lost $30,000 operating the team in 1932, this was not an intolerable price—for him, at least—to pay for scaling the heights of ownership in black sports. After barely a year, Greenlee's name was known everywhere black ball was played, and in black Pittsburgh the name was synonymous with the booming baseball scene. Indeed, if Greenlee could shrug off the loss of thousands of dollars, it was that much easier to do knowing that Cum Posey had lost his shirt, along with his reputation, in 1932.

Posey was shattered by the death of his East-West League. He had promised so much and delivered so little. Not only was his prestige badly damaged; he was close to bankruptcy. While Posey lost less than Greenlee, he wasn't in a position to grit it out. But grit Posey did, cutting corners to keep the proud Grays from folding. In late 1932, Posey took the team off salary, creating a gate receipt–sharing plan that netted little, given the paucity of crowds at EWL games. Then, over the winter, Greenlee struck again, taking several Gray players, including pitcher Leroy Matlock.

Worse, Greenlee's team was parading around as world beaters. The April 29 *Courier*, still cheerleading for Gus, called the Craws the "champions from the Steel City."

While Greenlee's losses were an omen, Gus could take bows all day for his accomplishments as a sports czar. The fever he had cultivated around Greenlee Field never waned; paid admissions in 1932 came in at 119,000, and Greenlee succeeded in expanding his purview by booking black college football teams, boxing matches, and big band concerts at the ballpark.

By 1933, Greenlee had also done for black ball what Posey could not: he put together a league out of more than idealism, Scotch tape, and narcissism. To be sure, Greenlee was a match for Rube Foster and Cum Posey in vanity, yet he was more opportunist than idealist. Greenlee really didn't care about grand concepts like racial purity or making black ball the focal point of the civil rights movement. While the black game couldn't help but be a social cause, for Gus it was just as much a personal cause and a business investment.

In many ways, this was exactly the kind of hard-eyed realism necessary to avoid the mistakes of dreamers like Foster and Posey. Gus's start-up philosophy for his updated Negro National League was refreshingly free of portentous dogma and centered on keeping salaries and expenses in line.

These were precepts all black ball teams could get behind—and even Cum Posey, who reluctantly came into the league as the price for getting dates against the Crawfords—and yet at the beginning, most black teams, battered by the Depression, couldn't commit to paying dues to any central authority. The only established teams Greenlee could interest in the league were the Chicago American Giants, the Baltimore Black Sox, the Detroit Stars, the Nashville Elite Giants, and inferior, filler teams from Columbus and Indianapolis.

With the *Courier* doing its part to see Gus through, the Crawfords began league play with a doubleheader sweep of Nashville at Greenlee Field. They took the opener, 7–5, as Josh backed up Leroy Matlock with three hits, then won the nightcap on a William Bell four-hitter. HERE 'TIS! the *Courier* etched over the box score, the "it" presumably meaning

Greenlee's league. The paper regularly printed NNL schedules, and its coverage seemed geared around the Craws'
league games.

If any reminders were needed that these games were important, the *Courier* furnished them often. In mid-May, when
the Crawfords completed a two-week road trip, the paper
crowed that they "have spanked and buried all . . . league opposition . . . seven straight in the Negro National [League] is
their record. Four from Nashville and three from Indianapolis. . . . As a matter of record the Greenlee clan's performance
would indicate that they are unbeatable."

Such friendly coverage would come in handy for Gus, especially since other challenges were rising for him. That season, a new team was created in Philadelphia from the remains
of the deceased Hilldale franchise. Fronted by the longtime
Hilldale owner, Ed Bolden, the team was actually organized
by Eddie Gottlieb, the Philadelphia booking agent and owner
of the semipro South Philadelphia Hebrew Stars basketball
team. In 1933, Gottlieb eased into baseball ownership, first
with a hardball mutation of the Sphas, then with the Philadelphia Stars, with Bolden bearding Gottlieb's ownership role.

Greenlee showed Gottlieb respect by scheduling Crawford
games with both Philly teams and even promised Satchel
Paige would pitch and Josh Gibson would catch in contests
against them. Gottlieb, who had a ruthless sense of ambition,
repaid Greenlee's kindness by taking three of Gus's best players, Jake Stephens, Boojum Wilson, and Rap Dixon. Gottlieb
also lifted Chaney White from Cum Posey's Grays.

But still Greenlee was bighearted, hoping to bring the Stars
under the NNL banner. As promised, the Craws went to
Philadelphia in June for one game against the Sphas, then
played a home-and-home series with the Stars. The Craws
had an easy enough time with the Sphas, as Lefty Streeter and
Paige combined on a seven-hitter and Josh banged out three
hits in a 5–2 win. But against the Stars, Porter Charleston
outpitched Paige, and the Craws could manage just one hit—

a fourth-inning single by Josh—and lost, 2–0, in the Greenlee Field game.

Smarting, Paige took the ball for the return match at Parkside Avenue Stadium and allowed just three hits through eight innings. He was leading 1–0 going into the bottom of the ninth, but then hit a snag. Third baseman Tom Finley opened the inning with a single and went all the way to third on an infield out. He then scored when Chaney White's grounder went through second baseman Pistol Russell's legs. With the game now tied, Biz Mackey bounced one to shortstop Obie Lackey, who went for the out at first and threw the ball over Oscar Charleston's head, bringing home White with the winner.

As it was, Greenlee's team was having enough trouble against teams in his league. When the Craws went to Chicago for a four-game set in late June, they won the first game, 17–3, with William Bell profiting from a homer by Josh. But they lost the next two, 15–10 and 3–1, as Willie Foster won both games, the first in relief and the next on a five-hitter called after six innings for darkness. It took a magnificent fifteen-strikeout 3–1 win by Satchel Paige in the getaway game for the Craws to come out of Chicago with a split. But when they came home expecting to feast on the lowly Columbus Bluebirds, they again stumbled. One out away from a 3–2 victory, Lefty Streeter gave up a two-run homer to center fielder Herman Andrews and the Craws fell, 4–3.

The team did hit its stride in early July, when they won four in a row from the Bluebirds and two of three from Detroit. By then, they were atop the league standings at 18–7, though the American Giants were right behind at 15–6. But by then, too, the NNL was a little smaller, having booted out the Grays. This was the culmination of a festering war of nerves between Posey and Greenlee. Clearly, as chastened as Posey was, from day one he had been chafing in a subservient role to Gus's, and no doubt still stewing over Greenlee's heist of Josh Gibson.

Looking for some way to tweak Gus's authority, Cum had waited until his team was out of contention; when they fell to 7–11, he may have figured he had little to lose by violating league bylaws against raiding other league teams and signed two players from the Detroit Stars. When the owners met on July 1, the Grays were thrown out of the league and Posey took his leave, though few league elders doubted he would in time be heard from again, when and if he could successfully rebuild the Grays.

For the time being, subtracting Posey clearly put Gus Greenlee even more in control of the league's affairs, and Gus had moved to ensure favorable notices in the black press by elevating two of his reliable allies in the press, John L. Clark and Bill Gibson, to key roles within the NNL power structure, Clark as Crawford and league publicity man and Gibson as a proxy at league meetings for Baltimore owner Joe Cambria. Yet nothing Greenlee could do made things any easier for the Crawfords on the field. As the season moved toward its halfway point, when a first-half champion would be named, the Craws still had not shaken the American Giants, and the drama grew thicker when the teams met for the final two games of the half-season with Pittsburgh a game behind and needing to sweep.

The first game was played at McKeesport, Pennsylvania, on July 7, and in a bit of daring Oscar Charleston bypassed Satchel Paige and started Bertram Hunter against the seemingly unbeatable Willie Foster, saving Satch for a possible clincher. Hunter did his part, scattering ten hits but holding the Giants to two runs. Still, the Giants led, 2–0, until Charleston cracked a two-run homer in the seventh. Then, in the ninth, Josh got a leadoff double, and with two outs, right fielder Anthony Cooper lined a hit to right field, scoring Josh for the gamer.

Now, with the NNL's first-half title designation on the line, the Craws seemed to be in a lock with Paige on the hill against the Giants' Sug Cornelius before five thousand fans at

Greenlee Field a day later. But Satch struggled, yielding what the *Courier* called a "smoking double" to Turkey Stearns in the first. Turkey was singled home by outfielder Nat Rogers and Alec Radcliff then tripled to score another run and came home on a Mule Suttles hit.

The Craws tied it at 3–3 after two innings, then fell behind again in the third when Stearns singled and was later driven home by Radcliff, but the Craws hung in until two miscues did them in. The first was by Josh. In the eighth, Suttles lumbered around third trying to score from second on a hit and seemed to be dead meat as Pistol Russell took the relay and pegged it to the plate. But Josh bobbled and dropped the ball, allowing the insurance run. In the ninth, Charleston led off with a walk. Josh, going with the pitch, slapped a hard grounder into the hole off first, and second baseman Jack Marshall ranged far to his left and snared it; but then he threw it into the dirt at first and Suttles couldn't dig it out. When the ball trickled away, Charleston tried to go to third, but Suttles scrambled after it, and his perfect throw to Radcliff shot Oscar down. Cornelius then ended the game by getting Judy Johnson to hit into a double play.

In reclaiming their all but lost legacy, the American Giants were accorded all the spoils due them as champions, or semi-champions. Even the parochial-minded *Courier* ran a two-column team photo under the headline COP HALFWAY HONORS IN N.N. ASSOCIATION RACE, and Chester Washington in his column hailed the American Giants' "sensational" play. In the Giants' surge, even Josh Gibson found himself snubbed. "Behind the bat," Washington wrote, "Larry Brown and Quincy Trouppe [the Giants' catchers] have played more consistently than Perkins and Josh Gibson of the Craws."

Actually, at this stage of the season, league statisticians on Gus Greenlee's payroll had been telling a different story. In late June, the *Courier* offered a team-by-team rundown of each club's top four hitters, compiling at bats, hits, doubles, and average. Gibson had a .373 average, third on the Craw-

fords behind Oscar Charleston (.450) and Cool Papa Bell
(.379), with four home runs in forty-five at bats, which tied
him with Charleston (in sixty at bats) for the league lead. Bill
Parkins came in at .344. (The circuit's top hitter was veteran
Baltimore catcher Tex Burnett, whose .625 mark was based
on ten hits in a mere eighteen at bats.) In the catching derby,
Larry Brown was at .343 and Quincy Trouppe didn't show
up at all.

Even so, Gibson's engine had yet to really kick in. As his
career lengthened, Gibson would make a habit of getting off
slowly and then becoming as hot as the August heat. Always,
though, whatever the month or season, his energy would be
primed for a release that could occur only when he was
standing in the batter's box. Even on a rare day off, he would
sit squirming like a caged panther in the dugout, obsessively
squeezing the handle of his bat. In a game in Indianapolis on
May 6, he was unchained and sent up as a pinch hitter for
Jimmie Crutchfield in the eighth inning, with two on and two
out and the game tied, 4–4. Josh, according to the *Courier,*
"hit the first pitched ball over the left field wall, scoring three
runs." The blow sent the Craws on to a 7–4 win.

Actually, the fact that Josh was being somewhat devalued
was partly the result of what was probably Gus Greenlee's
most inspired idea. This was the September 10 Negro league
all-star game, which came to be known as the East-West
Game because of Gus's conviction that black ball's structure
and its rituals must have a national reach, just like the major
leagues'. In fact, most everything about the black all-star
game was cribbed from the white All-Star Game, which was
first played in Chicago's Comiskey Park in July 1933 as part
of the city's World's Fair festivities and was an immediate hit,
punctuated by a Babe Ruth home run.

For black fans as for white fans, assembling the greatest
stars of the game on one field went right to the core of this
team game's appreciation for individualism. On the black
side, this was an especially resonant notion, given the abun-

dance of individual talent and grit required of any black player to be worthy of any sort of comparison with the best white players. Accordingly, Greenlee acted with genius when—unlike in the big league game, for which the players were chosen by sportswriters—he threw open the selection of the East-West Game performers to African American fans, who found a mail-in ballot on which to write the names of their favorite Negro-leaguers when they opened their local black weekly each summer. Also to Gus's credit, their choices could be from any black team, not just those enrolled in the NNL.

Greenlee, who copromoted the game with the *Courier* and the *Chicago Defender,* purposely selected Comiskey Park as the site of the East-West Game. As the game drew closer, it began to take on more and more meaning in the black community as it melded with the emerging black consciousness, which demanded black enfranchisement. Thus, black ball became a maypole of the civil rights movement, and the annual accumulation of East-West Game ballots became a profound symbol. This feeling was palpable on the eve of the inaugural game, when *Courier* sports editor William Nunn, caught up in the excitement of black ball's self-tribute, trilled in his column that the 1 million ballots delivered by black fans "made me proud that I'm a Negro, and tonight I'm singing a new song!"

Handed this gift, blacks had voted with care and with a poignant wish to honor the men who had labored the longest for their small slice of fame. The leading vote getters were not Satchel Paige or Josh Gibson but rather warhorses like Oscar Charleston, Boojum Wilson, Willie Wells, Cool Papa Bell, Mule Suttles, and Turkey Stearns. Among pitchers, Paige came in fourth behind Lefty Streeter, Billy Holland, and Porter Charleston. In the voting for catcher, the great Biz Mackey, now playing for Eddie Gottlieb's Philadelphia Stars, outpolled Josh.

As with much else about the first season of the Negro National League revived by Gus Greenlee, Gus's boys were hard pressed in the East-West Game. In what was essentially a contest between the Crawfords and American Giants—four Crawfords and seven American Giants players started the game—the West came back from 3–1 and 5–3 deficits to win, 11–7. Willie Foster, who pitched the entire game, outlasted Streeter, Bertram Hunter, and Chippy Britt. Mule Suttles, supplying the juice in the Babe Ruth role, hit a home run. Josh, who came in for Mackey in the fifth inning, went 1-for-2, made an error, and flied out to end the game.

Although his side went down to defeat, Greenlee profited handsomely from this terrific promotion. Despite rainy skies, which held the crowd to around twenty thousand—described by *Defender* sportswriter Al Monroe as "a howling, thundering mob of 20,000 souls"—this was still a huge success by black ball standards, and the promoters cleared some $8,000 in profits. (The players, on the other hand, received nothing beyond travel expenses.) And if the game was quite exciting by itself, the heavy press coverage ensured that its sheen would be preserved by black ball legend makers.

Indeed, Al Monroe seemed to realize that his reportage might be a peg around which Negro league myths would thrive. Stressing that he was being completely objective, he wrote in his game story:

> The contest was billed as the Game of Games, and gents, a baseball-mad throng . . . will attest to our story that its premise was fulfilled. This, folks, is our story, and we'll stick to it even when informing future generations that we were among those reporting the first of what by all manner of reasoning should become an annual event.

What's more, Greenlee may have been relieved that in the aftermath of the event few fans seemed to have a great hunger for doings in his league, even in Pittsburgh and even after Josh had caught fire. Although that season's statistics were never updated, in July a *Courier* dispatch on a Crawford doubleheader sweep in New York against a semipro unit called the Farmers contained the intriguing news that "Josh Gibson got three home runs in the second game, bringing his season total [in all games] to 27."

This claim could have emanated only from Greenlee's stat men, who did go on compiling Josh's numbers. Included in the home run total was one humongous shot in Philadelphia against the Stars that wound up on Forty-fourth Street outside Parkside Stadium. Another Gibson blast even allowed Greenlee to manipulate the league's championship. This came during the Crawfords' second-half rematch with the American Giants, which Greenlee and Giants owner Robert Cole had booked in Cleveland's League Park as a doubleheader on July 27.

Desperately needing to establish superiority, the Craws took the opener as Lefty Streeter, in a clutch performance, hurled a four-hitter and beat Willie Foster. In the nightcap, though, the Giants dusted William Bell and Harry Kincannon (Satchel Paige, busy on a private gig, was unavailable for the games) and surged to an 11–3 lead after four innings. The Craws fought back with six runs in the fifth and two in the sixth, and by the ninth they were down only 12–11. Then, as William Nunn reported in his *Courier* game story, " 'Josh' Gibson poled a long hit over the centerfield fence, the smash going for a homer," sending the game to extra innings. In the twelfth, the Craws pushed across the winning run against Willie Powell.

The sweep, combined with a subsequent 14–4 Craws wipeout of the American Giants, gave Greenlee a chance to pull a fast one. With coverage of these games heavy—because of his key homer, Josh's picture landed once again in the *Courier,* under the heading HERO ROLE—and with the crowd at the twin bill numbering seven thousand, Greenlee chose to use these games as proof that the Craws were as good as champs, with no further play-off evidence necessary. This conveniently ignored the Crawfords' ongoing tribulations, including a brutal doubleheader loss to the Detroit Stars and several defeats against the Philadelphia Stars, as well as the escalating tensions in the Crawford clubhouse.

These bad vibes were responsible for a hideous on-the-field eruption by Oscar Charleston. After the Craws had lost another doubleheader, in Birmingham, to the Nashville Elite Giants, they were losing again to Nashville the following day in Chattanooga when the volatile Charleston began arguing an umpire's call. Minutes later, Charleston tore his hat from his head and tossed it in the air in disgust, then pulled his team off the field; this resulted in a Giants victory by forfeit. At least Oscar kept his hands to himself and avoided spending a night in jail as he had in Indianapolis in his younger days after a similar dustup. Still, Charleston was involved in other incidents; when some of his own players challenged his authority, Oscar responded by yanking a pistol from his belt and sticking it in their faces to shut them up.

Few black ball fans knew of the Crawford dissension or of their troubles on the field since the league office—aka the Crawford Grille—happened to stop furnishing league standings. Thus, by summer's end, no one seemed to be quite sure of how the second-half and overall champions would be determined. On September 5, when the American Giants repaid the Craws by sweeping a previously scheduled doubleheader in Indianapolis by scores of 9–8 and 4–0, the *Afro-American* headlined its game story CHICAGO TOPS CRAWS FOR SECOND HALF HONORS and reported that the Giants had now won thirty-eight of their last forty games. But this was hardly an official judgment. A month later, when the Craws again went to Cleveland's League Park to play Nashville in a three-game set, Greenlee had convinced the *Courier* that the series constituted, as William Nunn wrote, "a playoff" and that the winner would in fact "meet Chicago for a series which will decide the Negro baseball championship."

On October 1, the first two games were played as a doubleheader, with Satchel Paige starting the opener against the Elites' Jim Willis. The Craws got on the board in the second inning when Josh—who played left field in the game—singled to right, went to second on a hit by Ted Page, and scored on Bill Perkins's sacrifice fly. Although Nashville tied it in the third, the Craws had a 4–2 lead going to the bottom of the ninth. But here Paige tired, giving up four singles, and with the score again tied, Charleston yanked Satch and brought in Leroy Matlock, who got out of the frame with no more damage done. Then, in the twelfth, the quicksilver Cool Papa Bell took over.

As Nunn wrote it up,

> The crowd . . . rose en masse as "Cool Papa" Bell, one of the greatest centerfielders in the game, caught a Willis pitch square on the butt end of his bat and drove a screaming liner into deep center field. And as the fleet [Bell] sped across home plate [with an inside-the-park home run], his flying spikes marked "finis" to as great a diamond struggle as we've ever seen.

In the nightcap, played under a dank and darkening sky, the Craws broke on top, 2–1, in the third, then made it 3–1 in the sixth when Josh doubled and came home on an error by shortstop Sam Bankhead. When Bertram Hunter set down the Giants in the bottom of the inning, the game was called for darkness; that gave the Craws a sweep and Gus Greenlee all the ammunition he needed to call off the championship round he had proposed with the American Giants. In Gus's mind, the logic was all on his side. For one thing, league people had become depressed by the steadily atrophying crowds at parks all around the league. When only three thousand showed up for that Crawfords–Elite Giants twin bill in Cleveland, for example, Gus canceled the game scheduled between the clubs for the next day.

Given this burgeoning lack of attention, it was clear that

practically no one but Gus and possibly Robert Cole gave a hoot about the league pennant race, and the honor was a dubious one anyway since only three teams—the Crawfords, the American Giants, and the Elite Giants—would complete their league schedules. So Gus simply let his team's two much-publicized sweeps in League Park speak for the state of his league. Rather than name a champion either for the second half or for the season as a whole, the NNL office named no winner at all. For two months the league and the result of its season were mired in rumors, nor was it reported for certain whether the Crawfords or other league clubs were perhaps playing somewhere in America on any given day up until the time snow began falling. Then, in mid-December, the issue no one cared about was decided when Greenlee wrote to the *Courier* with the news that the Pittsburgh Crawfords were NNL champs. Robert Cole, of course, begged to differ, but only one thing about the decision mattered: that Gus Greenlee had made the call.

These absurd machinations—the kind that made many baseball people regard the Negro leagues as an endless source of jokes rather than ballplayers—meant little to the hardy men of black ball, who simply played when they were told to and were grateful for the chance. For Josh, black ball's arcane attempts to legitimize itself and profit from it were trivial and as empty as the black ball concept of "big games"—in leagues where a new game of games seemed to be played every week.

Nor were his stats of much interest to him, though they were certainly a big deal to other people. Greenlee, who didn't care to keep track of his league's standings in 1933, released a meticulous set of Gibson stats for the season, showing Josh with fifty-five home runs and a .467 average, with 239 hits in 512 at bats—nearly a hundred points higher than the second-best Crawford hitter, Oscar Charleston, who was said to have hit .374. Josh, according to this accounting, had also scored more runs than any Craw but Cool Papa, who in fact acted more as a PR man for Josh than for himself, swearing years later that he had kept notes on every one of Gibson's homers that year and that the grand total was sixty-eight. Latter-day research, based on surviving data of Gibson's production versus league teams, is less delirious but by no means unimpressive; by these measurements, Josh hit .362 with six homers in thirty-four games and 116 at bats in 1933, and led the NNL in round-trippers, with one more than Mule Suttles.

For Josh himself, it was enough to know he could get to any pitcher and put a hurtin' on him, if not with a homer then in the field or with his feet, for a stolen base. What was important was that there'd be more games on the horizon, one after another, somewhere in the hemisphere, whenever Josh Gibson wanted to play some hardball.

Ted Page, who sometimes rode with Josh to games and played with him in Latin America, once recalled that if Gibson had a game in his sight, travel time meant nothing to him. "One weekend, I remember, we played a twilight game at Forbes Field in Pittsburgh. Afterward we jumped in two cars and drove the six hundred miles to St. Louis for a two P.M. game the next day. And the next day we drove three hundred and fifty miles to Kansas City for a doubleheader. It was a hundred and ten in the shade, but he loved it. That night Josh and I were sitting on the back porch of the hotel and we saw a kid ball game and we went and joined it."

By the end of 1934, when Josh headed off to Puerto Rico again for another season of winter ball, today's ball game was merely an appetizer for tomorrow's ball game.

8

A Player

Josh, he didn't know what to do with women.
　　　　—GEORGE GILES, KANSAS CITY MONARCHS,
　　　　1927–38, IN *BLACKBALL STARS*

My father was a player, man, as far as women were concerned. I met a lot of his women.
　　　　—JOSH GIBSON JR.

The secret life of Josh Gibson was never more evident than in his relationships with women. To his teammates and to the public that knew of his name, Gibson was a kind of great gelded creature, his seemingly eternal youthfulness a comforting counterpoint to his frightening brawn. On team bus rides, the more hard-boiled Crawfords would watch their language when Josh was within earshot, as if an off-color joke or crude comment about women might embarrass him. Only reluctantly did they begin to allow him to sit in on their regular card games in the backseat.

If Josh was aware of this deference to his youth and innocence, he may have enjoyed the refuge it gave him from the trials of his personal life, which could have destroyed any man's youth. Rather than signal his eagerness to join in on the bonding rituals of older men, he hid for now behind the protections afforded him.

Under that cover, Josh began his first meaningful liaison since Helen's death. Josh had been looking for a stable relationship after his meanderings on the road in the company of Satchel Paige. The indiscriminate sex and one-night stands during that blur of days had left him feeling empty and unrooted. Then, in 1933, he met Hattie Jones, a domestic in her late twenties whose rather stern demeanor and maturity offered ballast. To Josh, spending time with Hattie was a soothing retreat from a world in which he was expected to play a leading role.

In this partnership, Hattie was the dominant force, and she could be a ball breaker when she commanded Josh to take care of her financially. Eventually, after listening to her cawing, he agreed to live with her, though not as man and wife. Josh was unwilling to accede to this sort of arrangement so soon after the pain of Helen's death, nor did he seem eager to break what he may have considered a sacred bond with Helen by remarrying. In the spring of 1934 he purchased a two-story brick town house for $1,000 at 2157 Webster Avenue on Pittsburgh's north side, not far from where Mark and Nancy Gibson lived.

To those in the neighborhood, Josh and Hattie seemed the picture of a happy, young middle-class couple, with a car in the driveway and a pet bulldog that Josh named Bozo. Today, when Josh Gibson Jr. is asked about Hattie Jones, he laughs and says he remembers more about Bozo. "Oh yeah, he was black-and-white, he had a black eye. Hattie took care of Bozo when my father went on the road. I don't remember too much about Miss Hattie—that's what my sister and I called her, Miss Hattie. We'd go up there every once in a while to see him and Miss Hattie'd be there, and she was a quiet lady, at least around us she was. She was very dark skinned, and I'd call her average looking. But the bottom line is this: Hattie had no personality."

That the children never got too close to Hattie was no accident. As pliable as Josh could be when Hattie opened her mouth, he laid down an unconditional law regarding the kids: Hattie was not to even think about bringing them into the household and acting as a surrogate mother.

"Oh, no, no, no," Josh Jr. said, still flinching at the thought sixty years later. "That issue wasn't on the table. His life with Hattie was his private deal, and I guess he didn't want to disturb the life he'd set up for us."

Though this dictum could also be construed as a way of further isolating his memories and his responsibilities as a father, his son always believed the opposite. "In a way," he said, "I think he was protecting us. Maybe he thought Hattie wasn't up to taking care of us. And we were well taken care of by our grandmother and our aunts. My father would check in on us quite frequently, he could see that. He wasn't gonna mess around with his kids."

The unspoken corollary to this theory was that Josh may have believed that it was in the best interests of the children for him to keep away as well. The union with Hattie, after all, did little to tame his wandering eye and libido. While it did him good to know he had a woman like Hattie to come home to, even Josh Jr., who lived mainly on the periphery of his father's life, came to recognize where the man's weaknesses lay.

"My father was a player in every way," he said. "Later on, I saw it for real, but even as a kid I knew he had so many women he couldn't count 'em all."

The 1934 season emerged as another bumpy ride for the Crawfords, yet this fact would be difficult to discern from the many laurels bestowed upon the team by Negro league literature, including the claim that they were black ball's best team ever—that is, when the 1930 Homestead Grays weren't given that title.

The men responsible for these revisionist salutations were none other than Gus Greenlee, Satchel Paige, and Josh Gibson, the three men most responsible for saving black ball from extinction. Just as the popularity of the white game began to slump in the wake of Babe Ruth's retirement, the black game actually started to attract new devotees. The Depression, of course, was still battering both ends of the game, but African Americans had learned how to cope with such deprivations long before the effects of economic collapse were felt by the white working class. Now, with race and class distinctions less visible to much of the population, black ball, by its very survival, could make an even stronger case for inclusion in the sports landscape.

As if aware of this new deal, black fans came out in large numbers throughout the 1934 season, allowing Greenlee's tottering league to continue as though it were the bearer of black ball tradition. In many ways it was, since Greenlee's East-West Game had given black ball real recognition as a major league after its long days in the dark, and since Satchel Paige and Josh Gibson made a convincing case for major league status by themselves. The drawing power of these two magnificent names was never more evident than in the mid-thirties, when both of their legends were certified gold in black America—and had even begun to gain recognition in the white sports culture.

One reason why black ball history has been so susceptible to revisionism is that its seasons were often rewritten on the spot. Almost no one had any idea in 1934 that the Crawfords were a tempest of ill will and jealousy and that these qualities would soon destroy this Negro league centerpiece. The leading player in this epic drama was the unpredictable Paige, who followed his inner voices to ends that alternately exalted and desecrated black baseball.

Not that Paige should have had a social or, egad, a political conscience about black ball; such attitudes simply did not exist among black ball rank and file, not at a time when playing tripleheaders on Sunday wasn't a choice but an economic necessity. Still, seeing Paige being given leeway to skip games in order to enrich himself made his Crawford teammates wince more and more each season. Besides perhaps the priggish Jake Stephens, nobody really detested Paige; his droll affability and quick wit prevented that. But privilege for the sake of greed seemed a weak rationale on those endless sojourns aboard the Mack bus, when Satch's seat would normally be empty during weekdays and the Craws would be losing games to teams that would have been easy pickings for Paige.

The season began with a testament to the potency of the Crawfords at full strength. Pitted against the Kansas City Monarchs, Josh—who by now had displaced Bill Perkins behind the plate when Paige pitched—homered off the great curveball pitcher Hilton Smith. Paige gave up eleven hits but clamped down when he had to, and the Craws won, 6–4.

A few games later, the Craws pulled into Chicago for three games against the American Giants. They took the first, a tense 3–2 win with William Bell beating Willie Foster. Then, after Willie Powell won the second game, 9–2, behind home runs by Turkey Stearns and Mule Suttles, Paige faced Ted Trent in the rubber game. With Satch throwing blinding heat, all he needed was Josh's bases-clearing triple in the third to break open a scoreless game. With Paige striking out nine and giving up three harmless singles, the Craws won, 7–0.

The grumbling began when not only games but big houses were lost in ballparks that Paige routinely filled when he was billed as the starter. Since those overflow crowds produced the cash for Greenlee to give his players bonuses, it quickly got around that the players would not accept the same long absences that Satch had strung out in 1933, when he pitched in only thirteen league games and listlessly enough to finish with a reported 5–7 record. Consequently, Greenlee got Paige to curtail his barnstorming to pitch several important games, first against the Philadelphia Stars, who, soon after joining the NNL, had begun to challenge the Craws for supremacy in the East.

The Stars' big weapon was nineteen-year-old southpaw Stuart "Slim" Jones, a lanky carbon copy of Paige both in appearance and pitching skills. This pitching rivalry heated up in late May, when the two teams met in a three-game series at Greenlee Field. After the Craws won the opener, 3–0, behind Oscar Charleston's two-run homer and Bertram Hunter's two-hit pitching, Paige and Jones hooked up in a remarkable game. The Stars scored three in the first inning but Satch stiffened and threw zeroes for the next seven innings while the Craws fought back.

They were down, 3–2, when Josh came up in the fifth and, according to Chester Washington's *Courier* story, "thrilled [the crowd] with a long home run" to tie it. The Craws went ahead, 5–3, in the seventh, but Paige couldn't hold it. In the ninth, wrote Washington, "a fusillade of bats exploded in front of him." The Stars—shockingly—tallied seven runs off Paige, as Charleston refused to bring in a relief pitcher, and the Stars won, 10–5. Leroy Matlock saved the series for the Craws with a 7–5 victory in the finale.

Even though the Craws were stumbling, Josh required no warm-up period this season. His bat smoldering from day one, he was lethal throughout May and June of 1934. On May 31, after the Craws had won the first of a four-game set against the Bacharach Giants of Atlantic City, the Giants were up, 2–1, in the bottom of the ninth at Greenlee Field when Josh came up against Daltie Cooper with two outs and Cool Papa Bell on first. The result was reported by Chester Washington:

> "Josh" Gibson, a native son, came through in dime novel fashion . . . by smashing out a mighty homer. . . . Josh's healthy four-base wallop, which cleared the stands in right field, spoiled a perfectly good evening's pitching performance by Daltie Cooper, who had slow-balled the Craws throughout eight thrilling innings. . . . The Bacharachs and many of the

fans who began to leave the stands thought the game was "in the bag" for the visitors, until the resounding crack of Gibson's bat turned the tide of victory in miraculous fashion.

Josh's homers were as regular as a metronome now, marking each successive Crawford series. There was a three-run clout against the NNL's newest team, the Newark Dodgers, three homers in the first game of a doubleheader against the Cleveland Stars, a shot against Nashville, and another against Philadelphia. And yet, the 1934 season was not to be stamped by the image of a mighty hitter but by an ethereal pitcher, Satchel Paige, rubbing out hitters as fast as they could come to bat.

Rebounding from his mediocre 1933 season, Paige was probably at the absolute height of his powers in 1934, though even he suffered some humiliating defeats that year. He also had the good sense to reach back and throw extra hard when the most people were likely to hear about it. In the first half of the season alone, he beat the American Giants with three shutouts. Then, on July 4, in the first game of a doubleheader against the Homestead Grays at a teeming Greenlee Field, Paige threw his second Negro league no-hitter.

Mowing down eight of the first Grays, he whiffed seventeen in the 4–0 win (a mark which, in the absence of verifiable statistics, would stand as a Negro league record, though Smokey Joe Williams and Chet Brewer, of course, had each fanned more in a nonleague game in 1930), missing a perfect game by one walk and one error, becoming the first pitcher ever to no-hit Cum Posey's club. Buck Leonard, the superb first baseman, in his rookie season with the Grays, was so helpless against Paige that afternoon that he asked the home plate umpire to inspect the ball during one futile at bat, not knowing whether it was real or an illusion.

"You may as well throw 'em all out," Satch cackled from the mound, "'cause they're all gonna jump like that!"

What's more, Paige made that day's headlines even bigger,

if not better, by coming into the nightcap in relief in the seventh with the Craws up, 3–2. According to the *Courier,* "the stands went wild when the elongated Satchell [*sic*] leisurely strolled across the field, proceeded to execute his quadruple windup, and then struck out [Neil] Robinson." But facing pitcher John Strong, Paige let up and Strong doubled, opening the way for the Grays to score three and go on to win, 4–3.

Despite that setback, Paige's popularity was now out of sight. In the wake of his no-hitter, the *Defender* outdid the *Courier* by plastering Paige's full-form picture across two columns; in the weeks and years to come, his name was a constant in black newspaper headlines from coast to coast. This, in turn, gave Paige the power to ignore his Negro league attachments and further flaunt his independence.

Gus Greenlee could do little but stand by as Paige cut out on the Crawfords in August to pitch for the Colored House of David team—a spin-off of the bearded, Jewish House of David ball club representing the religious colony of the same name in Benton Harbor, Michigan. His destination was the *Denver Post* baseball tournament, an annual rite of small-time ball that attracted the top semipro teams from across the country, as well as hungry gamblers looking for action. Facing the Kansas City Monarchs, who also had gained entry to the tournament, in the championship game, Paige—wearing a fake red beard as a goof—won, 2–1, striking out twelve, and collected a cut of the gate as well as a share of the $7,500 first-prize money.

Although Paige came back to the Craws, Greenlee wasn't willing to take any chances on whether he'd be around for the East-West Game, which had a heavy advance sale and would pull in over thirty thousand fans when it was played on August 28. With Satch still somewhere between Denver and Chicago, Gus named Slim Jones, who finished second to Paige among East pitchers, to start against Chicago's Ted Trent.

Paige, who for all his fame finished behind Josh and top vote getter Oscar Charleston in the East-West fan balloting, did make it to Comiskey Park in time for the game but was a spectator for five innings of a scoreless game. He came in for the last three innings, and when the East scored the only run of the game—Cool Papa Bell, in a typical play, came all the way home from second base on a slow grounder by Boojum Wilson—Satch not only got the win but all the headlines.

Even though other players had performed at least as well—including Josh, who had a double and a single in four at bats—Paige dominated the press coverage of the game, which now extended into the white papers. Most notable was a *Chicago Times* piece that lionized Paige as "Black Matty," comparing him with the great white pitcher Christy Mathewson while failing to name even one other black player in the game.

All of which could not have escaped Paige's teammates. Although Paige did return to the Craws, the quiet rift between star and team was given voice. In Paige's absence, the Craws had again been topped by the American Giants in the first-half pennant race and now found themselves mired in third place in the second half. The matter of Satchel Paige finally boiled over when a strident item appeared in the *Courier,* unsigned but clearly the opinion of owners and players hostile to Paige. It read:

> Satchel is a great pitcher, but he can't be used as an example of colored baseball players. . . . Gus [Greenlee] exploited Satchel throughout the United States and forgot all about such men as Gibson, Matlock, Bell, Charleston, Perkins, the men who made the Pittsburgh Crawfords.

Whether Josh was a party to this sneak attack is unclear; he likely was not, but by now the mounting expense of subsidizing Hattie Jones, not to mention the care of his children, had certainly made him more aware of money. Though he was earning a top-shelf (by black ball standards) $300 per month, only slightly less than Paige—who of course made far more in his private gigs—he was getting ready to demand more from Greenlee for himself. All he needed was a little more nerve and the right opening.

The Paige contretemps remained submerged for now as the Craws tried to rally in the second half. By late summer, though, the Philadelphia Stars had taken over first place, and symbolically, Slim Jones had beaten Paige head-to-head in two of three games. Just as damaging to the Craws was a three-game sweep at the hands of the Stars and a double-header loss to the Bacharach Giants, though Josh kept on pace by homering in both of those series.

Still, the Craws hung in, winning four of six in a return match with the Stars in late August at Shibe Park, with Josh personally taking apart Slim Jones in the opening game, an 8–2 rout that the black *Philadelphia Tribune*'s Ed R. Harris condensed like this in his game story:

> In the [game], young Stewart [sic] Jones, the Stars' elongated and youthful twirler, was swamped under a barrage of Craws batting. . . . Did I say the Craws' batting? Take that back and put down instead the potency of Gibson's bat. [He] was the star of the day. He scored four times and drove in three runs. He hit two home runs over the Broad Street fence of the ball park, no small matter that.

In the next big series, a Labor Day twin bill with the American Giants at Greenlee Field, Josh ushered Paige to a 7–6 win in the opener with a homer and a double. But the Craws dropped the second game to Willie Powell, 7–4, and by the end of the second-half schedule—with won-lost records this time being kept—the Craws had come in third behind Philly and Nashville.

Still, if Gus Greenlee couldn't manipulate the standings, he could, given his reputation and his team, manipulate public interest in black ball. And so, rather than end the Craws' season, he extended it so that he could upstage his own league's championship round between the Stars and American Giants. This he did by booking Yankee Stadium for a benefit double-header featuring the Craws and Stars in a climactic nightcap following the American Giants and Black Yankees in game one (the Stars and American Giants having willingly put their "title" series on hold in order to profit from an event of this kind).

As Gus hoped, this Sunday spectacle became, next to the East-West Game, the season's high-water mark, and the chance to see Satchel Paige and Josh Gibson go against Slim Jones in New York brought over twenty thousand people and every major black paper to the big stadium. Satch, who got to the park late after driving to New York and falling asleep in his roadster in Harlem, gave up a run in the first on a ground out, then matched zeroes with Jones, who allowed not one hit until the seventh. When Jones fanned the side in the fourth, the fans gave him a standing ovation.

But the Craws tied it in the eighth, and now it was Paige's turn at theatrics. In the ninth, he loaded the bases with one out—then, with night closing in and cloaking the park and his pitches, he blew the ball by the next two hitters. With the last strike, reported the *Philadelphia Tribune,* "the fans nearly mobbed [Paige] as they rushed on the field to congratulate him on his superb work."

Although the war ended in deadlock, called right then because of darkness, this high drama of dueling fastballs in the twilight—Paige had twelve strikeouts, Jones nine—immediately became worthy of championship status, albeit nonofficial, for Greenlee's aims. If Gus couldn't claim outright victory this time, he could claim to have gotten all the attention; not by coincidence, few fans and reporters bothered with the Stars' triumph over the American Giants. (Not even the Stars seemed overly excited by it; they quickly agreed to play the Craws once again at Yankee Stadium in late October, when before another large crowd Paige beat Jones, 3–1, giving up five hits.)

Actually, Gus Greenlee had to be relieved that Paige had stayed around long enough for these big games. Right before the Craws ended their black ball season in late October, Paige had wandered again, to a semipro team in Bismarck, North Dakota. In this, Paige was following the lead of Double Duty Radcliffe, who had jumped the club in midseason to play first with the American Giants and then in Bismarck, where accomplished black players were being offered big money for a few months of barnstorming in the woodsy terrain of the upper Midwest.

While Paige's jump portended calamity for Greenlee, he once again returned in time for Gus's next marquee assignment: a series between a combined squad of Crawfords and Philadelphia Stars and another "all-star" white barnstorming team—this one fronted by a real star, the redoubtable Dizzy Dean, who was coming off a thirty-win season and a World Series victory with the St. Louis Cardinals.

Just like Paige, who was always eager to match skills with a bona fide big league pitcher, Josh was also anxious to stand in against a white pitcher with superstar credentials. Such cravings explained why teams of diffident whites were commonly pummeled by Negro league combines; Dean and the other white farmhands that accompanied him on these barnstorming gigs also weren't known to overtax themselves. Moreover, Diz knew a good promotion when he saw it, and though it no doubt shocked many of his buddies back home in Lucas, Arkansas, he was not adverse to building up black men as his equals on the diamond, no doubt with sincerity but also in the spirit of fun and profit, and in relative safety since he knew big league jobs weren't threatened by blacks.

For men like Dizzy Dean, having kind words for black players was a magnanimous gesture, but the name of the game for these exhibitions was still exploitation, and that went for the black players as well. Although these exhibitions did little to make baseball take a stand for pluralism—not in the way that, say, desegregating the white barnstorming teams might have—it was no small matter that Satchel Paige made around $1,200 splitting gate fees with Dean for two weeks' work. Josh made somewhere around $400, which was equal to more than a month's salary.

Not that Dizzy Dean was prepared to throw any game or groove any pitches, but when he faced the black team in several games played in Philadelphia, Pittsburgh, Cleveland, and York, Pennsylvania, he took his lumps with remarkably good humor. In one game, Paige struck out thirteen and beat him, 4–1. In another, Paige saved a win by coming in as a reliever and striking out the side.

But as it turned out, Dean's major nemesis—or dramatic foil—in these games was not Satch but Josh, who feasted on Dean's not-so-fast ball all series.

In Philadelphia, Josh poked three hits, including a triple. But it was in York that he made corn mash of Dean's pitches. In his first time up, Gibson knocked one over the center field wall. In his second, he hit one longer over the center field wall. This set in motion an affable piece of black-versus-white burlesque, as the good-natured Dean threw his hands grandly in the air, removed himself from the mound as Josh trotted the bases, and took up a position in right field for the rest of the game. Dean reportedly told Josh after the game, an 11–1 win by the Negro-leaguers, that if Paige and he were on his Cardinals, "We'd win the pennant by July Fourth and go fishin' the rest of the season."

This made for wonderful fireside reading in the black press and in future Negro league retrospectives, as would Dean's other splendid confrontations with Paige—the most memorable of which came later that winter when a stronger Dean-led team met a Negro league squad sans Gibson. In a thrilling pitchers' duel Paige came away with a 1–0 victory in thirteen innings, with Paige garnering seventeen strikeouts, Dean fifteen. However, it was during the Crawfords-Stars tour that the burlesque act for a few tense moments became an all-too-literal exercise in racial confrontation.

It began when Vic Harris was called out sliding into second base, argued with the umpire, and wound up pulling the mask off the guy's face. Reacting by rote, Oscar Charleston ran out to join the fray and got into a fight with a white player, which escalated into a bench-clearing melee.

In the sprawl of bodies—a hideous and potentially ruinous image for the cause of integration—most eyes turned to Josh, who was tangling with catcher George Susce. Partly to quell a particularly ugly situation, and partly to save Susce's life, Dean and Ted Page grabbed Josh by the shoulders, trying to pull him away. As Page later mused, "There was no telling what he would do to any man, it didn't matter who, when he got him in a crack like that."

But when Josh felt the tugging, he reached back and with the strength of a Brahma bull lifted Dean off his feet with one hand under the armpit and hurled Diz into the air and onto his back some ten feet away—all the while never letting go of Susce. Luckily, though, this strongman stunt worked to take the edge off things, since the sight of Dizzy Dean flat on his can—and seeing him in hysterics about it—broke everybody up, and the game continued without further incident.

For the black players who were on the field that day and for those who heard about it later, this one incident would have been worth the price of admission. The fact is, people had been waiting for the day of reckoning when Josh lost his cool. Even Oscar Charleston was scared to death of provoking Josh's anger; when Oscar got into a tiff with Cool Papa Bell and threatened to deck the reedy outfielder, Josh interceded on behalf of Cool Papa and Charleston backed off. That Josh finally lost it against baseball's best-known white pitcher was a major event. Josh seemed quite pleased by it himself.

"I can still see Josh today, right now, when that was over," Ted Page told author John Holway years later. "He was kind of scratched up and had lost his cap in the scuffle, but he had a big grin on his face, you know, one of those satisfied grins, like, 'Well, that was a good one.'"

9

Bronzed Bambino

That boy is worth $200,000 of anybody's money. He can do everything. He hits the ball a mile. And he catches so easy, he might as well be in a rocking chair. . . . Bill Dickey isn't as good a catcher. Too bad this Gibson is a colored fellow.
— WALTER JOHNSON, 1935

As the 1935 season began, the Crawfords, who had been able to deflect the reality of their also-ran status in the Negro National League by weltering in the publicity geyser of Satchel Paige the year before, faced an uncertain future knowing that Paige had left them high and dry again. This was hardly an unusual turn, of course, but it was more serious this time since Paige jumped the team before the season had even begun and apparently had no intention of coming back. Thus, as ambivalent as most of the Crawford players were about his constant duck-outs in the past, it could not have been comforting to know that the money spigot Paige could open for all of them might now be turned off all year.

Least comforted was Gus Greenlee, who had lived in fear of just such a development; even with Paige filling seats in those big games against Slim Jones, he had lost money again in 1934. With disaster looming on the field and at the gate, Gus and the Crawfords must have shared an almost audible common thought: God only knows how important Josh Gibson will be now.

Actually, Gus had only himself to blame for Paige going over the hill. When Satch married a waitress at the Crawford Grille the previous fall, Greenlee threw a gala reception there for Paige, an expensive affair at which Bojangles Robinson, Paige's best man, performed. But Greenlee, trying desperately to hold the line on player salaries, refused to give Satch a raise—and worse, had gotten a drunken and unaware Paige to sign a new contract for the same salary. When he sobered up, Paige told Gus where he could stick his contract and went back to North Dakota to play with the Bismarck team. Even that far away, Paige still made headlines, carrying his club to victories in several state tournaments, as well as the *Denver Post* tournament.

With Paige gone, Greenlee acted quickly to shore up his team, signing Birmingham first baseman Jelly Taylor, Nashville infielder-outfielder Sam Bankhead, and Chicago catcher Spoony Palm and second baseman Pat Patterson. No one, though, would be as important to the fortunes of the Craws as Josh Gibson. Accordingly, Gus Greenlee went to work, through his conduits in the black press, making sure that Gibson received star treatment.

To be sure, that was becoming easier all the time, as evidenced by Walter Johnson's unsolicited tribute, given on record to an important white sportswriter after the Craws went to Hot Springs for spring training. Johnson, the former pitching great of the Washington Senators known as Big Train, happened to catch a few black ball games and lauded Gibson in an interview with Shirley Povich of the *Washington Post*. Although

Johnson's words carried the seemingly mandatory disclaimer that Gibson had been born with the wrong skin shade, they were sweet music to black ball, especially given this rare incursion of the black game into the white press. And now, getting on the Josh Gibson bandwagon, the *Courier*'s sports page poured it on for the Craws' new headliner.

Avoiding any mention of Satchel Paige, the paper practiced the art of instant revisionism. The Crawford beat men simply left his absence unexplained, leaving the impression that Paige must have fallen off the earth. Meanwhile, the May 5 edition carried a large team photo of the club and touted the "important player trades" Greenlee had made. Right underneath was a piece of puffery with the headline CRAWFORDS SEE BIG YEAR IN BASEBALL, drawing on an obviously tailored Oscar Charleston quote about Josh, which read as if it had been typeset by Gus himself:

> Upon the broad shoulders and brawny arms of "Josh" Gibson, the Babe Ruth of [black] baseball, will rest a major part of the responsibility of bringing to the Pittsburgh Crawfords the National Association pennant for 1935, according to a statement made recently by Manager Oscar Charleston.
>
> Although pitching and fielding will play a large favor in whether or not the Craws can cop the league pennant, Charleston declared, "The batting of such men as 'Josh' Gibson, the bronzed Bambino, will either keep us in or put us out of the close race which the teams will fight this year."
>
> Gibson batted out 69 home runs last year, and 72 during 1933, but he is out to set a new all-time record and better even the mark made by Babe Ruth in his prime, in 1935. He has knocked balls even farther than Ruth, records show.
>
> "Josh," who is a Pittsburgher, is one of the most popular members of the club, and is anxious to start on his "home-run" parade when the Craws open with the New York Cubans in the Smoky City next week.

This, the first known citation of Gibson as the black Babe Ruth, was designed for maximum exposure and was an important milestone in Gibson's career and, later, his myth. Because the smartly placed and eye-catching home run totals were effectively fuzzed to prevent differentiation between league games and those against sandlotters, most future tracts about Gibson would fail to make the distinction as well.

Soon thereafter, in a practice that would endure for decades, black reporters engaged in Gibson retrospectives would as a rule fatten up the Gibson power-hitting chronicles. Using notes he had made seemingly eons before, the *Courier*'s Ric Roberts wrote in the *Sporting News* in 1972 that Gibson had slammed a homer in 1934 at Yankee Stadium against the Black Yankees, which he described as "a rifle-shot that rattled off the escarpments in front of the 161st Street Elevated Railway [which] would probably have traveled 700 feet had it been two feet higher. It was a 680-foot explosion!" The problem with this contention is that no evidence exists that Gibson hit such a homer. Indeed, the only recorded Crawford games at Yankee Stadium in 1934 appear to have been those against the Philadelphia Stars.

Again, Josh's stats against NNL teams in 1934, as reconstructed decades later, look quite impressive, though certainly less than immortal, by most standards: .295, a league-high twelve homers and thirteen doubles in fifty games and 190 at bats. But if Josh had been effectively cloaked by the showmanship of Satchel Paige while maturing, he now stood all alone as never before.

As it happened, Josh Gibson at age twenty-three was about at the height of his powers. He was surely so at bat, but almost as impressive were the newest refinements he'd made in his catching. To take advantage of his hair-trigger throws, Josh had worked out a pickoff system with both Judy Johnson and Cool Papa Bell to trap base runners. If a man came too far down the line from third, Judy would whistle and Josh would fire one down behind the runner.

The Cool Papa play was more tricky: If a man was on second, the entire infield would move up toward the plate before the pitch, giving the runner a long lead. Then, having made eye contact with Josh, Cool Papa would race in from center field and receive a sharp peg on a pitchout. An unwary runner would be caught dead.

Cool Papa and Josh, in fact, had their own communication system, which was made necessary because of the widespread signal stealing in the Negro leagues. As Bell once related, Josh was aware of the thievery and even with no one on base he almost never gave a sign that could be deciphered by any non-Crawford. According to Cool Papa, Josh would change up each game, sometimes giving the real signs not with the number of fingers he put down between his thighs but by the way he turned his mitt. And since Cool Papa had to know what pitch was coming, to aid his positioning in center field, Josh would take a moment to clue him in: if he held his mitt to his chest before the pitch, it was a fastball; if the mitt dangled at his side, a breaking ball. Somehow, the opposition never caught on to it.

The feeling around the NNL—which in its third season had congealed with eight relatively stable franchises—was that the Craws would need every edge they could get to be able to compete with the Philadelphia Stars and American Giants in 1935. Without Paige, this edition of the Crawfords would have little of the élan of the 1934 team for future baseball historians. And yet the players stunned Greenlee and possibly themselves by making a shambles of the first-half pennant race.

For Gus, this was like an elixir. Although he would still lose money on the team and Greenlee Field—around $10,000 all told in 1935—the Crawfords' domination made him feel as young as his players. In late May, in his role as NNL president, Gus went to Dyckman Oval in New York to oversee a league game between the New York Cubans and the Homestead Grays—having paid his penance for twitting Greenlee's authority, Cum Posey was able to take his still shaky club back into the league in 1935—and became incensed when a brawl broke out between the teams. Hurdling the railing of his box seat, Gus, according to the *Philadelphia Tribune,* "injected his stout frame into the fisticuffs . . . and helped the squad of policemen restore order," though he could only watch and wince later in the game when "a number of excited Cuban fans . . . gave the umpire a pop bottle shower."

Getting tough on players who before had caused such disturbances with impunity, Gus fined several players as much as $25 and suspended another for thirty days. He also cracked down on owners slow to wire the league's 5 percent commission due on each league game.

Clearly, acting tough was on Greenlee's mind in 1935. As the season wore on, news of Crawfords victories was accompanied in the black papers by accounts of Joe Louis's unstoppable path toward the heavyweight title with knockouts of Primo Carnera, Kingfish Levinsky, and Max Baer. Greenlee struck up a friendship with Louis, who became a regular at Crawfords games. And though he could ill afford it, Greenlee, perceiving the immense metaphoric value of a sport where black men competed against white men with their fists, spent more money to manage the career of a promising light heavyweight, John Henry Lewis. Gus's big plans for Lewis got rolling when he defeated former heavyweight champ James Braddock and former light heavyweight champ Maxie Rosenbloom, and later that year, on October 31, with Gus in his corner, Lewis decisioned Bob Olin to become the first African American to win the light heavyweight crown.

The Crawfords also ran up a string of victories. Josh got them off fast with a two-run homer in the rubber game of an early season series with the American Giants, a 14–7 Crawford rout. He collected six hits as the Craws took three of four from the champion Philly Stars, then jerked two out of the park against the Newark Dodgers in a victory on June 8.

The fates were also seemingly on the Craws' side. In a doubleheader against the Stars at Greenlee Field, they trailed, 5–3, in the ninth inning of game one but tied it up against pitcher-manager Webster McDonald on two errors. Josh then walked and went to second on Pat Patterson's hit, and both men moved up on a double steal, a favorite play of Josh's when he was the lead runner. Cool Papa Bell walked to load the bases, and Judy Johnson got Josh home with the gamer on a sacrifice fly. In the nightcap, the Stars led, 5–0, in the seventh, then the Craws scored six in the last three innings on a variety of screwups in the field and won, 6–5.

By then, the Craws had won seventeen of their first twenty games, and it was apparent that Paige's loss was being more than filled by two pitchers having the seasons of their lives. One, left-handed curveballer Leroy Matlock, would have the distinction of going undefeated, winning eighteen games in a row. Taking Paige's ceremonial place, Matlock took the ball on July 4 and, like Satch, beat the Grays. The other big arm belonged to Roosevelt Davis, who had knocked around the Negro leagues for a decade with little success but went 12–4 for the Craws in 1935.

The odd thing about the Crawfords' surge was that Josh had to catch up with his teammates, who were clicking on all cylinders. In mid-June, league statistics showed Gibson hitting a paltry .217, with three home runs in sixty at bats— which put him behind eleven other Crawfords in batting average, including Leroy Matlock, and one behind Sam Bankhead in homers. (The Craws top hitter, Jimmie Crutchfield, was tearing up the league with a .444 mark.)

But predictably, Josh warmed, slamming homers in consecutive games against Homestead, Newark, and Brooklyn. There were also three-hit games against the latter two teams. When the Crawfords met the American Giants at Cleveland's League Park in late July for a three-game set, Gibson was white hot. In a Sunday doubleheader, won by the Craws by scores of 17–2 and 12–8, Josh piled up four hits, including a double and homer in the first game and a homer in the second. Next, in a game against Nashville in Columbus, Ohio, he unloaded a homer and a double in one game, a 10–2 win, and a two-run blast in another, a 12–3 win.

This awesome destruction even had a distinct effect on the East-West Game. When the Crawfords dominated the fan voting at almost every position, Gus Greenlee had to placate the owners of other East teams by shuffling the Craw players to the *West* squad, allowing players from the other clubs to have some extended game time.

The result was that the West team was arguably the most talented assemblage in black ball history. This dream team put Josh Gibson, Oscar Charleston, Cool Papa Bell, and Chester Williams in the same uniform as Willie Wells, Mule Suttles, Turkey Stearns, and Sug Cornelius. But the expected mismatch became another of those wild games that made black ball so memorable.

Overlooked by the West's font of superstars was some pretty fair talent on the East team; the starting pitcher was Slim Jones, the third baseman Boojum Wilson, the catcher Biz Mackey, and the second baseman Dick Seay. But the team's driving force was two native Cubans: Luis Tiant and Martin Dihigo. These two superlative players—especially Dihigo, a pitcher by trade who could step into any position on the diamond—put in most of their time in the baseball scene in the Caribbean but were now attracting scores of Latins to Cuban games in New York, a crucial fan base for black ball. (Years later, Tiant's son, Luis Tiant Jr., would become another fan favorite, in the big leagues.)

Starting in center field, Dihigo, a future Hall of Famer, singled in the first of two East runs in the first inning. By the sixth, the East led, 4–0, and would have led by more had not Jimmie Crutchfield robbed Biz Mackey of a run-scoring hit in the third by spearing his long line drive *bare handed*. In the fourth, Josh led off with a double—but was thrown out by Mackey attempting to steal third. He also messed up in the fifth when, with Dihigo trying to steal second, he threw the ball into center field and Dihigo then scored on Boojum Wilson's single.

The West did come back in the sixth after a frightening play. With one out, Josh smacked a typical blur of a line drive toward the center field fence. Dihigo, his eyes trained on the ball, reached for it on the dead run, crashed into the wall as the ball clanged off the 400-foot sign, and lay motionless as Gibson rumbled into second. As the *Defender* described the scene, "the entire playing cast ran to the side of the stricken player. The crowd sat in silence as doctors, photographers, and newspapermen ran to where Dihigo lay."

Regaining his senses, Dihigo stayed in the game. Mule Suttles then walked and Oscar Charleston reached on an error to load the bases before Alec Radcliff singled to score two and Dihigo threw home wildly, scoring another, to make it 4–3.

Josh's roller-coaster ride of a game continued in the seventh when, with one out and Cool Papa Bell on third, he lofted a wind-twisted fly ball to short left that dropped between Fats Jenkins and Boojum Wilson. Though Bell came home, Josh, said the *Courier*'s game story, "won the booby prize by standing and watching them as the ball fell between them for a clean hit. . . . Gibson should have had a double on the blow. [After the throw home] Mackey threw to Seay to catch Gibson on his way into second."

Now, with the game knotted in the tenth, came what may have been black ball's wildest inning. First the East got four runs, only to see the West rally for four in the bottom of the frame, with Josh getting an important single. Finally, the bizarre and electrifying match ended an inning later. With the wondrous Dihigo now on the mound, Cool Papa walked and was bunted to second. Dihigo whiffed Chester Williams, and up came Josh, who already had two doubles and two singles, for a classic confrontation—except that Dihigo lost his nerve and, playing it safe, walked Gibson intentionally, to take his chances instead against Mule Suttles. For the venerable Mule, this was likely the only time in his career anyone was walked to get to him.

At thirty-four, Suttles had something to prove—that he was still as potent a long ball threat as the young buck from Pittsburgh who'd stolen his fame. And on a 1–1 pitch, he turned around a Dihigo fastball and sent it screaming over the right field fence to win the game. As Mule rounded third base, William Nunn reported in the *Courier,* "pandemonium broke loose. Suttles completed his trip home, the third-base line filled with playmates anxious to draw him to their breasts. Over the stands came a surging mass of humanity."

This crackling blow momentarily restored Suttles as the Negro leagues' answer to the white home run god. Nunn, proving how fickle the designation could be, called Suttles "the bronzed Babe Ruth of colored baseball"—a phrase still not cold from when it was applied to Josh only months before in Nunn's own paper but that had probably been first attached to Suttles. To Nunn, the homer was "a Herculean swat, one of the greatest in baseball." The *Defender*'s G. D. Lewis cast Suttles as "still the most dangerous man left in baseball. . . . He is the only man in organized baseball that is able to come through in a pinch except Babe Ruth."

For the proud Mule, the clamor was a moment of exhilaration and glory, and a reminder that black ball gods were numerous. But for him the moment was a transitory one. Although Suttles would play in the Negro leagues until 1948, and Turkey Stearns until 1942, never again would there be any confusion about who held claim to the title of the "black Babe Ruth."

As tough as the Crawfords were, the second half of the NNL season grew surprisingly tight. Indeed, as the New York Cubans, led by player-manager Martin Dihigo and veteran first baseman Showboat Thomas, closed in on and then passed the Craws in the standings, only Josh's molten bat kept 1935 from turning into another letdown.

Indicative of his performance was a mid-August game against the Grays at Greenlee Field. A Buck Leonard homer put Homestead up in the first inning and the Grays led, 2–0, after the second against Lefty Streeter. Playing without Josh, who was being given a rare day off, the Craws were dead on their feet, having gotten just two hits off Ray Brown, until Josh came up to pinch-hit in the sixth with two out and runners on first and third.

As covered by the *Courier,* "Brown pitched to [Gibson] with disastrous results. Gibson tripled to left and two runs came in." Thus resuscitated, the Craws went on to win, 3–2, on Pat Patterson's sacrifice fly.

Josh's turnaround from the first half could not have been more dramatic. In statistics compiled by the league from July 6 to July 31, Gibson led all hitters with a .529 average, and also led the league with six homers, nine doubles, and twenty runs scored in fifty-one at bats; remarkably, he struck out only four times and also had three stolen bases.

Still, the Cubans finished the second half at 18–7, the Craws at 18–9, and a best-of-seven play-off was slated to begin on September 13 to decide the league pennant. The first two games, played at Dyckman Oval and attended by a majority of Latin fans, portended doom for the Crawfords as the Cubans' Frank Blake took game one, 6–2. John "Neck" Stanley then won game two with a 4–0 shutout. (In the classic black ball tradition of chaos, the second game was held up because the umpires hired for the contest didn't know where the game was to be played and arrived a half hour late.)

When the series shifted to Greenlee Field, Josh went to work in the first inning when, according to *Defender* sportswriter Allan Macmillan, Gibson "ripped [one] off the left field side boards [for a triple], scoring Patterson who had previously singled." Staked to a lead, Leroy Matlock bested Johnny "Schoolboy" Taylor, 3–0. Dihigo won the next game to put the Cubans a win away from the flag, but Rosey Davis took game five. Now, back at Dyckman Oval, Leroy Matlock, with the season and his seventeen-game winning streak on the line, fell behind, 5–2, in the eighth inning.

But here Martin Dihigo's ego overtook his senses. Though Schoolboy Taylor had pitched well, Dihigo yanked the kid and put himself in to pitch with two men on. But with stunning suddenness, Oscar Charleston took Dihigo's first pitch out of the park. Now, with the game tied, Patterson doubled and Matlock reached on an error. That brought the great old warrior Judy Johnson to the plate, and he cracked a hit up the middle, winning the game and knotting the series.

Game seven was another stomach churner. Again the Craws fell behind, 7–5, in the eighth, against Luis Tiant. Then Josh hammered one over the left field wall. Charleston came up next and also took Tiant out of the park to tie it. With the Cubans fans stunned, Cool Papa Bell singled off the shell-shocked Tiant. Cool Papa then stole second and went to third on a slow infield grounder, and when the ball was bobbled by the third baseman, Cool Papa turned on the jets and streaked home with the pennant-winning run.

Once again, the end of the NNL season meant little to Gus Greenlee. Seeking an even greater high than winning the league flag fair and square, he signed on for another go-around with the Dizzy Dean All-Stars. This time, though, the rest of the NNL's Eastern teams wanted in and the black players on the squad—who included, besides the Crawfords' best players, Showboat Thomas, Ray Dandridge, Neck Stanley, and Schoolboy Taylor—were grouped under the name of the Colored League All-Stars. Growing in scope, the first games took the form of doubleheaders at both Shibe Park and Yankee Stadium, and these were played before crowds exceeding fifteen thousand.

The Philadelphia games reprised an old theme: Josh Gibson making life miserable for Dizzy Dean. As the *Philadelphia Tribune* wrote up the first game, "Josh Gibson stole the show. . . . Gibson punched three sizzling blows, a single, double and triple to drive his mates to an easy [7–1] win. He sent two runs across the plate and tallied another pair himself."

After the nightcap ended in a scoreless tie called for darkness after five innings, Dean finally got a measure of satisfaction in the first Yankee Stadium game, holding Josh to a harmless single in three at bats and blanking the Colored Stars 3–0 on eight hits. Bill Swift then threw a 1–0 shutout in the five-inning, darkness-shortened nightcap. Even so, Johnny Taylor and Leroy Matlock also pitched well at the stadium, and an optimistic black press was convinced that the Negro leagues' showing in these interracial matches had to count for something.

"[These games] serve more purposes than just declaring a winner of such games," wrote the *Tribune*'s Lewis Dial.

They show that the Negro ball player, if given a chance to play every day for 175 or 180 days like the white boys, can develop as well as anybody. These games also give the lie to the story that Negro diamond stars and whites can't play without unsatisfactory results. No better sportsmanship was ever displayed than that between the two teams. . . . [Brooklyn Dodger third baseman] Joe Stripp spent a good bit of his time over at the colored boys' dugout and Dizzy Dean hung around it quite a lot too. It was a great day for baseball in these parts. . . .

After the first game, Dizzy Dean said that Johnny Taylor has the best drop he has ever seen and here is what he said later. . . . "Yo'all played a great game. Yo'all saw mo' stuff todah than them there big leaguers saw most all season. I ain't had that much stuff on that ball since I pitched agin them buggin' [New York] Giants."

Black optimism could be understood, a lot more easily than Dean's fractured English. But as with so many other dreams of desegregation in baseball, this one too was an illusion.

. . .

Actually, the only real consequence of the Colored Stars was that the team offered the self-exiled Satchel Paige a back door through which he could walk back to the Crawfords. This occurred when the Dean series carried on into Pennsylvania and Paige—who, with his stint in Bismarck over, had eased his way back into black ball by throwing a few games for the Kansas City Monarchs at the tail end of the 1935 season—agreed to join the Colored Stars. This allowed Gus Greenlee to save face and not have to make the first move to get Paige back in a league uniform.

In his first outing against the Dean All-Stars, Paige blew away the pseudo big-leaguers, 3–0, in York, with all the runs coming on Josh's resounding homer in the first inning. Paige beat Dean again by the same score in Forbes Field, profiting from a Boojum Wilson homer.

By the next spring, Satch was back in the Crawford fold, with the pay increase he had wanted the year before. For the Crawford players, that meant a return to old ways that both enriched and tormented them before the tranquillity of 1935. Immediately, Paige was once more at the center of all Crawfords news, his every move drawing huge headlines in the black papers.

Josh, meanwhile, was again relegated to the small print, though there were days that he demanded attention. In a May doubleheader against the New York Cubans at Dyckman Oval, for example, Paige won the second game, but when the day was done the *Tribune* headline read JOSH GIBSON GETS 3 HOMERS AS CRAWS STOP CUBANS. At least on this day, the lead of the game story bypassed Paige in citing other Crawford heroes:

> Josh Gibson, husky catcher of the Pittsburgh Crawfords, Sunday clouted three homers, one of nearly 400 feet distance. . . . Gibson broke up the second game with a drive over the right center barrier in the eighth with one on. He collected

five hits in the two games. Sam Streeter, Crawfords' veteran hurler, stopped the Cubans with four hits and 12 strikeouts in the opener.

The Crawford pecking order was more accurately delineated in a June 13 item in the *Courier* billboarding an upcoming league game:

> When the Crawfords and the Newark Eagles meet at League Park in Cleveland, O., this Sunday in a double-header, besides the appearance of the great "Satchel" Paige, dubbed the league's greatest and most colorful pitcher, two of the greatest hitters in the league will be swinging for the respective teams.
>
> These men will be "Josh" Gibson, home-run hitter de luxe and catcher of the Greenlee-Charleston entry, and the mighty "Mule" Suttles [who had jumped to Newark that season].
>
> Then, too, there will be the personification of speed in "Cool Papa" Bell, fleet centerfielder of the Craws. He'll reach first base during the two games, and when he leaves there, you'll be looking at a "human express." Other outstanding stars will be Willie Wells, Bankhead, Charleston and others.

In reality, Josh came to Paige's aid frequently over the season. In early August, for example, Paige was in a struggle in the first game of a doubleheader with the Philadelphia Stars, holding a 5–4 lead in the ninth when Josh hit one completely out of Parkside Stadium, giving the pitcher some breathing room in the 6–4 win. Then, in the nightcap, he cracked a two-run shot to help Willie Foster, who had again jumped to the Craws from the American Giants, to an 8–5 triumph. Predictably, the headline in the *Tribune* that day read SATCHELL PAIGE LEADS CRAWFORDS TO DOUBLE WIN.

The problem for Greenlee was that, as in the past, Paige's presence seemed not to turn the key to victory. Sold-out houses aside, Paige was even less useful in 1936, causing discernible static on the field as well as in the clubhouse he still only occasionally frequented. With Satch reinstated as the Craws' ace and able to pick and choose his starts, the smoothly operating pitching rotation of 1935 was disrupted, to the detriment of Leroy Matlock and Rosey Davis; their rhythm and confidence shaken, both men suffered through mediocre seasons.

In fact, the delicate chemistry of the whole team that worked so well in 1935 was now gone. The Craws never got untracked and finished third behind the Washington (formerly Nashville) Elite Giants and the Philadelphia Stars in the first-half race, and only a game above .500. Not by coincidence, Greenlee began to focus more on another crusade that might overshadow the pennant race. Reconstituting the Colored All-Stars, he arranged for the team to compete in the lucrative *Denver Post* tournament, which in recent years had come to be dominated by black teams.

This version of the all-stars could fairly be called a dream team in itself, as it skimmed the cream from the top of the Craws (Paige, Gibson, Bell, Williams, and Streeter), the Grays (Buck Leonard, Ray Brown, and outfielder Jerry Benjamin), and the Philly Stars (third baseman Felton Snow, outfielder Wild Bill Wright, second baseman Sammy Hughes, and pitcher Robert Griffith). Facing the top semipro teams in the country in the early August tournament, the Colored Stars swept away four opponents in five days. Josh hit four homers and Paige won three games, the last a 7–0, eighteen-strikeout lark against a magnificently overmatched team from Borger, Texas.

The Borger team's state of mind was clearly not very good going in. Petrified by the thought of standing in against Paige's fastball, they wore specially made plastic batting helmets—a baseball first. But if the Borger boys had seen enough of Paige, the Denver promoters had also seen enough of black ball interlopers walking off with their tournament; never again would a black team be invited to compete.

Greenlee and the Elite Giants' owner, Tom Wilson, who split most of the $7,000 first-prize money in Denver, now made an arrangement of their own. With the Craws seemingly stalled and the Elites in a second-half tailspin—they'd follow up their first-half championship by finishing dead last—the two men agreed that there would be no league playoff this year; instead, the season's crown jewel would again be the East-West Game.

The strategy looked wise when the East squad, blessed again with the services of the Crawfords, tore apart the West, 10–2, before around thirty thousand fans. Indeed, to Gus's delight, Josh and Paige finished one and two in the fan voting, and though Paige was held back for a three-inning mop-up stint, Josh had two hard singles in his three at bats, scored twice, and drove in a run.

As it turned out, though, Gus acted a tad prematurely. Suddenly, the Craws came on strong in late August. They were victorious in a four-team round-robin tournament at Yankee Stadium, then went on to cop the now barren second-half title with a 20–9 record. Although Gus knew he had outsmarted himself, what he couldn't know was that his arrogant maneuvering had cost him his last chance at a league championship.

What's more, Greenlee took a huge, if unfair, hit in early September when the Crawfords played the white Brooklyn Bushwicks. The Craws lost the game, but what hurt more was when the *New York Mirror* hit the stands the next morning and carried a stinging attack on the team by gossip columnist Dan Parker.

The lead item in Parker's "Broadway Bugle" column that day reported that

gamblers got to several members of the Pittsburgh Crawfords, champions of the Negro National League, at Dexter Park last Wednesday night and made a clean-up, taking the short end of 9 to 6 odds against the Bushwicks. The Bushwicks won

7–0. One description of the game read: "What angered Manager Oscar Charlestown [sic] was the awkwardness with which his club conducted itself." Awkwardness is hardly the word for such superb acting.

The Negro leagues had been craving attention in the white press, but this kind of publicity was the last thing the black game needed in its attempt to gain legitimacy. For Greenlee in particular, exposure of his gambling roots was potentially ruinous. Which was why John L. Clark, Greenlee's flack and NNL secretary, immediately fired off a telegram to Parker demanding that he back up his allegation. At first, Parker smugly wired back, "In reply to your telegram . . . I am not in the detective business." But a week later, after every player on the team signed an affidavit denying any involvement in or knowledge of a fix, Parker retracted the charge in print, writing that someone "had steered me wrong" about the reputed fix and that "I hereby make amends to the Crawfords for casting suspicion on them, unjustly."

In truth, as the garrulous Double Duty Radcliffe related many years later, Brooklyn was indeed an obstacle course for visiting black ballplayers trying to steer clear of gamblers. After a Crawford loss to the same Bushwicks at Ebbets Field in 1934, he said, a mysterious man came into the locker room. "A fellow named Stewart. I heard he'd bet a lot of money. He used to follow us everywhere and bet on us. He gave me two hundred dollars. He told me to keep one hundred dollars and buy the boys some beers with the rest. But nobody would accept anything, so I kept the whole two hundred dollars."

The players' wariness about gamblers in the midst of the Crawfords was palpable and was no doubt made more so by Greenlee, who wanted to invite no suggestion that black ball was contaminated by the same forces he dealt with in his prime business. All the same, the damage done by Parker was real, since the web of black ball numbers men and the suspicion they aroused would be an issue in the coming integration debate. Realizing this, John L. Clark, dripping with moral outrage, wrote in the *Courier* that Parker, "by making light of the investment that has been made in organized Negro baseball," had "done more to harm the game than anyone ever has."

For Josh, the season assured him only a greater fame. In August, the last figures released by the league office credited Gibson with no less than a .457 average, tops among regular players, and his fourteen home runs in ninety-four at bats were twice those of the next man in line, Boojum Wilson. (In an extensive reconstruction of the 1936 season by Negro league historian Jim Riley, Gibson's numbers are spicier still: .444, twenty-two homers in forty-five games and 151 at bats, and only eight strikeouts.)

Of more importance, the fact that Satchel Paige could walk out on the team and be rewarded so handsomely for it gave Josh the nerve he needed to drive up his own price. And while Paige's next act of sedition would eventually lead to the breakup of Gus Greenlee's team, the moment Josh Gibson made his stand was really the day the Pittsburgh Crawfords began to die.

10

A Complex
Temperament

For catcher [on Cum Posey's All-American Baseball Club] we have the easiest position on the team to fill. "Josh" Gibson of the Pittsburgh Crawfords is in a class by himself among colored receivers, and is the peer of all catchers in the game today. We take advantage of this opportunity to express our sincere opinion, sad as it may be, that "Josh" Gibson is the only Negro player of the 1936 season whom we are certain could step right into the National or American League and make good as a regular without the usual procedure taken by white players through minor leagues.
—CUM POSEY, PITTSBURGH COURIER,
OCTOBER 17, 1936

In the usual manner, Gus Greenlee sent Josh a contract renewal during the winter, with a nominal raise that brought his salary up to $250 a month. Gus no doubt expected it to be signed and back on his desk without delay, as soon as Josh got home from Puerto Rico. But when days and weeks passed without the contract in the return mail, he knew he had a problem on his hands. If Gus had put the pieces together, he would have known the problem was beyond his power to remedy.

There was, first of all, the drainage of Greenlee's financial base, which had grown from seepage to a hemorrhage. Gus could still put up with blowing a few thousand each season to continue to lord over black baseball, but in 1936 the ground began to give beneath his kingdom on the Hill. Rumors abounded that his numbers business had taken a beating, that he had had to pay off big on several winning numbers. This happened at the same time that a new generation of blacks came of age pledging to disown the grimy underworld within their community and the mobsters who for earlier generations had served as heroes.

Greenlee now found his financial base eroding, and with police informers infiltrating his numbers parlors, the vice squad began to bust his cronies regularly, almost as soon as they set foot in the Crawford Grille. When other numbers men in black ball's ownership bloc began to divest their gaming interests and looked to go legit, Greenlee could only cling to his fading reputation to try to stem his losses. And though he continued staking John Henry Lewis as he defended his light heavyweight crown, when Josh requested that he bump up his salary to the $300-a-month level, which was in the Satchel Paige stratum, Gus refused.

For Greenlee, the decision was based as much on the public perception of Josh Gibson as on his lack of cash. Like almost everyone else, Gus believed he knew Josh to the bone and that his rock-solid catcher, when it came to the ways of real men, was as soft inside as the ice cream he devoured. As Gus saw it, Josh may have thought it was cool to show him up in the Satchel Paige manner, but he felt that if he put the screws to Josh he could bring him around.

This much became evident when March arrived but Josh's contract hadn't. With Greenlee himself unwilling to publicly slam Josh, he yanked his puppet strings in the black press, sending John L. Clark to his typewriter. Clark first tried to downplay the holdout while at the same time attempting to shame Gibson into relenting. Buried near the end of a combined preview of the Crawfords' and Homestead Grays' chances for 1937 in the March 6 *Courier*, Clark inserted these paragraphs:

> The ace holdout is none other than "Josh" Gibson, and the reason has not been determined. Rumor has it that some eastern club has offered him a job as manager. Still another story is told that he prefers to wear a Grays uniform. In the several conferences Greenlee and Charleston have held with the hard hitting receiver, neither of these angles have been confirmed. Even the pinochle figures which Gibson mentions in connection with salary have thrown no light on his intentions for 1937.
>
> Negotiations are at a standstill. The Crawfords' salary list has reached the top. And unless Gibson resigns from the "common agreement" group, Greenlee will have no foundation for compromise or trade. Gibson must make the next move.

What was most absurd about this take was the reach by Clark that Gus Greenlee—who of course had originally gotten Josh to sign with the Crawfords mere hours after he had signed with the Grays—was playing by the rules of some kind of unwritten but implicit common agreement among Negro league gentlemen, while Gibson was not. But what was most significant about the remarks was that the scent of the Grays had pervaded the story of the holdout.

In fact, Cum Posey was holding the ace card in the Gibson stakes. The wily Cum had always been mindful to be kind to Josh and to go overboard in his praise for him. Each season, when Posey selected his All-American team in the *Courier*, Josh was covered with laurels; the most effusive example of this was when Posey, announcing the 1936 team, pronounced Gibson the only Negro-leaguer fit for the majors, a judgment that would have been challenged by many other black ball mavens.

Posey's goal clearly was to get Gibson back in Homestead flannels, and at the tail end of the 1936 season he made his move, getting Josh to play with the Grays for a couple of games during a lull in the Crawfords schedule. Because Josh had returned to the Craws promptly, Greenlee had thought little of the mini jump, equating it to one of Satchel Paige's brief loan-outs. But with Josh refusing to give an inch in his salary demand, Posey again entered the picture—and unlike the chastened man who'd had to eat his pride and endure five years of kowtowing to Greenlee, this was a much stronger Cum Posey.

In fact, probably the most critical factor in the course of Josh Gibson's career was that Posey, against all odds, had kept the Grays in business through the pit of the Depression and the consequences of his own blunders. To accomplish this, Posey had to make a strategic change in his black ball perspectives. Seeing the black game cling to the perverse form of Gus Greenlee, Posey resolved to play it Gus's way. In effect, he went out and got a Gus Greenlee of his own. When the Grays came back into the NNL in 1935, he had a new co-owner, Rufus "Sonnyman" Jackson, a black racketeer who owned Homestead's hottest nightclub, the Skyrocket Cafe, as well as several of the district's best-trod brothels.

Although Jackson clashed with all of Posey's stated ideals about black role models in business and sports, he was an ideal partner for Posey in several respects. Most important, Sonnyman's finances, ill gotten or not, took the Grays off the critical list, allowing Posey to put his suffering players back on full salary. More subtly, Sonnyman's presence changed the Grays' old bluenosed, Boy Scout image—farcical as that image had been, given Posey's womanizing and his players' traditional drinking, brawling ways. With the numbers king of Homestead now attending league meetings, speaking Greenlee's language, and moving in the NNL's upper echelon—he was elected league secretary in 1937—Posey's time was freed, which enabled him to concentrate on baseball matters.

Change of image notwithstanding, Posey's teams were still pretty drab, still coldly efficient, still a well-organized molding of the right players to the right positions. But not since the early thirties were the Grays a black ball dynamo. In 1934, Posey could only give voice to his desire to regain black ball sovereignty by wistfully planting a pro-Grays item in the *Courier*. The item read:

> Loyal followers of the Grays feel that the Crawfords have no right to the spotlight position which the Greenlee men now occupy. They simply cannot bring themselves to believe that a team which has been organized only three years should compare or compete with the most representative product of Negroes in Pittsburgh for the past twelve years—the Homestead Grays. They will concede that there must be some good reason for the weeklies and dailies to devote columns of space to this new child in baseball's family—but even so, they refuse to forsake the old friend for the new.

When Satchel Paige tossed his July 4 no-hitter against the Grays that year, the *Courier* reported that Posey had swallowed aspirin tablets by the handful in the stands during the game. Posey had grown more distressed and more incredulous about his position vis-à-vis Greenlee in the time since. He also could not forget how John L. Clark had maligned him in the press for his "childish pouting." When the Grays had been kicked out of the NNL, Clark had written that Posey's conduct "was no surprise to old observers of the diamond pastime. [The Grays] were expected to violate some rule or regulation before the season closed."

By 1937, Posey's slow burn over these indignities had

grown into a plan to remedy his team's flaws and take vengeance on Gus Greenlee. That way, of course, was through Josh Gibson.

But Posey, who had learned what it felt like to be ostracized by the Greenlee camp, did not move in the once routine Negro league fashion of signing Gibson out from under Gus. Instead, acting on the up-and-up, he made Greenlee an offer to trade Josh to the Grays for the colossal (by black ball standards) sum of $2,500. So that Gus could have some warm bodies along with the cold cash, Posey broadened the deal: Gray catcher Pepper Bassett and third baseman Henry Spearman would go to the Craws if Gus would throw in oldie but goodie Judy Johnson with Gibson. The black press, warming to the rumors of the gigantic deal, began speculating on the "Punch 'n' Judy" trade, meaning Gibson and Johnson.

This wasn't the only proposal directed to Greenlee during Gibson's holdout. Ed Bolden, the Philadelphia Stars' titular owner, also dangled some players and cash in front of Greenlee to persuade him to move Josh. But Gus knew Josh was an invaluable commodity and shuddered at the consequences of losing the black Babe Ruth. And so Gus let the offers slide and, as spring training approached, waited impatiently for Josh to crack under the pressure of the ongoing stalemate.

Josh, though, was reveling in his ability to make time stand still. As Gus had feared, Gibson had ripened as a man and hardened in his convictions. Hardly bullied, Josh took pride in the fact that no Negro league player had dared to hold out this long, not even Satchel Paige, who often exhibited his independence by stepping down in class in order to avoid, rather than fight, the powers that be. When John L. Clark snidely dubbed Gibson a "perpetual holdout," it sounded to Josh as if it was Greenlee and his camp who were cracking.

And they were. In the March 16 *Courier*, a now less civil Clark composed a remarkable seven-paragraph "analysis" of the situation, which was reprinted in many black papers. This piece, which mixed faint praise for Gibson and a backhanded slap at Cum Posey and Sonnyman Jackson with Clark's bile, demonstrates how black ball could deviate from its ostensible veneer of unity when business as usual was challenged; black owners could surely be hard on their own if Josh Gibson could be called out as some kind of ingrate. More valuable still, Clark's column, for all its sophisms, also managed to provide an accurate reading of Josh's interior being, even though Clark didn't know the half of it. Under a headline reading JOSH GIBSON TURNS OUT TO BE NO. 1 HOLDOUT IN NATIONAL LEAGUE LISTS, Clark wrote:

> The most aggravating holdout in the Negro National League happens to be none other than Josh Gibson, first string receiver for the Pittsburgh Crawfords. Not so much because Gibson has demanded an unreasonable salary but on account of a complex temperament developed in the past year, and the inclination of other owners to tamper with this player. . . .
>
> Gibson started off with a stunning salary figure. He followed by saying that he could secure this salary without any trouble for managing an eastern club. Questioned as to whom made the offer, conflicting stories were told and Greenlee decided to do a little investigating. . . . Greenlee intends to have a warm session with the owners who have gotten into the practice of tampering with [Gibson] and thereby caus[ed] dissension and player problems.
>
> Gibson, mentioned often by writers on daily papers last year as good timber for the major leagues, has been a member of the Pittsburgh Crawfords since 1933. Each year, he had had a great deal to say about his salary figure—because he showed improvement each season. He is a good receiver, considered the best in the loop, hits hard, often. Is on the alert and has a way of getting the best a pitcher has to give. Strangely, he is one of the best base runners to be found anywhere.
>
> He is an asset to any club. But not the kind of asset that

more colorful and less capable players might be. With all of his ability, he has not developed that "it" which pulls the cash customers through the turnstiles—although he had been publicized as much as Satchel Paige.

With this shortcoming charged against him, the complex which has engrossed him, and the inclination to play two ends against the middle, it is likely that Greenlee will sell or trade Gibson to the highest bidder.

Clark's comments must have been the first any player, and certainly any black ball fans, had ever heard that Josh was *(a)* less than the second most valuable player in black ball, next to Paige; *(b)* anywhere near as publicized as Paige; and *(c)* a particularly complicated human being. How Greenlee and Clark knew the last was a mystery, though it seems likely the diagnosis was not meant to describe anything beyond Josh's stubbornness about money.

Still, it was becoming harder now for Josh to conceal the particulars of his life away from the field. He was older now, and if he still wasn't comfortable telling people about his painful past, he was no longer concealing his private life. More and more, he would bring Miss Hattie to the ballpark and introduce her to the other players and their wives, though some of these people questioned Josh's apparent need to attach himself to an older woman so unlike himself; some even blamed Hattie for his new money hunger or resented her for undermining his old innocence and humor.

But it was not Hattie's doing that Josh had begun to drink some. For that, many would blame outfielder Sam Bankhead, with whom Josh had been keeping steady company. Bankhead, who was known for his humor and his seeming wisdom about all things under the sun, had a serious affection for the bottle. In the two years that he had been with the Crawfords, Bankhead, a five-seven 175-pounder who turned thirty-one in 1937 but still played as if he had a high-tension wire running through him, had become a kind of self-appointed buffer for Josh; if you wanted to ask something of Josh, you had to go through the briny little Bankhead, who'd sort out the okay requests from the leeching ones, at least as Sammy saw them.

To Josh, Bankhead served as a father confessor, a baseball coach, and a drinking crony. And from about 1936 on, he was practically the only human fixture in Josh's life. "I know that as far back as I can remember," said Josh Gibson Jr., "Sammy was a constant. I'd see a lotta guys come by our house with my father when he dropped off a payment. Satchel, Cool Papa, Buck Leonard. All them great players. But the only guy whose face I got to know was Sammy's. I don't think they were inseparable, 'cause my father didn't get that close to nobody. But they clicked out of mutual respect."

As he took on more of Bankhead's hard edge, Josh's manner and his moods began to change. And while his bouts of playful egotism were still perceived as just that, there were times when his remarks would get barbed and cut at people's hides. During one of the games against the Dizzy Dean All-Stars the previous autumn, Webster McDonald, who threw mostly junkballs, tossed in a pitch that Gibson caught with a bare hand. McDonald, the Philadelphia Stars' player-manager and a twenty-year black ball veteran, called Josh out to the mound. When he got there, McDonald was fuming.

"Don't ever humiliate me like that again!" he rebuked Gibson. "Don't you be catchin' me with no bare hand."

Josh laughed, squirted tobacco juice on the mound, and blithely told the old pro, "Web, you ain't got enough on it to break a dish."

Gus Greenlee, who had been taking note of these changes in Gibson, clearly believed Josh was being misled, that the pushing and tugging by those he trusted had made him more confused than complex. Thus he felt he was safe in siccing John Clark on him. By having Clark inform Josh of his "complex temperament," Gus at first apparently hoped to convince Josh he was acting screwy and thus restore the naive kid in him: maybe a scolding was all Josh needed to bring him back down to earth.

But if Gus read Josh's insecurities correctly, he definitely underestimated Josh's ego, his pride, and his capacity to feel slighted—as well as his intelligence, since, as to most Negroleaguers, it had become evident to Josh that the black ball owners may have been losing money but they were still living off the players.

In misreading Josh, Greenlee made the same mistake that Cum Posey had in 1932. He had also been careless by neglecting to keep an eye on Cum. But by the time Greenlee learned that Posey was willing to meet Josh's price and to shower Greenlee with $2,500, he had lost the war.

On March 27, Gus accepted Cum Posey's cash-and-trade deal at the league's annual meeting in New York, which gave Greenlee a chance to put a favorable spin on this huge public relations debacle. He went about it by reminding everyone who was still NNL boss man.

Orchestrating his reelection as league president, which was not in doubt, he rigged press coverage to play up his election and his address to the owners on the hot-button issue of white booking agents. Despite the fact that Gus had empowered men like Eddie Gottlieb, the Philadelphia Stars owner and promoter of nearly all black ball games in the east, Greenlee, reported the *Tribune*, "sounded the opening gong on a 'finish fight' with Eastern bookers. [Greenlee] stated that the league had reached such a point in prestige and demand that former arrangements would be discarded, and the league would take its proper place in the world of organized baseball."

In fact, no such alterations would take place. But the speech accomplished what Gus wanted, boosting him on the national black ball stage to such a degree that this "news" partially obscured the Gibson trade. GREENLEE NAMED PRESIDENT OF NATIONAL ASSOCIATION AS JOSH GIBSON GOES TO GRAYS was the *Tribune*'s headline, for example. The *Courier* gave

Gus his due, but also ran a full-figure photograph of Josh beneath the heading GRAYS' PRIZE.

Next on the Greenlee agenda was the impossible task of transforming Pepper Bassett, the catcher Posey had tossed into the deal, into a man who could make the fans forget Josh Gibson. In truth, Bassett was a pretty good ballplayer, but the gimmick Greenlee seized upon to hype him showed how silly the mission was. Bassett had promoted himself through his career by catching some exhibition games while sitting in a rocking chair. Now Greenlee had a multicolored rocker built for Pepper to do the same in selected nonleague games. From the chair, Gus swore, Bassett could "knock a gnat off a dwarf's ear at a hundred yards."

Bassett made Gus look good by hitting .444 and was the starting catcher in the 1937 East-West Game, though he went 0-for-3 in the East's victory. Notwithstanding Bassett's play, and Greenlee's quest to give him superstar credentials, there was another reason why he was in the East-West Game—at the time, Josh, as well as most of black ball's real stars, was playing in a far different arena, far from home.

This development was yet another tidal wave of trouble Greenlee had failed to see on the horizon. Cum Posey, on the other hand, was able to handle this, the Negro leagues' most perilous crisis, in a way that both elevated himself and toppled Greenlee—which was no small feat, given the fact that Posey lost Josh almost as soon as he got him.

Posey may have thought he was dreaming when Gibson, like the prodigal son, walked into the Grays training camp in Jacksonville, Florida, on April 1. On that day, Josh was installed in the cleanup spot in the order, right behind Buck Leonard, a move that at once made the Grays a formidable power. Before, except for Leonard and leadoff hitter Jerry Benjamin, the team's center fielder, the Grays were mediocre at bat, and in 1936 their league record had been a combined 22–27. But with Gibson in the order, Vic Harris, who was managing the Grays, now had the catalyst that would make base hits and runs materialize.

Harris's decision to bat Josh cleanup was based on sound reasoning. Looming behind Buck Leonard, whose tightly controlled swing made him a base hit machine, Josh would be able to feast on a steady menu of meek serves by overly cautious pitchers. After Buck, a left-handed hitter, Josh would come at pitchers from the other side, posing an entirely different set of problems. And because the hitters lower down in the order would come up with Buck and Josh so often on base, they too would benefit from pitchers trying to shave the strike zone too fine.

But more than this strategy of bats and balls, Leonard recalled a more important aspect of Gibson's arrival. "He made the whole team better, more confident," Leonard said. "He put life into us. We felt like major-leaguers then." For Leonard in particular, being close to Josh Gibson had the effect of a buff cloth on a pair of polished shoes. Almost inevitably, this great underappreciated hitter became yoked to the black Babe Ruth and was dubbed "the black Lou Gehrig."

On April 8, in a game against the Miami Clowns, the Grays offered a glimpse of the excitement they would provide for much of the next decade. According to the lead story filed from Miami in the *Courier,* one that seemed to shift the paper's allegiance and hyperbole from the Crawfords,

The mighty 1937 machine of the Homestead Grays rolled to [a 10–7] victory here Saturday, paced by the two home run smashes of Josh Gibson, former Crawford star, and by Buck Leonard, outstanding first sacker. . . . The Grays battered the Clown pitchers for 13 hits, Gibson gathering a double and two homers [and] Leonard, rated one of the best first basemen in the circuit . . . was credited with a triple and a home run to round out the day's work.

The box score of the game sat under the heading TOO MUCH JOSH!

Now, game stories even about Gray defeats carried a seemingly mandatory mention of the relocated top dog of black ball. Covering a doubleheader against the Newark Eagles—the new home of Mule Suttles—the *Defender* wrote up the game, an 8–4 Eagle win featuring a three-run homer by Suttles, with the précis that "Leon Day, on the mound for the Eagles, held the hard-hitting Grays with Josh Gibson and company to six hits and fanned four."

Unlike with the mercurial Crawfords, the hype was not wasted on the emerging Grays. In the instant it took to sign Josh, they were a made team. Double-digit run totals became common. Even when Buck Leonard missed a few games in June, the Grays raged on behind some frightful performances by Josh. In a doubleheader against the Washington Elite Giants at Griffith Stadium, he had two hits in the opener, then went 3-for-3 in the nightcap with a homer and two triples.

Two weeks later, the teams met again in a four-game series divided between Griffith Stadium and Greenlee Field, and with Leonard back in the lineup, Vic Harris flipped the two big men in the order, with Buck behind Josh. As Vic saw it, hitting third in front of Buck would make Josh even more menacing and prevent pitchers from intentionally walking him—the exact practice that made Babe Ruth more dangerous hitting in front of Lou Gehrig.

Forced to compete against this lineup, the Elite Giants rolled over. The Grays took three of the four games, the first two by scores of 21–4 and 8–1, though the latter was close until the sixth inning. Then, the *Courier* reported, "Josh Gibson, the big catcher, and one of the hardest hitters in the game, sent a homer over the right field fence with [Ray] Brown on to win the game." In the third game, Josh merely collected two homers and a triple in the Grays 8–3 win.

By then, the Grays had raced to the top of the NNL standings. Josh, according to league figures, was hitting at a .391

clip with a league-high seven homers. Buck Leonard was leading the circuit with a .478 mark, and the formerly sapless Grays were hitting .344 as a team, by far the highest in the league, with ex-Crawford shortstop Chester Williams (.389) and even Ray Brown (.378) among the leaders.

But then, on June 10, Cum Posey probably thought his world had fallen apart. On that day, stunning news came in the black press that Gibson had gone AWOL. Breaking the story in the June 12 edition with the headline GRAYS TO LOSE JOSH TO ISLAND BALL CLUB, the *Courier* reported these details:

> The gilded paradise for ball players of the Negro National League in San Domingo continues to attract stars of all teams. Josh Gibson, the home-run king of the league, announced here Tuesday that he would leave Thursday evening for the islands.
>
> Gibson, catcher for the Homestead Grays, is the first of their number to leave. . . . The high price of $2,200 will be paid for seven weeks' work, according to a report.

Mortifying as this turn of events was for Posey, he had already ensured that he would survive that season's raids from the Dominican Republic league, which had begun in April. Hit hardest by the poaching, Gus Greenlee had only delusions that he could do the same.

The Grays had moved to the head of the black ball class at a time when almost everyone in the black game was preoccupied, and nearly paralyzed, by the Dominican raids. For Greenlee, it was a time in which he could do little else but come more and more unstrung. The episode began when the Crawfords went to spring training in New Orleans and were met by mysterious men in white suits and Panama hats— who, Greenlee found out too late, were hell-bent on taking some of black ball's best known ballplayers to the tropics.

The raids were made possible by the 1930 revolution that

brought dictator Rafael Leónidas Trujillo to power. Having nationalized the American-owned sugar and rum industries, Trujillo suddenly had a lot of money available to sign American players to play summer ball, their existing contracts notwithstanding. For Trujillo, this was both a public relations boon and a political necessity, since the Dominican masses were really the ones obsessed by baseball. It made sense for *el presidente* to own a ball team in the league, but it made even more sense that it be a winning team.

Later, Trujillo's political rivals for power would face a firing squad, but at first his regime was fragile, and baseball became a political tool; the two other teams in the league were operated by men in drab russet uniforms who hoped to create a groundswell that might carry Trujillo out of office in shame. They too went after black ball stars, as well as the best players from Cuba and Puerto Rico.

Accordingly, the season there began with a mix of Latinos and African Americans engaged in spirited competition. Not by surprise, though, Trujillo's agents had lured the biggest names to his team, Ciudad Trujillo—called after the capital city, which at the time he had renamed from Santo Domingo. And yet the mass defections and the whole tempestuous affair might never have gotten off the ground if not for the ministrations of the biggest apostate of all, Satchel Paige.

As might have been predicted, Paige was the first to jump. Offered the mind-numbing sum of $30,000—half of which was his to keep, the other half to disburse to other players he could get to make the jump with him—Paige was the ringleader of the walkout. In short order, he induced no fewer than seven Crawford teammates—including Cool Papa Bell, Sam Bankhead, and Leroy Matlock—to catch the same boat.

Seeing this evacuation, other Negro-leaguers signed up in what became a giant meat market. San Pedro de Macorís got Chet Brewer, Pat Patterson, Showboat Thomas, Schoolboy Taylor, and others to join the two magnificent Cubans, Martin Dihigo and Luis Tiant. Santiago de los Caballeros got Spoon Carter and George Scales.

Josh too was an object of desire on the island, of course, and of frequent calls from Paige to come on down. But having sunk his energies into his holdout, and as pleased as he was with the contract Cum Posey had given him, Josh fended off the advances.

At the same time, Posey and Sonnyman Jackson took drastic measures to keep the people in Panama hats away from the team. During a Grays-Crawfords game at Greenlee Field in May, Sonnyman spotted two Latin men in the front row and had them not only put out of the park but arrested on suspicion of player theft. One of the men, who were quickly released, turned out to be a Dominican consular employee from New York named Luis Mendez, who while offended at being treated like a criminal did not deny he was indeed at the game to court Gray players.

Such paranoia was rampant leaguewide. Gus Greenlee too had suspicious-looking (to him) Latins ejected. And Gus moved rapidly to put a lid on the migration and punish the renegades. On May 1, he instructed his latest puppet commissioner, Ferdinand Q. Morton, to issue an ultimatum: the defectors had to return to their teams or else. When nothing happened, Greenlee collaborated on a statement with the president of the new Midwest-based Negro American League, Robert Jackson. Saying that the Negro leagues were "far larger and more powerful" than the defecting players, Gus set a May 15 deadline. When that came and went, he banned the turncoats "from organized baseball in the United States for life." Said Greenlee: "When they return to the States, they will have nowhere to play."

For Greenlee and his retainers in the black press, public enemy number one became Satchel Paige, whom the *Courier* scorned as a man who had "proved again that he is about as undependable as a pair of second-hand suspenders." The headlines that once told of Paige's pitching feats now focused on the lifetime ban against him and his cohorts.

In retrospect, this outraged huffing and puffing was an overreaction that could only backfire on Greenlee. In effect, the loss of this coterie of players was a three-month sabbatical, which would end by the time the NNL stretch run began. Playing the whole thing down may have worked to the league's favor, building up the anticipation of the players' return. But Greenlee was reasonably apoplectic. With all of this coming so soon after Josh turned his back on him, Gus's pride was on the line. And while his league carried on without much effect one way or another from the defections, his team was wrecked and fell into the NNL basement, from which it wouldn't escape for the rest of the season.

Gus had no trouble getting the other owners to rally behind him and to share in his outrage, Cum Posey included. While Posey was not overly distraught over Gus's woes, he had to join in the league's punitory moves, knowing the threat the Grays were living with. Indeed, as united as the league high command was, and as paranoid, keeping Josh out of harm's way was a doomed cause. With just too much money to turn down, Josh belatedly agreed to play with Ciudad Trujillo.

But unlike Paige, Josh felt he owed Cum Posey the courtesy of an explanation. And, unlike Greenlee, Posey knew he could not cajole his star into changing his mind. Instead, over a box, a compliant Posey did something that was considered heresy around the league. He gave Gibson official permission to take the sojourn, a fact he wanted known in light of Greenlee's failed attempts to bully his men to come back.

Fed the news by Posey, the *Courier* reported the desertion in the most mannerly of terms:

> Gibson . . . is the first [Gray] to leave. It is understood that he will leave with the consent of the Grays' management. . . . Gibson plans to leave by plane on a bee-line for Miami, then

to the islands. Apparently no effort will be made to stop him. Efforts on the part of other league clubs and owners to bring back players have been useless. A test case was tried here in Pittsburgh a few weeks ago when two representatives were arrested. The case was dismissed.

Other teams in the league have lost one or two, and the new raid that has begun has left them with a scare but no idea how to stop them.

Unable to stop Josh from going, Posey had taken the next best step, telling him in advance that all would be forgiven later.

To hear Negro-leaguers tell of the Dominican interlude, it was as if Rafael Trujillo was willing to serve the *americanos'* heads on a platter if they failed him. This tale of terror and intrigue is part of black ball's most beloved lore, though it was created by a simple misunderstanding: that being put under allegedly around-the-clock guard by armed soldiers was a threat to their freedom when in fact it was actually Trujillo's way of pampering and protecting them.

As usual, Satchel Paige was the main purveyor of these tales, which at the time seemed all too real. Because Trujillo wanted to shield the Americans from the seamier attractions on the streets of Ciudad Trujillo and to keep their minds on baseball, his troops ringed the hotel where they lodged, occasionally firing shots into the air in an inspirational fervor while shouting, *"El presidente! El presidente!"* When the players went to the ballpark and left it, they were also escorted by the armed chaperones.

A number of the men who were holed up at the Hotel Inglata for the duration of that hot summer held their teammates and friends back home spellbound for years with romanticized tales of imprisonment and fear. One who did not contribute to the narrative was Josh. It wasn't just that he was never big on fables; the truth is that he had no reason to tell survival tales, since for most of his seven-week stay he was feeling little in the way of discomfort. Or, for that matter, much of anything at all.

He was bunking again with his main man, Sam Bankhead, and those two, at least, had little difficulty evading the rifle squads long enough to do a thorough investigation of the town's red-light district. One of the non-Americans on the team, the Cuban Rodolfo Fernandez, laughs about the concentration camp stories, recalling how the Americans were, as he saw it, treated royally while he and the other Latin players had to live in squalor and fend for themselves. Free to roam the streets at will, Rodolfo often met up with Josh and Sammy in the local *tavernas*. He would go bottle for bottle of *cerveza* with the duo until he could no longer stand erect, at which point Gibson and Bankhead would take another case back to the hotel or to a cathouse.

The amazing thing was that, if Paige can be believed, Satch himself, though a notorious night crawler, never found his way out of the hotel or even to Josh's room to hoist a few. But then, this was classic Josh Gibson, somehow keeping his carousing a very private matter, between only himself and Sam Bankhead. If his other teammates still believed he was in his room all the while, living his days as a monk, he really had reason to giggle about it now. Besides, as Gibson remarked to Sammy on occasion, he was shocked himself by how much he could drink and not become sloppy or even walk funny. One day, he would tell Bankhead, he'd be as good at it as Sammy was.

"Never happen, Josh," Sammy would say. "Never happen."

In time, Bankhead would wish that he had been right.

11

A Martyr to
the Cause

*There's a couple of million dollars' worth of baseball talent on
the loose [in the Negro leagues], ready for the big leagues, yet
unsigned by any major league. There are pitchers who would
win 20 games this season for any big-league club that offered
them contracts, and there are outfielders who could hit .350,
infielders who could win quick recognition as stars, and there
is at least one catcher who at this writing is probably superior
to Bill Dickey.*

> —SHIRLEY POVICH, WASHINGTON POST,
> MARCH 16, 1938

Being able to stand up and focus his eyes after a night of
drinking had rewards for Josh in the Dominican Republic.
Bathed in the burning heat that always loosened up his joints,
he hit a league-best .453 in his seven weeks of highly paid
carousing, though, oddly, he had more triples than homers,
three to two.

As it turned out, Rafael Trujillo needed every one of Josh's hits, as well as the league-leading eight wins in ten games racked up by Satchel Paige. Because as powerful as the Ciudad Trujillo team was, the league race remained close all the way, so close that Trujillo had to impose his dictatorial survival instincts on baseball. When antigovernment riots erupted during games in San Pedro de Macorís midway through the season, he ordered the games stopped and ruled his team the winner by forfeiture.

By season's end, Los Dragones of Ciudad Trujillo, at 18–13, just got by Santiago's Aguillas Cibaenas by three and a half games and San Pedro's Estraellas Orientales by four. In the round-robin play-off that followed the regular season, it came down to Ciudad Trujillo versus San Pedro for the championship, and the events surrounding this series framed many of the monologues of dread told by the men interred on the island. Before the series began, they were taken en masse from the Hotel Inglata to spend the night in the local jail, again, for their protection. In the lockup, they dined on arroz con pollo and red wine, yet in the tall tales it sounded more like a last meal of bread and water

More alarming to the players were the scenes at the ballpark, where troops lined up, bayoneted rifles against their chests, along the opposite stands. Caught in this web of banana republic intrigue—and, so they believed, in a possible cross fire—Estraellas Orientales, with its mostly Dominican lineup, blew past the jittery Americans in the first three games, beating Paige and Leroy Matlock in two of them, although Ciudad Trujillo did come back to square the series at three games apiece.

Now everything was on the line in Ciudad Trujillo's Estadio Quisquey as Paige took the mound to the sound of rifle shots being pumped into the air by whooping soldiers. Waiting for the smoke to clear, Paige surveyed the scene with, he later professed, his knees knocking. "I had it fixed with Mr. Trujillo's polices," he wrote in his memoirs years later. "If we win, their whole army is gonna run out and escort us from the place. If we lose, there is nothin' to do but consider myself and my boys as passed over Jordan."

Actually, the game that followed more than lived up to the mythmaking. Paige fell behind, 5–4, in the seventh inning, and, he later said, "You could see Trujillo lining up his army. They began to look like a firing squad." If Paige really believed that, it must have stoked him and the team. Satch himself sparked a rally in the home seventh with a single. Sam Bankhead then took one over the wall to give Los Dragones a 6–5 lead, which stood up when Paige clamped down with two perfect innings, striking out five of the last six men he faced.

According to Paige and other raconteurs, the postgame celebration came not at a victory parade through the streets organized by Trujillo—not eager to go through another close call, Trujillo ended the organized ball on the island, dashing the dreams of a generation of Dominicans—but on the dock to which they had all made a mad scramble right after the last pitch, counting the minutes until they could leave for home.

The truth was that the players trickled home, and some stayed on the island for days rather than go back to an unsure future and face the wrath of the Negro leagues for their desertion. Paige, in fact, hung out on the Devil's Island of his memoirs for several weeks, pitching exhibition games while he negotiated long distance, through the press, with Gus Greenlee to pay him more than before; Gus, however, insisted he would consider lifting the lifetime ban on Paige only if Satch took a pay *cut*.

Pleading for understanding, Paige was both truculent and contrite. "I would be willing to . . . live in the jungles rather than go back to the league," he said in one breath, then in another that "I am pretty sure when I get back to America I will not be a stranger to the NNL. . . . If I was such a bad fellow, why did such men as Josh Gibson, Matlock, Bankhead, and Cool Papa Bell and others follow me?"

As for Josh, he faced no wrath from his team's owner. During those seven weeks Cum Posey had made sure to keep ladling praise on Gibson; in the July 10 *Courier,* Posey announced his "all-time Grays team," allowing him to hail Josh three separate times in the categories of catcher, best right-hand hitter, and hardest hitter.

Because Posey maintained that he had given Josh a waiver on the lifetime ban, Josh eased right back into his second life as a Gray. This left a red-faced Gus Greenlee unable to maintain a unified front on the league's policy toward the jumpers, even though Posey had voted in favor of it. This was the first breach of Greenlee's authority within the NNL, and because he couldn't do a thing to stop Posey, it set an important precedent in the eventual weakening of Gus's powers—no doubt as Cum Posey had known it would all along.

Still, Josh was subject to some form of de facto punishment; Greenlee declared that all of the jumpers would be ineligible for the August 8 East-West Game. Gus would not budge on this point, and Josh's absence opened the way for the rocking-chair catcher, Pepper Bassett, to play. It also allowed Posey to take a potshot at Greenlee. Previewing the game in the August 7 *Courier,* Posey groused that "Josh Gibson, the greatest player in the history of Negro baseball, is barred by an edict of the president of the Negro National League. We do not criticize this move, although we think the league members should have been consulted."

By excluding Gibson, Posey went on, Greenlee had asked for trouble. "Unless the East sends their strongest lineup to Chicago, do not be surprised at a Western victory." Posey's disingenuous concern was unjustified; the East, behind a Buck Leonard homer and strong pitching by the Crawfords' Barney Morris, won, 7–2.

As he cozied up to Posey, Josh didn't seem troubled that he had distanced himself from the rest of the outlaw band he had joined on the island. When they returned home in late July, they had no alternative but to keep together. Playing exhibition games under the name of the Trujillo All-Stars—

when Satchel Paige came back from the Dominican Republic
and hooked up with the team, they renamed themselves the
Satchel Paige All-Stars—they toured across the Midwest.
With the built-in lure of Paige and the team's status as out-
laws and international champions, they drew immense crowds
and publicity in the black press. In August, the *Denver Post*
tournament temporarily lifted its sanctions against black
teams to allow the All-Stars entry, whereupon they breezed to
victory.

Cum Posey, trying to rehabilitate his image as a loyal member of the league, proudly made note of Gibson's absence
from the outlaw team, trumpeting Josh's loyalty to the circuit. "Josh Gibson returned to the Grays this past week,"
Posey wrote in the July 31 *Courier*. "Josh refused to join the
[Trujillo] club. . . . He was approached time and again to join
the club but positively refused even after some of the players
assured him that they were given permission by some official
of the league [to do so]."

Posey's posturing, of course, was monumentally hypocriti-
cal. But he could afford to gloss over his own heresies on behalf of the league now. With Josh boycotting the Trujillo
All-Stars, Posey savaged the team, not because he was holding a grudge against the players but because it gave him a
chance to rail against the league office, which had made the
team's existence and its popularity possible.

"We are very, very suspicious that there is something very
putrid in Denmark, insofar as the trip west by the players
who returned the past week from San Dominica [*sic*]," Posey
wrote.

The one thing which causes us to be suspicious is built on fact.
Why was so much money and time spent to keep these players from going to San Domingo and then when they return
allow them to go unmolested to play . . . throughout the West
and to participate in the Denver Tournament. It is no worse to
have them in San Domenica [*sic*] where they are practically for-

gotten than to have them playing in the United States where they are competitors.

Disingenuous as Posey was, his departure from the league's hard line against the jumpers ultimately led to its disappearance. As a result, Posey's power would burgeon, mainly because his team was on top of the black ball world again. Even with Josh in the tropics for two months, the chemistry he had created led the Grays on to unbroken success. When Josh put his Homestead uniform back on, the team had already taken the first-half flag with a 26–6 record, three and a half games better than the Newark Eagles, and they were about to make a rout of the second half.

When Josh reentered the lineup for a July 20 doubleheader between the Grays and Washington Elite Giants in Baltimore's Oriole Park, Posey faced little opposition. Still, when Gibson's name appeared on the lineup card, Vernon Green, the Elites' vice president and road manager, refused to let his team take the field. For around ten minutes, the Elites sat in the dugout while, according to the *Afro,* "team officials argued over allowing Josh Gibson . . . to compete in any league games until some definite action was taken by league officials."

Actually, the protest was more the result of confusion and indecision by the league office than contempt for Gibson. As the *Courier* noted, "[Gibson] returned last week, but as yet no action has been taken by the league concerning the status of returning players, thus the Elite manager, Biz Mackey, complained of his presence in the lineup."

Posey could clearly see that Gus Greenlee was beginning to reconsider the league's position on the lifetime bans, now that Paige, Cool Papa, and the other Crawfords were back on home soil. And Cum guessed correctly that Gus would be a paper tiger about it in the end; rather than cracking down on Gibson, he used the situation to send a signal to Paige and the rest that they could follow Josh back into the league in 1938.

Thus, while the Elite Giants filed their protest with the umpires pending league action—permitting the Grays-Elites twin bill to go on—nobody expected the protest to be upheld or the entire matter to be dealt with at all.

Now free and clear to play without the slightest worry hanging over his head, Josh went 1-for-2 with a walk and a stolen base, though the Grays went down to a rare defeat in the opener, 8–4, when Ray Brown was strafed. The Grays righted themselves quickly in the nightcap, as soon as Gibson came up for his first at bat and blasted one. The *Courier* reported that "Gibson's clout . . . sailed over the left field wall and [was] said by park attendants to be [one] of the longest drive[s] seen in the park's history." Unfortunately, it wouldn't count; the Grays were ahead, 6–3, in the fourth when the game was halted by darkness.

Josh carried on his usual late-summer barrage when the same two teams played in early August. After the Grays won the first two games, 8–2 in Charleston and 7–4 in Columbus, the clubs went to Fairmont, West Virginia, where Josh added another benchmark performance. The *Afro,* covering the Grays 8–4 victory, reported, "Saturday's game featured Josh (Fence Buster) Gibson, who hit three home runs over [the] centerfield fence in four times at bat." All of the dingers in this, his second recorded three-homer game against Negro league competition (he may certainly have had many such games in total, and was known to have a four-homer game against a semipro team in Zanesville, Ohio, in the thirties), came off pitcher Andy Porter, who was good enough to turn in eighteen Negro league seasons.

The last two games of the series drew around ninety-five hundred fans to a doubleheader at Cleveland's League Park. The opener was the closest the Elites would come to winning, but again Josh made the difference, this time with a shot into the alley in the first inning. The *Defender,* in its game story, related the hit in a paragraph that was made almost poetic by a typographical error that seemed like a fitting description of Josh:

> The Homestead Grays made two tallies . . . when [Vic] Harris sent a sizzling smash through the box and scored when Gosh Gibson crashed one against the left center field bleachers for two sacks. Slow fielding by [Bill] Wright gave Gibson an extra base and as the infield relay went wild at the plate Gibson slid across safe.

The Grays went on to win, 3–2, behind Ray Brown, then ran away with game two, 5–0, with Louis Dula getting the victory. Then, in a late August doubleheader in Chicago against the American Giants, the Grays' one-two punch drew the attention of the *Defender*. The lead of the paper's game story read:

> Cumberland Posey's Homestead Grays came to town Sunday and when they left, they toted away both ends of a sensational double-header with the American Giants.
>
> The scores were 4 to 2 and 5 to 3, but these figures don't half tell the story. They don't say anything about the prodigious wallop that Josh Gibson, hefty home run slugger of the Grays, lofted clear over the left field fence in the first game. Neither do they tell of the one Buck Leonard hoisted over the right field wall . . . in the second affair.

There were several other electric moments in these games. In the first, Josh hit a screamer that smacked against the left field wall on the fly. While the Chicago outfielders chased the ball as it caromed back toward the infield, Josh tore around the bases, holding up at third at the last second rather than trying for an inside-the-park homer. Leonard then singled him home. Then, in game two, Buck came up in the sixth with the bases jammed and was struck out by the old pro Willie Foster.

Clearly, the stodgy old Gray style had given way to a new brand of high-voltage baseball that fans craved. Late in the season, when the Elite Giants moved to Baltimore, Posey broadened the Grays' purview by scheduling some home games in D.C.'s Griffith Stadium. In the process, he entered into an agreement with Senators owner Clark Griffith that split gate and concession income between the two teams. Now the Grays could call *two* major league ballparks home. In 1938, the Grays would divide their home games between Forbes Field and Griffith Stadium, though Posey had plans to eventually make D.C. a permanent base. Accordingly, whenever the Grays played in D.C., he had a big *W* stitched onto their uniform shirts.

After the deal was struck, Clark Griffith began issuing apparently earnest plaudits about the caliber of men like Josh Gibson and Buck Leonard, and even reflected on a long-ago meeting with the father of the Negro leagues. When Griffith was manager of the Washington Nationals in the 1910s, he said, the team shared a train ride from Chicago to St. Louis with Rube Foster's American Giants. Because the train was so crowded, Griffith's team had no sleeping quarters. After he told his plight to Foster, Griffith said, Rube allowed the Nats to use upper berths in the Giants' Pullman car. Griffith relished telling people that the white team slept in the space where the black team normally stowed its luggage.

Griffith also began to hang around the Grays dugout and to inch closer and closer to Josh. "Gonna hit a homer for me today, Josh?" he'd chirp, loud enough for everyone on the bench to hear. In time, word spread that Josh was Griffith's pet.

But if black ball people got the idea that Griffith planned to carry the ball on the still-orphaned concept of big league integration, it would soon become apparent that Griffith's hyping of black players had much more to do with the effect of the Grays on his money coffers than it did with his conscience or sense of justice. As lowly and unprofitable an attraction as the Washington Senators were, Griffith could reasonably count on something like $50,000 per season from Grays games, and some years that was the difference between solvency and bankruptcy for Griffith.

As always, Josh Gibson's solvency was bolstered by his forty-ounce Louisville Slugger and his quickly growing legacy, which was swelled by another colossal shot that 1937 season. In this unverifiable scenario, Negro league hands tell of a titanic blast in Yankee Stadium against the Black Yankees—another one that in some versions went clear over the roof—that was recovered by a fan and given to Black Yankee outfielder Clint Thomas. When Thomas was later interviewed on Ed Sullivan's radio program, Sullivan, according to lore, paid him $50 for the ball and kept it until the day he died.

Despite the seven-week hole in Josh's Negro league season, Cum Posey's flacks had no compunction about swelling Gibson's home run total in the usual fashion. When the Grays split a doubleheader against the American Giants in late September in Oriole Park, the *Afro*'s coverage served as the conduit.

"The opener was a battle of home runs," the paper said. "Josh Gibson, Grays star catcher, open[ed] the parade by poling one out of the park in the third. The ball traveled some 425 feet and landed on a housetop across the alley from the field. It was Josh's seventy-fourth smash of the season."

NNL stat keepers, who were known to keep hours at the Crawford Grille, had some amazing figures on Gibson as well, though not ones Posey's people were willing to accept. Gus's minions had kept track of only eleven games he had played, and these "official" figures credited Josh with a .500 average (21-for-42) but—despite his spree of big flies in the second half—only seven homers, the exact number of home runs he'd had when he cut out for Ciudad Trujillo; now he was said to have finished second, by five, to Mule Suttles for the league lead.

This flimflammery, which may have been a kind of retroactive punishment aimed at Josh for jilting Gus, would be repeated in 1938 as well, as Gus was struggling to hold on to the last of his power. But now, with Gibson at his disposal and with his team beginning to establish itself as a dynasty, Cum Posey knew he would be able in time to grab control of black ball's information lines and erase Gus's fingerprints from them once and for all.

There is little to suggest that Josh especially cared what the stat men were up to; he had to be genuinely flattered, however, that he was accumulating name recognition in the white baseball world on a level second only to Satchel Paige's. Following the hymns of Walter Johnson and Clark Griffith, late in 1938 came another paean, from Leo Durocher. When the Grays barnstormed against a white team fronted by the Dodger shortstop and incipient manager, Leo "the Lip" watched Gibson pound three homers in the eight-game series and delivered this soliloquy: "I played against Josh Gibson in Cincinnati, and I found out everything they said about him was true, and then some. He hit one of the longest balls I've ever seen. He caught hold of one of [Jim] Weaver's fast ones, and I'll bet you it's still sailing."

Before long, white sportswriters would begin to take note of such words about black men and begin to wonder in print what in hell the big leagues were waiting for to sign them. Only then would the cause for integration get serious.

As Cum Posey had figured, Gus Greenlee's posturing ended as soon as the men of the Trujillo All-Stars—which was essentially the Crawfords roster—returned to the league looking to reclaim their jobs. Since the All-Stars had outdrawn league games, Greenlee had lost his leverage anyway, and the Craws' stint in the NNL basement had convinced him that amnesty for the players was a good idea.

As a last conceit, however, he assessed each of the expatriates the nominal fine of one week's pay, a move Posey supported but feared would lead to a potential replay now that other Latin summer leagues were putting out feelers about the availability of Negro league players. Posey counseled in his column, should any players attempt to jump, "do not allow them to hold a club over your head by threatening to depart."

As for the Dominican jumpers, most walked back to their old teams. But one who didn't was the man Gus needed the most, the redoubtable Satchel Paige. Inexplicably, Greenlee held to his stance of the previous year, refusing to pay Satch more than $350 a month, which made Paige the most famous Negro league holdout and the target of invectives by black sportswriters still loyal to Greenlee. The newest of that lot, the *Courier*'s Wendell Smith, insisted that Paige was "not the pitcher he once was. He is getting to the point where batters can distinguish between a pea and a bullet. There was a time when they couldn't see it."

But, as with his standoff with Josh, Greenlee was doomed to fail. Paige, as was his custom, simply stepped down a notch in competition and went to play for the summer in the Mexican League. And he was not alone in this course of action. When Paige got to Mexico City and joined the Agrario team, he found Cool Papa Bell roaming the outfield; he too had become fed up with Greenlee's penury. In response, a weary Gus could only hand down two more lifetime bans, which just underscored Greenlee's eroding power base.

Gus pressed on with the season, with an aging and dying team. In a desperate attempt to attract fans to Greenlee Field, Gus stooped to hiring Jesse Owens, the great black Olympic track hero, to run against a racehorse on the field before games. Meanwhile, Cum Posey was drawing fans to two big league parks and plotting his return to power, using Josh Gibson to his advantage every step of the way.

As he had the year before, Josh occupied the better part of Posey's writings during spring training. Posey went so far as to devote an entire column to a question-and-answer interview with Gibson. This encounter shed little light on Josh's personality, but was enlightening about his take on his career, the traces of his ego, and his impish challenge to an old teammate and running mate. One excerpt went like this:

Q. How does colored baseball at the present time compare with colored baseball at the time you broke in during 1930?

A. It is better now. We have a league now which we consider well organized. I feel as though I have something to play for now, besides just making a payday.

Q. What did you consider your best year?

A. 1931.

Q. What pitcher had best control of any pitcher you ever caught?

A. Smokey Joe Williams.

Q. Who was the smartest pitcher?

A. Two of them. Sam Streeter and [William] Bell.

Q. What park do you prefer to play in of all parks?

A. Polo Grounds of New York.

Q. No use asking you why as I know it is on account of the short left-field stands.

A. Right field, too.

Q. What was the hardest ball you ever hit?

A. Last year at Farmers [East Orange, New Jersey], and in 1930 at Yankee Stadium.

Q. How far did you hit them?

A. At Farmers I hit the ball over the left-field fence and over a two-story station outside the park. At Yankee Stadium I hit the ball on a line into the bullpen in deep left field.

Q. Where do white fans appear to appreciate colored baseball the most?

A. Dexter Park, Brooklyn; Farmer, East Orange, New Jersey; Belman, Phillipsburg, New Jersey; and in Philadelphia.

Q. Have you played against many major-league players?

A. Too many to remember—Hornsby, Foxx, Dean brothers, Pepper Martin, Whitehead, Hack Wilson, Manush, Ted Lyons.

Q. Did you ever hit a home run off Dizzy Dean?

A. Yes, in York, P.A.

Q. I guess that's all, Josh.

A. No, that's not all. Why don't you ask me how I think I will come out when I face Satchel Paige this year? [At the time, Paige had not yet gone to Mexico.]

Q. That's interesting to everybody. Satch against Josh. What do you figure?

A. I look to break even, two out of four. One thousand in a pinch, providing Charleston don't say, "Put him on."

Posey followed up this attempt to humanize Josh with a dispatch on April 16 that read:

Josh Gibson furnished another good reason why we rate him as the best Negro baseball player of all time, when he appeared at Memphis, Tenn., with the Grays on April 3rd. Josh accounted for all the Grays runs with two home runs, a single, batting in four runs and scoring three [as the] Grays won over the Memphis Red Sox of the Negro American League 7 to 3.

Working their way through the South, the Grays next faced the NAL champion Kansas City Monarchs in Houston and won, 9–5. Under the headline JOSH GIBSON AND HIS BAT BEATS KAYSEE, the *Defender* described the game's turning point this way: "Josh Gibson's home run in the seventh with two men perched on the sacks put the Homestead Grays . . . far enough out in front so they could not be overtaken by the Kansas City Monarchs."

This was followed by a 4-for-4 day against the Atlanta Black Crackers. The Grays then opened the NNL season with a doubleheader in Philadelphia. With Josh catching both games and slamming a homer in the first, the *Courier* aptly wrote that the Grays had "jumped all over" the Stars, sweeping the two games by scores of 11–3 and 6–2 and giving fair warning that both the team and Gibson would be juggernauts in 1938. Taking on the Washington Black Senators, a short-lived entry in the NNL, Homestead had four homers in game one, a 10–8 win that led to a five-game sweep. Against the more formidable Baltimore Elite Giants, the Grays took three of four games, losing only a game called for darkness after seven innings, 6–5, while putting away the remaining games by scores of 16–3, 6–0, 6–3, and 13–1.

By July, when the Grays had eliminated any semblance of heated competition, the league released its set of batting average statistics. Josh was hitting .375, Buck Leonard had a league-best .480 average, and Buck had reached a milestone of sorts by winning notices in the Negro papers as the "black Hal Chase." By this time, such comparisons between black players and major-leaguers suddenly sounded less chimerical and more demanding of answers to baseball's race evasions.

It was during the 1938 season, in fact, that the attentions of white sportswriters fomented the first few ripples of the integration wave. Actually, the first sounding on the subject may have come as early as July 1935, when Gene Coughlin of the *Los Angeles Post-Record* noted,

It's about time for organized baseball to pull its head out of the sand and take a gander at a nation and a people it has not seen clearly since 1889, or thereabouts. . . . The master minds of the national pastime are pretending that the only people who have a right to play baseball . . . are members of the Caucasian race. . . .

It occurs to us that if Joe Louis can excel in the heavyweight field; if Jesse Owens and Ralph Metcalfe and Eddie Tolan and others can lead the field home in track meets; if Brice Taylor and Willis Ward and Duke Slater can win All-American recognition as football players, then why is it not reasonable to assume that colored athletes could become stars in organized baseball, even topping the performances and records of Ty Cobb and Babe Ruth?

But the earth really moved, at least under the Negro leagues, when in 1938 two of the more consequential white writers upbraided the lords of the white game for ignoring obvious big league material playing in their own ballparks. In these tracts, Josh Gibson was a constant. In March, columnist Shirley Povich of the *Washington Post* wrote delicately but emphatically of the "couple of million dollars' worth" of black talent to be had, and the instant big league potential of the black catcher named Gibson who may be superior to Bill Dickey.

In September, the *New York Daily News* sports editor, Jimmy Powers, made his pitch, relating the by now wide-spread black ball lore about Josh's Ruthian home run totals and venturing that "this man [Gibson] would be worth $25,000 a year to any club in baseball."

A week later, Powers wrote another column in which he named seven black ball players, headed by Josh, Buck Leonard, and Ray Brown, who he believed could step right into the New York Giants lineup and take the team to the pennant. At once, the black papers played it up as an epiphany. The *Courier,* in a state of near delirium, ran photos of the players with the slug "Here's Jimmy Powers' 'Dream Team' for the New York Giants."

Such high-visibility notices encouraged black writers to become more militant and to meet the issue head-on. Just before the 1938 season, the *Courier*'s Chester Washington, brandishing a hypothesis similar to Jimmy Powers's, wired a telegram to Pittsburgh Pirate manager Pie Traynor, which read:

KNOW YOUR CLUB NEEDS PLAYERS STOP HAVE ANSWERS TO YOUR PRAYERS RIGHT HERE IN PITTSBURGH STOP JOSH GIBSON CATCHER B. LEONARD 1B AND RAY BROWN PITCHER OF HOMESTEAD GRAYS AND S. PAIGE PITCHER COOL PAPA BELL OF PITTSBURGH CRAWFORDS ALL AVAILABLE AT REASONABLE FIGURES STOP WOULD MAKE PIRATES FORMIDABLE PENNANT CONTENDERS STOP WHAT IS YOUR ATTITUDE? WIRE ANSWER

Pie Traynor did not bother to reply, nor did he need to. Indeed, for all the crackle of impatience in 1938, some black journalists knew full well that the prize was nowhere near and would not be until there were many more white voices and many more days of Negro league progress to make the case. One highly influential black writer, Dan Burley of the Negro Associated Press, cited another complication: the ambivalence of black owners pledged to the cause but knee deep in the business of baseball apartheid.

"I have a sneaking suspicion," Burley wrote tartly, "that the moguls of colored baseball, in their hearts, don't give a single thing about colored players getting into the big leagues. . . . That's why you don't hear them agitating so much [for integration] and personally I don't blame them. Of course it's hard on the players who, after all, must eat."

Another black voice, the *Afro*'s Art Carter, was harder still on black ball's high council, decrying the owners' delusion that they had evolved as highly as their players. The Negro leagues, Carter said, should fight the integration fight, but "the job would be so much simpler if we clean out our own setup first and start putting out real ball clubs, with efficient methods . . . and then see how quickly those race bars would come down."

And so, for the time being, most white owners could ignore these first calls for reform. It fell to Clark Griffith, the Grays' landlord in Washington, to put the matter to rest, however, by raising a point that must have resonated for every Negro-leaguer. "I know the time will come when the ice will have to be broken," he said, adding that the black man chosen first "will hear caustic comments. He will be made the target of cruel, filthy epithets . . . and thus become a sort of martyr to the cause."

If it occurred to Josh that white aggrandizement required a certain attitude in *him,* or that it would help his chances for a possible big league promotion if he avoided plebeian temptations away from the field, he gave no evidence that he was listening. Lost beneath the constant blush of victory and flattery, his hidden drinking went on unabated. Not only had he removed the red flags that once cautioned him about following Nancy Gibson's path; he was beginning to allow his new habits to intrude on the game.

Although Josh again garnered the most ballots among East players for the East-West Game, on the day the game was played he turned up AWOL. Quickly, Cum Posey quashed any unsavory scuttlebutt and announced that Gibson had come down with an unspecified last-minute injury. Privately, Posey had learned that Josh had been drinking, slept through his alarm clock, and missed his train to Chicago.

Posey, who was far more interested in upholding Josh's reputation than Josh seemed to be, had to walk on a hairline when confronting Gibson's roistering. On the one hand, keeping it out of sight was good for business and good for Josh's image. Yet because Posey practically encouraged drinking on his team (in this world excessive drinking was considered a manly art), neither he nor Josh thought a problem existed beyond Josh's ability to get to games on time. As a result, Posey's response was a side game of cover-up.

For now, Posey told Josh he had saved his neck in Chicago and Josh promised it wouldn't happen again. But Posey, apparently impervious to the potential effect drinking might have on Josh's well-being, only made things worse after the Grays captured their second straight pennant. It was then that Posey, celebrating the demise of the Pittsburgh Crawfords, took Josh's advice and picked up his carousing buddy Sammy Bankhead off the remains of Gus Greenlee's club, which Greenlee was in the process of folding.

The Crawfords' passing was a big story in Pittsburgh and in black ball that winter, with reason, since it brought an end to black ball's most gilded and manic era. In Homestead, meanwhile, hidden beneath the astounding success of the Grays, a more personal kind of black ball tragedy was in its genesis.

From the Conroy
Pre-Vocational School
yearbook, 1928: Young,
gifted, and innocent. And a
natural on the ball field.

Nineteen-year-old
Josh and the love of
his life, teen bride
Helen Mason, at
Ammon Field, 1929.
A year later, tragedy
marred the picture.

Josh's children, Josh Jr. (left) and twin sister, Helen, with their aunt Rebecca Mason, circa 1934. Only occasionally was Josh there to hold their hands.

3

"Samson" Gibson broke into the Negro leagues in 1930, blasting home runs for the Homestead Grays—including the longest-ever hit at Yankee Stadium.

4

5

Gus Greenlee, racketeer owner of the Pittsburgh Crawfords, shook up black baseball by getting Josh to jump from the Homestead Grays to the Crawfords in 1933.

With the Crawfords, Josh formed a "Murderer's Row" of future Hall of Famers with (left to right, in uniform) third baseman Judy Johnson, manager Oscar Charleston, and pitcher Satchel Paige. In the middle is light heavyweight champ John Henry Lewis, who was managed by Gus Greenlee.

Although known for his hitting, Josh was a talented and underrated catcher with a fine arm. Pitching great Walter Johnson once favorably compared Gibson's skills to Yankee catcher Bill Dickey's.

8 The young Gibson (second from right, top row) was heavily influenced by hard-drinking outfielder Sam Bankhead (second from left, middle row, flanked by Cool Papa Bell, left, and Oscar Charleston).

Josh, who regularly played winter ball in Latin America, cavorts on the beach with Crawford teammate Ted Page in San Juan, Puerto Rico, in 1939. Gibson won the most valuable player award in the Puerto Rican League several times.

When it came time to play in the tropics, Josh (middle, top row) sometimes looked woozy after partying all night, as during this stay in Cuba. But if he could stand, he could hit.

11

12

By the late thirties, wear and tear and alcohol had begun to take a toll on Josh.

Josh returned to the Homestead Grays in 1938, whereupon he became frequently mentioned in the black and the white press as a candidate to play in the major leagues. But there would be many roadblocks ahead.

The heart of the Grays' potent batting order featured the "Thunder Twins," Josh (second left) and future Hall of Fame first baseman Buck Leonard (middle). Other powerful bats belonged to Sam Bankhead, Dave Hoskins, and Jerry Benjamin.

13

At Josh Gibson Night, Washington, D.C., 1943, Grays owner Cumberland Posey presented Josh with a set of luggage and an oversized bat.

14

Gibson's physical and mental pain were eased by his beautiful mistress Grace Fournier. But it was Grace who hooked Josh on heroin.

15

In an epic confrontation, Josh and Satchel Paige faced each other in the 1942 Negro World Series. Satch won the war.

16

17

Even in declining health, Josh gave it all he had. Always an aggressive base runner, here he slides home during the 1944 East-West Game in Comiskey Park.

In 1946, a terminally ill and bloated Gibson still led the Negro leagues in homers with eighteen and hit .36l.

18

JOSHUA (JOSH) GIBSON
NEGRO LEAGUES 1930-1946
CONSIDERED GREATEST SLUGGER IN NEGRO
BASEBALL LEAGUES. POWER-HITTING CATCHER
WHO HIT ALMOST 800 HOME RUNS IN LEAGUE
AND INDEPENDENT BASEBALL DURING HIS
17-YEAR CAREER. CREDITED WITH HAVING
BEEN NEGRO NATIONAL LEAGUE BATTING
CHAMPION IN 1936-38-42-45.

Long gone and all but forgotten, Josh was given his due when he was enshrined in the Hall of Fame in 1972.

12

A Household Word

The broadcasting stations of New York City heaped limitless praise on Negro players and Josh in particular in advertising the four-team [Negro league] doubleheader at Yankee Stadium on July 23. There is no doubt that many of the fans who attended on this date came to compare Josh with sluggers of the Hank Greenberg, Jimmy Fox [sic], Joe DiMaggio, and Bill Dickey type.

—CUM POSEY, PITTSBURGH COURIER,
AUGUST 5, 1939

By all rights, the 1939 season should have belonged to Josh. At age twenty-seven, he was at his physical peak, his bat as hot as it had ever been and his skills as crisp as the creases of the tailor-made seersucker suits he had begun wearing to the ballpark.

"I'll never forget one ball he hit that year," said Gene Benson, who played center field for the Philadelphia Stars. "We was playin' in Griffith Stadium and we had the Grays beat by a couple runs in the ninth inning. A fellow by the name of Henry McHenry was pitching for us. A good curveball pitcher. And he threw Josh a beautiful curve that really fooled him because Josh kinda bailed out as it came in. But even though he took one hand off the bat, he swung and hit the ball back up over my head in center field. No exaggeration, the man hit it up in the stands with one hand."

This was also the year, at least as best can be pinned down, when Josh blasted the fourth of his most fabled home runs. Not incidentally, it occurred, like the "500-mile" homer in York, Pennsylvania, outside the ring of press coverage. But there are still monuments today in nearby Monessen, Pennsylvania, commemorating the landing site of the 512- or 575-foot (depending on the teller of the story) meteor he evidently hit against a white semipro team. Adding some eyewitness testimony is Buck Leonard, who had no trouble isolating this shot from dozens of similar blows he saw from the on-deck circle.

That day, Leonard attested, Josh "hit the ball out of the park in dead center field and it landed on the side of a mountain. We could see the boys looking for the ball on the mountain out there."

Years and years later, Josh Gibson Jr., retracing his father's steps, went to Monessen to check out this myth, pacing off 512 feet from where home plate had been in what is now a weed-strewn coal field. "Them people there, they know all about that home run," he said. "What happened was, the mayor of the town saw my father hit it and they stopped the game and the mayor went out there with a tape measure to where the ball landed. That's like the biggest thing ever happened in Monessen."

By now, with Satchel Paige having renounced his Negro league citizenship, the black papers, especially the *Courier*, did not lose a beat in turning to Josh as the Pegasus of their cause. Continuing the brash advocacy journalism of the year before, the *Courier* launched a frontal assault in July 1939 by sending a reporter to a Pirates–New York Giants game at Forbes Field to question Giants manager Bill Terry and some of his players about the issue of baseball integration.

Terry's response was curt: "No, I do not think Negro players will ever be admitted to the majors. . . . The problem of mingling socially with the other players and traveling about the country together makes it impossible for us to admit the Negro player. I think they can be more successful with a league of their own."

However, the paper did make headway when it put the question to the great first baseman Mel Ott. Said Ott: "I've heard a great deal about Satchel Paige and Josh Gibson, but I haven't had an opportunity to see them. From what the other big leaguers tell me, they must be good enough for the majors."

But there was a bonanza of good copy from another future Hall of Famer, pitcher Carl Hubbell, who had barnstormed against black teams. Normally a taciturn man, Hubbell ran off a long and fervent testimonial to the new black ball king, not so much for his bat as for his other skills:

> I've seen a lot of colored players who could make it up here in the big leagues. First of all I'd name this big guy Josh Gibson, the catcher. He's one of the greatest backstops in the history of baseball, I think. Boy—how he can throw! There seems to be nothing to it when he throws. He just whips the ball down to second base like it had a string on it. He's great, I'm telling you. Any team in the big leagues could use him right now.
>
> But with all that, the thing I like best about him is that he's as fast as greased lightning. You know, after a few years a catcher usually slows up considerably from bending down so much. But that guy—why, he's never slowed down.
>
> Gibson came to bat [in one game] and laid down a bunt that rolled almost to the pitcher. And do you know that he beat the throw to first! Yes sir, I've seen a lot of colored boys who should have been playing in the majors.

Such prose, which was routinely shrugged off by the big league powers, was like sweet honey to the black ball forces. The *Courier* splattered the Hubbell quotes all over sports page one, trumpeting that "Hubbell, one of the greatest pitchers of all times, was loud in his praise of Josh Gibson, probably the greatest catcher in baseball, and a member of the famous Homestead Grays." The remarks also formed the basis for a sidebar touting the Grays' top guns. "If and when the major leagues open their doors to Negro ball players," the piece began,

> there are two young men going about the country these days who will, in all probability, lead the sepia parade into the big league fold.
>
> They are Josh Gibson and Buck Leonard of the Homestead Grays!
>
> Anywhere that Negro baseball is played the names of Gibson and Leonard are household words. From coast-to-coast they have left their fence-bustin' marks for other potential sluggers to shoot at as well as battered the home-town mound idol from his local perch day in and day out for the past eight years.
>
> These two powerful sluggers are to the Homestead Grays what Babe Ruth and Lou Gehrig were to the famous Yankee team of 1927. . . . [Gibson] is in the prime of his career, captain of the team and generally regarded as the best catcher in baseball with the possible exception of Bill Dickey. . . . Josh wields a potent war club. Two years ago he pounded out 61 home-runs against all types of pitching, and whaled the horsehide for a .355 mark.
>
> Big league pitchers who have played against him rate Josh with the best in the game. Dizzy Dean, Carl Hubbell and countless others have spared no words in singing of the big catcher's greatness.

Cum Posey, who was of course managing this PR onslaught, contributed to that July 12 edition with a lead item in his "Posey's Points" column. Wrote Posey: " 'Josh' Gibson hit two home runs and a double at Red Bank, New Jersey, July 12th. [Smokey] Joe Williams says, 'Joe Louis's right and Josh Gibson's big bat are bad news; you can't slip up once.' "

Posey's press releases were now practically running as is in black papers, providing much of the news about Gibson and his nonpareil team. A typical example was a piece that ran concurrently in the *Courier,* the *Afro,* and the *Newark Herald* touting a hugely publicized Grays–Philadelphia Stars double-header at Yankee Stadium in July. It read:

> Since leaving their training camp in Orlando, Fla., the last of March, the Grays have played in every state east of the Mississippi, compiling an imposing record of 97 wins out of 111 games played. . . . Josh Gibson, world's greatest catcher and distance slugger, has 42 home runs, 13 of them in league games; Buck Leonard, star first baseman, has 31 home runs to his credit, 8 in league competition; Jerry Benjamin, outfielder, has stolen 27 bases. Then there's Sammy Bankhead, with one of the greatest throwing arms in the game today . . . and their formidable pitching staff of Ray Brown, Red Ferrel [*sic*], Big Train Parker, Mountain Walker, Ducky Partlow and Specks [*sic*] Roberts.

Josh made much of this hyperbole seem commonplace. His most awesome power display of the season came during a spine-tingling twin bill the Grays and Stars played at Griffith Stadium in mid-July. With the Grays down, 5–2, in the fourth inning of the opener, Josh lined a two-run shot over the left field wall to close the gap. In the seventh, it was 7–6, Philly, when Josh tripled high off the fence to send home the tying run. Then, in the bottom of the ninth, Josh again faced Henry McHenry, whom he had recently victimized with his one-handed homer in the same stadium.

No doubt remembering that blow, McHenry now tried to get him out with heat, but as the *Afro*'s Sam Lacy reported,

"Josh worked the count to three balls and two strikes before he met one of McHenry's fast balls squarely on the nose and sent it on a one-way trip against one of the tiers—six rows from the top—of the uninhabited bleachers."

In the nightcap, the Grays fell behind, 2–0. Josh came up with two men on in the second inning and promptly blasted yet another ball out of the yard. And though the Stars came out on top, 6–5, scoring in the top of the seventh before darkness ended the match, in writing up the doubleheader Sam Lacy mentioned no other players on either side until he had massaged Gibson for seven paragraphs. This was his lead:

> If for no other reason than that Josh Gibson, peerless catcher of the National League, crashed out three home runs and a triple which missed by inches being a fourth, customers at Sunday's twin bill . . . left Griffith Stadium fully satisfied with the show. . . .
>
> No matter the results of the games, the real story revolves around the manner in which Gibson seized and held the attention of the 3,500 fans on hand. . . . Heralded by the local press, mainly because of the high tribute paid him by Walter Johnson [who] rated him "as good as Bill Dickey," Gibson did all that was asked of him in the way of living up to those notices. The way he handled his pitchers and the manner in which he threw to the bases were incomparable, and his response to the praise given him for his batting was likened to the rare instance when a baby does for company what he does at home.

The effect of this nonstop attention manifested itself in odd ways. Gibson naturally was voted to start the East-West Game, but he received fewer ballots than a number of other players, including Buck Leonard, Mule Suttles, Sammy Hughes, Pat Patterson, and Willie Wells, who got the most of all. One explanation for this was that so many fans took Josh's selection as a fact that they simply skipped over the catcher's line on the ballot.

Certainly, Gibson's heroics were appreciated by black ball's barons, who much preferred Josh's good-company-man image to Satchel Paige's habit of making them look like fools. It seemed as if there was nothing more important to the black game than making sure Gibson's name was known in every household, both black and white. In fact, the Gibson bandwagon was becoming so overloaded that at least one black opinion maker believed that objectivity was being sacrificed in the bustle.

In the July 29 *Afro,* Sam Lacy—who had apparently cooled down from his overheated coverage of Josh's three-homer day at Griffith Stadium—sounded a lone sour note in the Josh Gibson chorale. Lacy penned a column headlined GIBSON IS NO DICKEY that read:

A great hitter? Yes. A great catcher? No.

That seems to answer the riddle about Josh Gibson, regarded by many as the leading catcher in colored baseball; a riddle that was born when Walter Johnson, former Big Train of the majors leagues, passed the hand to the Homestead Gray receiver after seeing him in action.

From that night when Johnson . . . was so greatly impressed by the performance of the big Pittsburgh star that he immediately ranked him on a par with Bill Dickey, crack backstop of the New York Yankees . . . a controversy has raged among local followers of the diamond game over the comparative merits of Dickey and Gibson. Toward the end of deciding for themselves, upward of 3,000 persons were on hand recently when the Homesteads [played] in the nation's capital.

What they saw should have convinced them that Josh is a good catcher, but not a truly great one, and—on the other hand—that the big, jovial fellow is a truly great hitter, not just a good one.

As for placing him on a level with Dickey, that is entirely another matter. . . . Gibson can hit. . . . He can throw. . . . And from all indications Josh is a good receiver. He seems to have the goods when it comes to cupping the offering of his pitchers.

But what he showed local fans in the business of taking care of those all-important high fouls wasn't much. Three balls which should have been easy putouts for even an ordinary catcher were allowed to go astray. Two of these rolled off the toe of his mitt and the third he missed entirely. . . .

In view of our strong desire to see qualified colored players in big league baseball, it is natural that we would find every merit there is to be found in the work of [black players]. But when it comes to comparisons, we must [be cautious]. Josh is unquestionably a great hitter, but for all-around play, he's no Dickey.

Still, these objections, which were accurate, were hardly noticed. In fact, Gibson's appeal was such that Cum Posey made an extraordinary request of black ball pitchers vis-à-vis Josh when—even with Buck Leonard waiting behind him—pitchers began to routinely walk him intentionally. The boiling point for Posey was reached when he saw Gibson passed three times by the Black Yankees in a game at Yankee Stadium on July 23, even though the Grays blew the game open early. As Posey pointed out in his August 5 column, radio stations in New York had helped to publicize the game. Yet if fans came with the idea of comparing Gibson with big league sluggers, Posey wrote, they "did not get this opportunity and many went away from the park disappointed" when Josh never got a chance to cut loose.

To prevent future disappointment, Posey suggested selectively suspending normal baseball strategy. "We have no fault with that style of inside baseball which calls for walking a batter as dangerous as Gibson with players in scoring position," he wrote, adding,

We do find fault when cases arise as they did on July 23rd, when Gibson was passed on four straight balls, three times in one game, once deliberately with the score 8 to 2 in Homestead Grays' favor in the late innings. . . .

It is our contention that the cause of Negro baseball would

have been advanced had the pitchers pitched to "Josh" at all times after the game was apparently lost. This would have given the fans some measure of excitement in an otherwise very drab game.

Whether or not it was a result of Posey's ability to manipulate the league's statistics charts, Josh's numbers soared in 1939; by season's end, he had a .440 average, second to Baltimore's Wild Bill Wright, who was credited with a .488 mark. And after two years of Gibson being placed behind Mule Suttles in the home run race, this year the numbers left no room for argument: Josh reputedly hit sixteen in league games, to the Mule's ten.

And yet, 1939 did not belong exclusively to Josh after all; in the end, his newsprint space was crowded by the continued recriminations about the death of the Pittsburgh Crawfords and the Lazarus-like return of Satchel Paige.

Cum Posey's vendetta against Gus Greenlee was completed when Posey maneuvered in 1937 to form a majority bloc of owners prepared to oust Greenlee from the league presidency. Although Posey had taken Greenlee to task for years for allowing white promoters to book league games, when Greenlee made his grand stand against them, Posey formed an alliance with the Philadelphia promoter and Stars owner Eddie Gottlieb, who was concerned that Gus might really move against him.

Gottlieb brought to the bloc the New York Black Yankees, who were being booked by the late Nat Strong's associate, Bill Leuschner, and when the Newark Eagles' Abe and Effa Manley joined them, Posey had a Greenlee-proof majority coalition in a six-team league.

By the end of the 1937 season, Greenlee must have felt the rug moving beneath him. Crippled by the Dominican incursion, and with every league team losing money, Gus was voted out of office and replaced by Baltimore's Tom Wilson, a pliable man whom Posey could control. Then, during the 1938 season, with Satchel Paige and Cool Papa Bell refusing to play for him, the Crawfords went bankrupt and Greenlee was forced to sell off his best players.

Deep in debt, his numbers business withering, his investment in John Henry Lewis finished after John Henry moved up in his weight class and was KO'd by Joe Louis in less than one round, Gus had no choice but to divest himself from the Craws. In 1939, he put the club under the aegis of his younger brother Charles Greenlee, who then peddled it to a group of white businessmen in Toledo, Ohio, where the fabled Crawfords finally died in obscurity.

To many black ball aficionados, folding the Crawfords was not nearly as sinful as Gus's shuttering of Greenlee Field in December 1938. But when he sold the grounds to white construction interests, who began to demolish the onetime palace of black ball within weeks, even Greenlee's most staunch allies turned against him.

Incensed that a ballpark that had once been a symbol of black enterprise was now a symbol of failure, Greenlee's old *Courier* flack John L. Clark—who had lost his role in the league when his patron went down—blasted Greenlee for failing to operate the park "with a purer racial interest" and surmised that in light of the Crawfords' death, "Pittsburgh is no place to attempt big things for Negroes . . . Greenlee Field joins the list of banks, industries and other enterprises which should not be again attempted in this city for the next 100 years."

Harsh as that indictment was, it was evident that, with the Grays gravitating toward D.C. as their home base, black Pittsburgh would soon be without a team. For Gus Greenlee, the cruelest irony was that his vision and drive, which had saved black ball, also preserved the forces that eventually unseated him. Now, as black ball began to experience a second renaissance, he and his onetime crown jewel were nowhere to be seen. Small wonder that when he was heard from again, Gus would be out for some vengeance of his own.

Even though Cum Posey was unquestionably the power behind the NNL, he was hardly secure on the throne when a
major crisis once again rocked black ball. Not surprisingly, the
crisis had to do with Satchel Paige, who had become a hot
property once again. For a year and a half, Paige had lingered
in a kind of professional death, or so it seemed, after he hurt
his whipsaw right arm while pitching in the Mexican League.
Once he was back home, rumors of the injury, which Paige
had kept concealed, made him persona non grata in the black
ball universe; having had to put up with his eccentricities and
disloyalties before, club owners now snubbed him as repayment.

Paige did find work, signing on with a lower-level adjunct
team of the Kansas City Monarchs called the Travelers, which
inevitably took on the name of the Satchel Paige All-Stars. At
the start, Paige, his arm still throbbing, could do no more
than put in a couple of innings at first base or simply stand in
the coaching box. And yet word that he was back drew the
usual enormous crowds to these games throughout the Midwest. And along the way, Paige found rebirth when his arm
came around and he was once again able to run his Trouble
Ball by hitters.

When his healthy arm was documented in the black press,
the NNL, which had relinquished all claims on him only
months before, suddenly wanted dibs on him. The first claim
was made by the Newark Eagles, by dint of the $5,000 deal
Abe and Effa Manley had made with Gus Greenlee, which
had never been completed when Paige skipped to Mexico.
Repudiating this entreaty, Paige gleefully ripped the league
during this war-nervous time for what he said were its ele-
ments of Hitlerism, and instead took up J. L. Wilkinson's
offer to join the Monarchs.

That effectively put the junior Negro league on the map,
and by the end of the 1939 season the Monarchs—whose
popularity had been pretty much confined to the Midwest
barnstorming trails—were playing regular dates in venues
such as Yankee Stadium before huge crowds wanting to see

the great showman in action. This encroachment into their territory enraged NNL owners, for whom the only solution was to get Paige back in their league. The Manleys, even with their tenuous claim, promised to go all out with their case, which would lead to a showdown in 1940 that would bring black ball to the brink of civil war.

By then, Paige would be even more important to the black game and especially to the NNL, which in its time of need would look around and find that Josh Gibson was nowhere in sight.

The paramount importance of having the Paige-Gibson tandem intact was underlined in August of 1939 when the *Courier* again ventured to Forbes Field to put big-leaguers on the spot about integration. This time the paper got favorable responses from several Chicago Cub players, including Clay Bryant, Augie Galan, and manager Gabby Hartnett, and the St. Louis Cardinals' Pepper Martin, all of whom yoked Josh and Satch, as if by reflex. Hartnett's comment was typical. "Every now and then one of my players will name an outstanding Negro player whom he has played against in exhibition games," he said. "They usually rate Paige and Gibson with the best in the majors." Said Galan: "I think Satchel Paige and Josh Gibson could really go places in the majors, and would be an asset to any team in big league baseball."

Dizzy Dean, who was also called upon to reprise his old hymns about Paige, now wove Josh into the tune: "Gibson is one of the best catchers that ever caught a game. Watch him work [the] pitcher. He's tops at that—boy-o-boy, can he hit that ball! . . . I don't know much about Dickey, but I agree with Walter Johnson when he says Gibson is worth $200,000."

Jimmy Powers too was heard from again. The *New York Daily News* sports editor hyped the second of two East-West Games held in 1939, which was played in Yankee Stadium on August 27. As a result, a good number of whites swelled the gate, to around twenty thousand.

Powers, in this landmark of racial crossover coverage—

printed in the Sunday edition of the nation's largest-circulation paper and accompanied by a photo of Josh—urged that "baseball fans with open minds [go] to the Yankee Stadium this afternoon." For those who did, he wrote,

> Surely, somewhere on that diamond, you will see [black] men worthy of a major league trial.
>
> And if you concede they are of major league calibre, you must agree all this concern for "minorities" in distant lands is so much political or financial tub-thumping and that here, at home in America, we have fellow citizens who merit our attention, and whatever excess indignation we have to spill—first!

Powers then began his Gibson paean, the fictional aspects of which—outdoing that of the Gibson coverage in the black press—introduced to many whites a black superstar to rival Satchel Paige. Powers wrote:

> I have seen personally at least ten colored ball players I know are big leaguers, but who are barred from playing by . . . Jim Crow laws. . . . Probably the best ball player scheduled to appear at the Stadium today is Josh Gibson, a catcher. Josh is 27 years old, 6 feet 2 inches, weighs 210 pounds and has bigger shoulders and arms than Joe Louis!
>
> Here's how Josh got into baseball. In 1928 a team known as the Pittsburgh Crawford Juniors was returning in a truck from Yatesborough, Pa., where they had played a game. They were rounding a turn when suddenly a baseball came flying over an incline and smacked into the radiator.
>
> Roy Sparrow, coach of the Junior Crawfords, hopped out of the car to see what damage had been done. He looked about the landscape and finally spied a diamond 500 feet away. There were a group of schoolboys on the lot and one of them seemed particularly shamefaced. He was carrying a bat as big as a wagon tongue.
>
> "Did you hit that ball?" Sparrow yelled.

"Yes," mumbled the boy timidly. "What you gonna do to me, Boss?"

"What am I going to do?" said Sparrow. "If you can drive a ball 500 feet I'm going to sign you up!"

And Gibson was shanghaied on the spot.

Within one year, Buck Ewing, catcher of the Homestead Grays, broke his finger and Gibson got his chance to go behind the plate. In 1932 Josh was transferred to the Crawfords. In 1936 he established a record of eighty-four homers (twenty-four more than Babe Ruth's total) in 170 games. In '37 he was sold back to the Grays.

At the rate he is traveling, Gibson is liable to beat his own homer mark this year! . . .

I am positive that if Josh Gibson were white he'd be a major league star. He has a perfect disposition for a ball player. Timely in the clutch, but dependable and cool when doing the mechanical job of catching. He never kicks on decisions. He is popular with fellow players as well as umpires. Unlike Satchel Paige, the famed pitcher whom Joe DiMaggio insists is also a big leaguer, Gibson does not eat fried food. He follows a sensible diet, eggs, meat, vegetables and salads. He is never out of shape.

Salaries in the colored circuit are not high but Gibson has averaged $5,000 a year. In proportion to drawing power, Gibson is a $25,000 player. He'd be worth every cent of that to any major league club.

Some day some owner will come along with enough courage to sign a fine young catcher like Josh Gibson. Then baseball will be a true NATIONAL SPORT!

Josh, who had gone 0-for-3 in the West's 4–2 victory in Comiskey Park three weeks before, teased the crowd in the stadium. Twice he sent West outfielders ranging 400 feet or so into the left center field "Death Valley" to grab his line drives. Two other times up—Cum Posey or no Cum Posey—he was walked intentionally.

Then, with the East up, 6–2, in the eighth, he came to bat with the bases loaded; this was one time there would be no intentional walk to defuse the dramatic moment. Josh faced Indianapolis pitcher Johnny "Slim" Johnson, and the *Afro*'s Harry B. Webber described the scene this way:

> The great crowd expected great things from the famous Homestead Grays' catcher. He connected and hit a long fly out Turkey Stearnes's [*sic*] way [in left field]. The latter misjudged and missed . . . Gibson's fly, so Josh took three bases and Ed Stone and Willie Wells of Newark and Wild Bill Wright of Baltimore raced in. . . . Gibson came in on Leonard's single and it was all over.

The *Courier*'s take was more vivid:

> The ball came a-hopping across the plate. Josh took a sweeping cut. He put all of those 200-odd pounds behind his swing. Wood crashed against leather. The ball soared high, disappeared in the ether, and then landed in the runway back in deep right field. All three of his mates scored and Josh ended up panting at third, with the roars of the crowd ringing in his ears.

The *Courier* headline, playing off one of Powers's remarks, read JOSH BACKS UP JIMMY.

The rest of this dreamlike season played out according to form. Against Philadelphia, for example, Josh's two-run triple—a "Gibsonian swat," said the *Courier*—broke open the game and sent the Grays to a 15–9 win. And yet, aping the methods of Gus Greenlee before him, Cum Posey reacted to some late-season losses by releasing no second-half team standings. However, Posey did agree to a challenge by Tom Wilson's Baltimore Elite Giants—who claimed to have won the second-half flag—and the teams engaged in a play-off round sponsored by the New York Yankees. The best-of-seven series was scheduled to climax at Yankee Stadium, with the winner to receive the Jacob Ruppert Trophy, named after the Yankees' millionaire owner.

Homestead took the first game, 2–1, at Philadelphia's Parkside Stadium, and when Josh cracked a two-run homer in the first inning of game two in Baltimore, the series looked to be all Grays. But this Elite Giants team featured some pretty fair hardball players, including right fielder Wild Bill Wright, the league's leading hitter; third baseman Felton Snow; short-stop Pee Wee Butts; and a stocky young Italian–African American catcher named Roy Campanella. And as the home-town *Afro* reported, they "show[ed] fire and defiance to the vaunted reputation of the highly touted Grays."

Coming from behind, the Elite Giants turned the second game around. The key play came in the sixth. With the game knotted at 4–all, Campanella struck out, but Josh let the pitch get away from him. He scrambled after the ball, picked it up, and as Campy tried for second, threw it into center field, allowing Snow, who'd been on second base, to score. The Elites held on to the lead and won, 7–5.

When the teams went back to Parkside Stadium for game three, the Grays must have felt snakebitten. Although the Elites pitcher Sammy Bird gave up fifteen hits, the Grays could do no better than a 4–4 tie going into the seventh. Bal-timore also was lucky in facing Josh when he could do the least harm. As the *Afro* wrote it up, "Josh Gibson had the misfortune of coming to the bat with no one on [three] time[s] and each time he came through with a single. [He also hit] a home run to open the second inning." The Elites then broke it open with five runs in the seventh and won, 10–5, with Campanella notching a homer, a double, and three singles.

Baltimore now stood a win away from the putative title as the series shifted to Yankee Stadium for game four. Played on September 20 before fifteen thousand people, this one devel-oped into a tense pitching duel between two superb south-paws, the Grays' Roy Partlow and Baltimore's Jonas Gaines, who matched zeroes for six innings. The Elites broke the seal in the seventh when Wild Bill Wright doubled and left fielder Bill Hoskins singled him home. Then Hoskins went to second on an error and came home on a single by the red-hot Campanella.

The Grays made a bid in the eighth when, with two outs, Gaines walked Vic Harris, Josh, and Buck Leonard. Reliever Hank Hubert then came in and got Henry Spearman to pop out to second to choke off the threat. Hubert then retired the Grays in order in the ninth, and Baltimore took the game and the Ruppert Trophy by holding the "fence-bustin'" Grays to three hits.

Still, Cum Posey had learned the fine art of attention diverting from Gus Greenlee. Immediately after the series, he formed and began to heavily hype a postseason NNL barnstorming aggregation called the Negro League All-Stars. This team was copromoted by Posey and his brother Seward and Cuban promoter Emelio deArmas, who owned the Santa Clara team that Josh regularly played for over the winter. Together, they scheduled a two-month-long series against the Cuban League's best players, with a number of games in the States before the All-Stars competed in the Cuban League. By some reports, Gibson hit eleven homers and batted .456, a league record, in leading the All-Stars to the island's title.

As intriguing as these doings may have been to baseball fans—by now it was clear that hopes for big league advancement by Latin players were inextricably linked to the black ball cause—for Josh the money and adulation that he always accrued from his Caribbean excursions had now reached a peak. And as he bounced to the next tropical stopover, Puerto Rico, marking the new year and decade, he was also about to enter a whorl of new and better highs that would keep reassuring him that he would never have to walk the humble earth again.

13

Gone South

Let me tell you something about ballplayers. Every black ballplayer that could do anything here in the States had to play in Latin America. All you got to do is ask a ballplayer, hey, did you go to a Latin American country, and if it's, no, I didn't go, then he wasn't that good. You can count on one hand all who went over there for five years or more. And Josh, man, he was king down there, he had a name everywhere he go. He still got a name.

—WILMER FIELDS, HOMESTEAD GRAYS, 1941–49

It was during the tail end of the decade that Josh Gibson Jr., nearing his tenth birthday, began to slowly enter his father's world. As part of his belated effort at fathering, Josh took his son to Grays games to act as a batboy and brought him along on some road trips. The boy would go through life clinging to fleeting memories of these precious hours.

"For one thing, I used to hold his jewelry when he was

playin'," the son said many moons later, still sounding as boastful as he no doubt did telling about it as a child. "He wouldn't keep his rings and his watch in his locker, man. He was distrustful of people, so he'd have someone hold 'em for him. I'd be sittin' in the dugout or be out on the field collecting the bats. And one day before the game he pulled me over and he told me, 'Look here. If I get hurt out there, don't worry 'bout me. Just come out there and see if there's anything valuable in my pocket, and if there is, you take it before anyone else does.'

"That was funny. I mean, he had a helluva sense of humor. But there was a serious side of it, too, 'cause after that he had me hold his stuff and I don't think my father trusted too many people to do that. I also think that was his way of sayin', y'know, he loved me, that he wanted me there in his life."

Josh refused to alter Josh Jr. and Helen's stable living arrangement with the Mason family, but he was clearly making more time to come and see his boy. "I wouldn't say I felt alienated from him [in my younger years] but as I got older I wondered sometimes. I mean, people would ask me, 'When's your dad comin' home?' and I didn't know how to answer that. But I know I was goin' to school and I was being raised real well by my grandmother. I knew who my father was and what he was doing because he used to send me articles from the paper from them Latin countries.

"But let me tell you something. When we knew he was comin' over to our house, the whole neighborhood got ready. They'd be standin' outside the door. That's when I was on top of the world, man.

"But he didn't cut me no slack either. He whupped me one time, boy. I had called my sister a four-letter word, and I forget where he was at, Puerto Rico, Cuba, whatever, but my grandmother couldn't do nothin' with me, I was actin' up, and she told me she was gonna wait until my father came home and tell him. Well, my God, maybe it was four or five months before he came home and I thought she had forgot all about it. But then my father took one of them expensive alligator belts he got down in the Latin countries and he came at me. And I tried to make it up the steps but he caught me across my behind. And that was enough, man. He had no more trouble outta me after that.

"But he protected me, too. When I got a little older, there was a bunch of guys, the neighborhood bullies, up at the school where I went, Schenley High, causin' me problems. So my grandmother told my father about it and he went there and turned over the whole cafeteria. He raised hell and told them, don't be messin' with my son no more. And, I mean, everybody stopped eatin' and just stared. And the guys that was hasslin' me, they ran out of the cafeteria. Yeah, that was the end of that."

One explanation for this overreaction might be Josh's deep guilt about not being there nearly enough; whether it was disciplining or defending his son, Josh seemed to overcompensate for what was in fact alienation. But for father and son, stolen moments of kinship were not to be trifled with or analyzed. If the guideline of their relationship was that less was more, both of them understood the equation.

It is significant that when Josh Jr.'s memories of the man whose name he bore were shaped, so many of them coincided with Josh finding some time between stops in the tropics. For many Negro league stars, and especially for Josh, these stays often were extended beyond winter ball to year-round habitation. For Josh, it wasn't only the cool breezes, cold beer, and hot women that made him feel so comfortable in the meridians known in black ball as "the Latin countries."

For the lucky ones who were invited to take the boat ride south, the destination wasn't any particular country but the realization of every black man's fantasy of gaining respect and riches. Here, as in the States, talented men of color played ball for wealthy men of color, but, to many, freedom itself was the issue, or at least one that was as strong as the lure of money. Black ballplayers used to living in the ghetto, where they were lost in lower-class black humanity, could live in opulent hotel rooms or in bungalows in the countryside. Treated like movie stars or visiting potentates, they found themselves surrounded on the streets by mobs of adoring fans. Almost never did they have to pick up a check or pay for the use of an automobile or be circumspect about their off-hours behavior.

Unlike the Negro league burghers, the Latin owners paid no mind to social compacts. Although Cum Posey did nothing to stop the drinking and carousing of the Grays, he and the other black ball owners maintained the same charade as the white big league owners that their players were virtuous and even saintly. In the tropics there was no such hypocrisy. Just as Gus Greenlee was a bootlegger, and the Yankees' Colonel Jacob Ruppert owned a brewery, many Latin owners made their fortune from beer or rum, but they thought nothing of handing their players a case of booze for a winning hit or a well-pitched game. Latin aficionados who won bets on a game would buy rounds at the bars and openly hand money to the players right on the field. And since games were played only on Saturday and Sunday afternoons and because there was less travel time between league cities, the *americanos* would often have little else to do but drink.

For his part, Josh Gibson was all too ready to spend his off days in a drunken stupor. By the winter of 1940, he was all the more ready to numb himself with alcohol as a way of escaping thoughts of the badgering Hattie Jones.

In the past, Josh would sometimes bring Hattie with him to the islands for the winter, to share the simple pleasures of life there. But lately, as he had grown more sour tempered and snippety as a result of drinking, things had become acrid between them, apparently because Hattie nagged at him to stop the boozing. Recalling this period, Josh's sister-in-law Rebecca Mason told of Josh being in a lather about his common-law wife.

"He used to come over just to get away from her," she said. "I don't think he ever brought Hattie over, in fact. If the children were sick or something, my mother would call Hattie to come over and look at them if Josh was out of town. But it was like he had told her she couldn't, and he would come over when he got back home.

"But this one time he came over and he was just beside hisself, just sputtering. And my mother said, 'What you runnin' over here for? What's wrong?' And he said, 'Oh, Hattie makes me sick. I ain't never going back to that woman.'"

Hooks Tinker heard the same kind of scuttlebutt back on the Hill. "I heard things," he said. "I heard some things about how she didn't treat him too well, didn't treat him right. I heard the woman was untrue to Josh and he just went berserk."

Josh's habit of finding solace inside a beer bottle did not make him all that different from many other ballplayers, black and white. The difference was in the largeness of his appetites and urges and the delusion that his habits carried no risk. Thus, he was only too eager to broaden his roistering by dabbling with another brain-numbing substance, marijuana. Once again, he was not the only player sampling the native reefer, but he was alone in going a toke over the line. And as good as he was at hiding what he was doing, people began to notice that something was going on with him.

One was Dick Seay, the nimble Newark Eagle second baseman who played that winter with the Santurce Cangrejeros, who had made Gibson player-manager. Decades later, Seay told author John B. Holway about Josh's increasingly bizarre behavior. Recalled Seay: "He never did smoke. But in the bars he'd go into the men's room. Twenty or thirty minutes later he'd start talking simple like, you know? We'd say, 'What's wrong with the fellow?' I'd go in the men's room, look everywhere, but I never could find what he was doing. I don't think it was liquor. I think it was marijuana—we used to call them reefers at that time.

"He used to come to my house in the morning, six o'clock,

say, 'Come on, let's go to the *picarina*'—a little tavern. I'd say, 'Heh, Josh, it isn't open this time of day.' He'd just lay on the bed and fall asleep by himself.

"One time after he had gone to bed, he went down to the main plaza in Puerto Rico. He was taking off all his clothes. They called the police, and they came for him with a wagon. They all knew him. One thing, he was afraid of policemen. They put him in back, and all three policemen rode up front. He ripped the spare tire right off the back of the wagon. Just pulled it off. It sounds unbelievable, but he did it. He was a strong man."

Another version of the story was that when the naked Gibson was intercepted by the *policía*, they asked him just where he was going, and Josh supposedly mumbled, "I'm going to the airport." In this rendering, the cops took him in and, in lieu of charging him with being a public nuisance, the city and league authorities suspended him from playing and ordered him, no doubt gently, to go home to the States.

This may have been the case, since Gibson was not around for the last several weeks of the Puerto Rican League season; with no other dependable catcher on the Santurce team, Dick Seay had to go behind the plate—as well as take over as manager—as the club fell out of contention and finished behind the Guayama Brujos, which had Satchel Paige, Ray Brown, and Leon Day. (Buck Leonard was also present in the league, playing with Los Indios de Mayaguez.)

But while he was still in his Santurce uniform, Josh's ability to recover from his binges continued apace. Indeed, as his consumption of booze and marijuana increased, so did his hitting stats, according to league records. After starting off slowly, Josh's batting average climbed to .380 with a league-high six homers, one more than Petrucho Cepeda had hit playing for Guayama, before Josh's early and possibly forced departure.

On the island, Josh wasn't called the black Babe Ruth; he was Trucutu, which was the name of a Superman-like comic book hero in the local papers.

The only real problem he had was when he stood in against Paige, a pitcher Gibson could never quite figure out. Paige played a side game of psych-out by talking trash to hitters, and as resistant as Josh was to verbal ragging, Satch had a way of getting under his skin. Even though they had faced each other only a few times, mainly in the early thirties before Josh came to the Crawfords, both seemed to know that any confrontation between them would be seen as a meeting not only of black ball's two greatest performers, but of its two opposing alter egos.

Josh didn't mind that kind of pressure, but Satch was better suited to it.

"'S'matter, Josh, too hot for ya?" Paige would guffaw when he'd rush one by him. Josh would grin and act unconcerned, but rarely would he get into a game of call-out-and-dare at the plate. Against Satch, one out of four was a good day's work; with these odds, Josh could only lose. Still, he was game for the private challenge he had issued with his cheeky words to Cum Posey in the *Courier* about how this confrontation would be a thrill—provided Satch didn't put him on, that is.

At the time he made that remark, and whenever he took any playful jibes at another player, Josh probably believed his good-natured innocence would buffer his bravado so that he would not be taken too seriously. But when he got in against Paige, even in a meatball league in Puerto Rico, there were sure to be Negro-leaguers watching and fans salivating, and nothing could be more serious business. And as he seemed to know, he couldn't handle it.

Thus, in the most crucial innings played in Puerto Rico, when Josh first encountered Paige, he went 1-for-4, hitting a single in a four-hitter that Satch won by the unbelievable score of 23–0; in their second go-around, Paige won, 6–1, and Josh again was 1-for-4; Santurce got closer in the third meeting, losing 3–1, but Josh could do no better than the usual single in four trips. In their final duel on the island, Satch blanked him in four at bats and won, 4–2.

But now Josh had more on his mind than his newfound nemesis, Satchel Paige. Far more urgent to him was the unpleasant task of having to tell Cum Posey he was about to walk out on the Grays for the second time in three seasons. For Josh, again the latent urge was money, though it seems likely he was in no great hurry to come back home to Hattie, after failing to muster the courage to order her out of the house they shared. Once again the money was being proffered by Latin American baseball dilettantes, but Posey could hardly believe it when he heard that the offer would take Gibson all the way to Caracas, Venezuela.

At first, Cum believed Josh was once again exercising his now well-practiced strong-arm negotiating tactics to pull more money out of him. And in fact, Posey could have conceivably matched the Venezuelan bid on Gibson, $700 per month, a $1,000 signing bonus, and free lodging and expenses—at least the salary, though it would have required doubling his previous wages, making Gibson the highest-paid player in black ball. But Posey soon came to understand there was more than money involved in all this.

After meeting with Josh several times and hearing him express his sincere conflicts about leaving, Posey knew that Josh had to get Latin America out of his system before he'd be gung ho for Homestead again.

And so Posey let Gibson go to Caracas, for what he believed would be a three-month spring–early summer season that would leave Josh available by July, and said nothing by way of reproof in his *Courier* writings when the Negro league season began. But what Posey did not know was that Caracas was just the first stage of Gibson's tropical tour. In July, fresh from hitting .419 in the Venezuelan League, Josh wired Posey with more bad news: he had accepted another offer—an astonishing one at that, from Jorge Pasquel, the beer king of

Mexico, who with his four brothers operated the Mexican League, as well as the league's Veracruz team, Club Azules. For a Trujillo-like salary of $6,000, Gibson would enter that league's competition in July and stay until its conclusion in November; he would be clearing nearly $1,000 a month.

This was just a first step in Jorge Pasquel's master plan to bring major league baseball to Mexico. He believed that if he attracted the best Negro league players with huge salaries, major-leaguers would eventually follow, which would force the big leagues to sue for peace on terms that might give Mexico a big league franchise. This pipe dream had tons of money behind it, and while the league had lost Satchel Paige when he hurt his arm in Mexico City and refused to come back, Cool Papa Bell had stayed on and the Pasquels had doggedly kept the revolving door to the Negro leagues going.

Now, in 1940, black ball stars were crossing the border in significant numbers. Among those who were signed and disbursed around the league were Newark's Leon Day, Ray Dandridge, and Willie Wells, Baltimore's Wild Bill Wright, New York Cuban Schoolboy Taylor, and Kansas City's Chet Brewer. And, unlike in the case of the Dominican raids, Cum Posey was also burned by the Mexican incursions, losing Bill Byrd, Roosevelt Davis, Bill Perkins, and Sam Bankhead. Not by coincidence, Josh's decision to play in Mexico had a Bankhead connection.

Up to this point, Posey had been so convinced Josh was going to return to the Grays in July that he wrote as much in his column. But by then, Josh had joined up with Bankhead in Veracruz, the centerpiece team in the Mexican League. Over the coming months, God only knows how much Mexican beer those two consumed, but stories soon began to filter back to the States about cases of the stuff sitting in the locker room, taking up space normally occupied by players, and of Josh and Sammy leaving the floor so strewn with bottle caps and empty bottles that the Veracruz players had to step over and around the mess or risk getting a cleat caught and turning an ankle.

Everywhere the two great Grays went, the stench of beer marked their presence. And, in Josh's case, at least, the highs of Mexican cannabis were probably not left unexplored.

Back home, Cum Posey was riled but caught in a trap, one he had originally set for Gus Greenlee. Having gone on record that Greenlee should have played down the Dominican incursions rather than going hog-wild and making the league look bad, he now had to follow his own advice. In fact, Posey barely mentioned Gibson's absence. Although the assessment of lifetime bans was discussed by the owners, none were handed down and Posey had much to do with that.

Actually, Posey was in a position to act unfazed in 1940, at least publicly, since his team, with Robert Gaston and Josh Johnson at catcher, didn't miss a beat and won the flag it had lost with Gibson catching the year before. Besides, Posey's and everyone else's attention was diverted by the war over Satchel Paige, which came to a head in June 1940 and obscured almost everything else that happened in black ball that year.

When Paige continued to resist Newark's half-baked claim on him, Abe and Effa Manley, by now reeling from the Mexican raids, made good on their threat to raze the NNL if Tom Wilson, the league president, didn't compel Paige to report to Newark. The issue led to the two leagues meeting in an emergency session at Harlem's Woodside Hotel on June 6. By then, the Manleys had gotten chits from the owners of the New York Cubans and New York Black Yankees to remove their teams from the league, along with the Eagles, if no action was taken. The situation, as the *Afro* pointed out, "threat[ened] to disrupt the [NNL] schedule . . . and split the loop," which would "throw the league into complete discord."

After two days of bluster and bluff, the Manleys knew Paige was a lost cause, but instead of storming out of the league they brazenly signed two players from the Negro

American League—apparently to show that if J. L. Wilkinson could steal Paige, they could pilfer that league's players. While neither Cum Posey nor Wilkinson—the powers behind the two leagues—approved of this tit-for-tat extortion, in the end the Manleys' power play succeeded, at least partly. The Eagles were allowed to keep the two players as the price of peace between the leagues.

But while there would be peace in the NNL, Posey's league was now so fragmented that true harmony would never be restored, which, in the end, would only damage the integration crusade.

For Paige, though, it was sweet victory. Not only had he gotten his way again; he was able to cite, with great irony, the recent defections of such "gentlemanly" players as Josh Gibson to prove his case that he was not such a bad guy.

What's more, all the fuss brought Paige even greater recognition among both blacks and whites. And once the black press began to cover his every move in big, bold headlines, he effectively shifted the balance of black ball power to the NAL. Paige was also treated to a trilogy of flattering, if still strained and condescending, profiles in the mainstream white press over the next year and a half, in the pages of *Time, Life,* and the *Saturday Evening Post*. Only Joe Louis could boast the same credentials among African American athletes.

Josh Gibson, meanwhile, had found a paradise of his own, though the temptations he yielded to in Veracruz were of dubious value to his health. As for his bat, it remained in robust health. After joining Club Azules de Veracruz, which also had Dandridge, Wells, Ray Brown, and Schoolboy Taylor, he hit .467 with eleven homers and thirty-eight RBIs in twenty-two games, striking out only six times in ninety-two at bats. To Josh, the thin air and strong ocean breezes were a home run hitter's nirvana. And he could easily laugh right along with Jorge Pasquel when the owner approached him after he'd gotten a double, triple, and two singles in one game and playfully chided him, "Hey Geebson, I got Weelie Wells and Dandreedge for seengles and doubles. I got you for dee home runs."

Gibson's bat was never far from his other owner's mind, either, and Cum Posey's public civility in the matter of Josh's Mexican jaunt continued into the off season. Although Posey couldn't imagine that Josh would stay away from the Negro leagues for more than one year, he began to lobby for his return by writing in his column that the Grays' financial picture had brightened to the point where he would be able to pay Gibson the large salary he deserved. And for all of the tropics' seductions, it seemed Josh had gotten his fill of Latin America and was now ready to come home to his rightful place in the Negro leagues.

There was, after all, reason for him to believe that, even at $6,000, he had been cheapening himself as an African *American* ballplayer by playing in exile, when he could be aiming for the fences at Yankee Stadium, Forbes Field, and Griffith Stadium. Even with nothing coming from the first calls for big league integration, that movement seemed inevitable now, requiring only a little more time and effort.

With these arguments ringing in his ears, Josh came home in January. He visited Posey's office and walked out with a new Grays contract that would pay him $500 a month, which an ecstatic Posey announced was "the largest salary ever given to a colored player." (Josh's earnings still weren't in Satchel Paige's league, however. Paige's salary was merely a base figure; most of his annual income of around $40,000 still came from side deals for a cut of the gate on his barnstorming tours.)

A month later, when Josh was due to report to the Grays spring camp in Orlando, Florida, Posey, who must have felt as if he was riding on a yo-yo when it came to Gibson, experienced a déjà vu nightmare; just as in 1932, when Josh signed with the Crawfords only hours after signing with the Grays, damned if he didn't do it again.

In early March, possibly with some persuasion from Sammy Bankhead, Josh suddenly felt he needed still more time away from the Negro league wars, as well as from Hattie Jones. If any additional persuasion was needed, Jorge Pasquel furnished it with an offer of $6,400 over the full season, plus the usual all-inclusive expenses paid. When the Grays took the field in Orlando, Josh was again wearing the uniform of Club Azules de Veracruz.

Smarting now, Cum Posey—who had gotten neither Bankhead nor Perkins back and had lost Roy Partlow to Veracruz as well—was sick of the Mexicans, sick of being treated like Gus Greenlee, and especially sick of being slapped in the face by Josh Gibson. "Personally, we were the fall guy once more as we were in 1932," Posey wrote, adding that he was sure that on both occasions Gibson had used him "to get more money elsewhere."

However, having learned that newspaper jeremiads were useless against Josh, Posey took a more serious step. He filed suit in Pittsburgh District Court on the Hill, asking for damages he said were caused by Gibson's absence from the Grays.

Suits of this kind had been filed before in black ball's long history of contract breaking, few with any success. But Posey's suit was more earnest than most. Assaying the value of Gibson's home at 2157 Webster Avenue in Pleasant Valley at $10,000, he sued for that amount and asked that the deed be turned over to him to satisfy the damages. And Posey won round one when, in early May, Judge Thomas Marshall upheld Josh's Grays contract, returned judgment for $10,000, and ruled that Gibson must return to Pittsburgh within six days or risk possible forfeiture of his house.

It is arguable whether Posey really would have gone the distance with the suit and taken Josh's home, as that would have turned Josh against him forever. Posey's real intention was to convince Josh that he was serious this time about protecting his legal rights. And in fact, Posey fed to the black press a story, unverified, that when Josh heard of the verdict he tried to leave Mexico, only to be told by Mexican authorities that he would be jailed if he did.

Clearly, Posey worked hard to fight the Mexicans. According to the *Courier*, the Gibson defection even came close to causing an international incident, after Posey filed protest with the U.S. State Department, as Gus Greenlee had when Satchel Paige had jumped to the Dominican Republic. "However," said the paper, "when the big fuss started [over Gibson], this Government launched a gigantic 'goodwill' program in Latin America. It's doubtful [the government] will become involved in the situation now, because we aren't going to do anything in Mexico but spread good will."

But just as Gus Greenlee and John L. Clark had failed to shake Josh by pounding away at his "complex temperament," Posey found out that Gibson was in fact too complex to scare either by harsh words or court order.

For one thing, as irresponsible as he had been, Josh knew that Posey knew he hadn't acted out of malice or used him to up the ante for the Latin teams. For another, he knew Posey would likely back down rather than lose him for good. And with Hattie occupying the house, Josh had his doubts about whether he even wanted the place. Then, too, Josh passed word to Posey that he would be back, unqualifiedly, for the 1942 season. And while this didn't exactly soothe Posey, Cum eased off the lawsuit and eventually let it drop.

In the interim, with the NNL in dire need of this major league–ready star, the only Gibson playing baseball in Pittsburgh the first two years of the decade was Josh's younger brother, Jerry, who, possibly to prevent comparisons with Josh, tried to make his name as a pitcher. Playing for the Caraopolis Grays, a local semipro team, he threw a no-hitter in 1938; he eventually moved up to the NAL Cincinnati Tigers for an unmemorable season in 1943, before ending a career that was no more than a sidebar.

For Josh, facing down a man like Cum Posey was just his latest conquest. Now well into his conquest of the Mexican League, he was laying waste to league pitching, hitting .374 and slamming thirty-three homers in ninety-four games, with

124 RBIs, thirty-one doubles, and only twenty-five strikeouts in 358 at bats. After he led Veracruz to the championship, a Josh Gibson Appreciation Day was held at the city's Escambron Stadium. In ceremonies before a capacity crowd and attended by the league hierarchy and government officials of Veracruz from the mayor on down, Josh was presented the league's MVP and home run champion trophies.

These rites were part of Veracruz's pitch to get Josh to come back again in 1942. But after Josh again decamped for the Puerto Rican League for the winter, presumably keeping his clothes on in public this time, he kept his word to Posey. Perhaps this was also the signal that he had tired of living in the oxymoronic fast lane in siesta land and that he needed to be reawakened by the vibrancy of the inner city, not to mention Negro league pitching. Could he still hit the best black pitchers? Maybe he worried about it.

Without these challenges in somnolent Veracruz, it had taken just a few short months for Josh to balloon up to around 230 pounds, and for the first time signs of his heavy drinking began to show just above the overburdened belt around his waist. This wasn't evidence of a softer or weaker Gibson, but of a bloated one—a drinker's belly that had been built with much dedication.

Many years later, Sam Bankhead's widow, Helen, spoke with great wonder and disgust about the Veracruz experience to author William Brashler. Helen, who had accompanied Sammy there in 1941, recalled how he and Josh, continuing their drinking contests, lined up the empties, stacked them in pyramids, and counted them, with the figure at times going into the dozens. This would happen sometimes during games, but more often in the hollow of night, with the two men doing nothing but going bottle for bottle until one passed out and the other claimed his victory. Helen Bankhead, who was helpless to crimp this demented routine, said she was so sickened by it that she swore off booze right then and there and never touched it again in her life. But her husband's addiction only worsened.

While both Gibson and Bankhead were somehow able to awake the next morning, or by late afternoon if there was no game, and stand up straight and sturdy, it may well have occurred to them that their party was getting just a little out of hand. Whatever the reason, by January 1942, Josh began negotiating with Posey and signed a contract that paid him a salary of $750 a month plus bonuses that brought him up to a leviathan $1,200 a month, a figure that matched those being paid on the big league level. If it had been Josh's intention to take advantage of Posey to make more money, it certainly seemed as though he had done a superb job. (Satchel Paige, whose salary was at least $200 a month less, still made far more in total, by virtue of his outside appearances.)

With this contract signed, Posey and Sonnyman Jackson took no chances that it would go awry. They set up an early-warning defense system around the Grays, their sights trained on the crowd to interdict any Latins who might get too close to Josh. Early in the 1942 season, Jackson spotted a Latin man in the stands at Griffith Stadium and asked him if he was Mexican. The man said yes, identified himself as A. J. Guina, an employee of the Mexican consul. Jackson then asked if he was trying to sign Grays players.

When Guina, whose honesty was admirable but none too smart, said he was, Sonnyman had him put out of the park and then roughed him up on the street, which led Guina to file assault charges. Unfazed, Jackson vowed, "I don't care if they send Pancho Villa; they're not gonna get my ballplayers."

They didn't. And now, with the defectors returning and with Josh the Basher back to provide a valuable symbolic counterpoint to Satchel Paige's merry limp, the Negro leagues could proceed to what would be remembered as their salad years. But the terrible pity was that Josh's days at the table were now numbered.

14

Josh Versus Satch

*Paige and Gibson are two of baseball's greatest stars and
when the Grays' home run slugger faced the Monarchs' famed
slinger with three on and two out and the [Grays] trailing
2–0, in the seventh inning, the 5,219 fans in the park thrilled
to the "storybook" duel.*
— AFRO-AMERICAN, SEPTEMBER 19, 1942

In the wake of Josh's return, almost all of black ball's
Mexican runaways followed him back home in the winter of
1942. This exodus in reverse was due not so much to Gibson's example but to the cataclysmic events of December 7,
1941, which made it imperative for them to be home for the
duration of World War II. After Pearl Harbor and the mobi-
lization of the armed forces early in the new year, the players
either came back voluntarily or were ordered to do so by
their draft boards.

Over the next four long and terrible years, when over
170,000 black men and women entered service, Negro-

leaguers and white major-leaguers wore the same uniform at last, that of the army, navy, and marines, albeit in segregated units. Two notable exceptions, ironically, were black ball's dynamic duo, Satchel Paige and Josh Gibson, both of whom were declared 4-F. With Satch, it was because of flat feet. With Josh, in what was another clue to his impending decay, it was because his knees had become scarred and creaky from the rigors of catching almost every day for a dozen years. (Buck Leonard also was disqualified, because of a bad back.)

Of the Negro league teams that would lose key players, the seemingly cursed Newark Eagles would suffer the most, contributing Leon Day, infielder Larry Doby, and outfielder Monte Irvin during the course of the war. But Kansas City also lost its share, including pitcher Connie Johnson, outfielder Willard Brown, and the great first baseman Buck O'Neil. Others around the black game to go included Sammy Hughes, Dick Seay, and Homestead third baseman Howard Easterling.

Still, Gibson definitely had an effect on the homeward flow, since he had lifted the upper limits of the Negro league salary scale several notches for his confreres. Indeed, Gibson's raise to a big league–level salary happened just as bigger coin suddenly began to appear in abundance around the black game.

The war years would give the Negro leagues their first sustained success at the box office in their history. Black fans, given employment in defense plants, now not only had more disposable income but shared the dream that racial unity in war would carry over to the home front. While this optimism proved to be premature, in retrospect it was this mutual sacrifice that provided the last great heave forward for the cause. In the more mundane realm of games played by men for money, men like Josh Gibson came to understand that, as Cum Posey had said, African Americans might soon receive the sacraments of the big leagues if they were visible in the congregation where they belonged.

Now patriotic fervor in the black community melded with the cause of black baseball; black ball itself could afford to strut a little, given the void left by the absence of true megastars in the white game. As Williams, DiMaggio, Feller, Greenberg, Doeer, and others went off to war, the majors were forced to get by with factory seconds, including a one-armed outfielder and a one-legged pitcher; the white game sunk so far that the heretofore win-starved St. Louis Browns won the 1944 World Series.

In black ball, the continuing domination by the Grays and the Monarchs was a comfort to black fans, which translated into huge crowds and larger paydays for all Negro-leaguers.

Not by coincidence, the owners put aside their petty squabbles for the duration of the war to enjoy their prosperity. Seeing this era of good feelings coming, they had readmitted the Mexican wayfarers to their teams with, as before, a nominal fine, $100 this time, which for Josh at least was now tipping money. For the 1942 season, Josh and Sammy Bankhead were back on the prowl in Homestead, and as a bonus Cum Posey re-signed thirty-eight-year-old Cool Papa Bell, who appeared in his first Negro league lineup in four years, playing part-time in the Homestead outfield.

Posey got so caught up in his good fortune and the spirit of the times that he presented a gift to his team before the season, a brand-new bus on which to make their journeys across black ball. And though Cum was a bit put off by Josh's new girth, he reassured fans that all was the same with Gibson.

After the Grays went to Raleigh, North Carolina, for spring camp, Posey wrote:

> Josh Gibson, sensational home run catcher, rated the top receiver in Negro baseball, will return to the Grays' lineup [this season]. Gibson has been playing in foreign lands since 1939, but returned home this season. . . . Gibson is heavier in weight, but just as shifty as ever, and expected to set new batting records this year for the Negro National League.

This was the black ball spin on the return of Josh Gibson. And Josh made it stand up when he homered in his first at bat of the new season and looked for all the world like an even better analogue of Babe Ruth now that he was as overweight as the Babe.

To the Grays, however, the return of the old players to the lineup required some adjustment. Veterans still made up the foundation of the club, men such as Buck Leonard, newly acquired Boojum Wilson, Howard Easterling, Jelly Jackson, Chester Williams, Lick Carlisle, and pitchers Ray Brown, Roy Welmaker, and Edsell Walker. But Josh was only semi-familiar with the newer men who had stepped in so ably, including speed-burning outfielder Dave Whatley, catcher Josh Johnson, and pitchers John Wright, Wilmer Fields, Red Ferrell, and Specs Roberts.

Josh especially took a liking to Fields, a large and jovial man who attended Virginia State College in the off season. Fields's light skin and faintly Asian features earned him a pet name from Josh, which over time became variously "Chink," "Chinkie," or "Chinkapink." Josh allowed the bright young man a seat on the bus next to him and, as Fields recalled, filled his head with so much baseball shop talk that it was like a college-level education in itself.

"Boy, he was like an encyclopedia. He knew all the pitchers, all the pitches, all the little things to look for. But the main thing was, he gave me encouragement all the time," Fields said. "He'd tell me, 'Chinkie, you gonna win this pennant for us.' Coming from him, that meant a whole lot to me.

"When he came back, I didn't know what to expect. The guys on the team kept tellin' me about the home run in Yankee Stadium, the one that went four hundred and fifty feet, and Christ, he was a living legend and all. But soon as we met, he was tellin' me, 'You can do this, you can do that,' and what I was doin' wrong. He took the time to make me a better pitcher.

"Josh was a great team man, that's what I remember most

about him. A great ballplayer and a great human bein'. I can't say I ever saw the guy mad at anybody. Never. Oh man, I think about him all the time. What a man he was."

In exchange for being allowed to join this select company, Fields, by Josh's edict and by dint of his light skin, was designated to place the food orders of his teammates in redneck diners. Fields, his knees still knocking, related the time Josh got the munchies at 4 A.M. on a dark road in West Virginia and had the bus pull over to a truck stop. Fields, it seems, scored the food all right, but without warning, another, and darker, Gray pitcher—whom Fields still suspects was put up by Josh to do it—came into the diner and screeched, "Hurry up man, we's hungry," whereupon the cook chased the two of them out, ax in hand.

"I wouldn't put it past Josh," Fields said with a full grin. "He had that kinda sense of humor."

Josh, of course, was given a wide, wide swath, to accommodate not only his size but his status. Quickly, the Grays learned that there were rules for the team and another set of rules for Josh. Though no one on the team begrudged this double standard, Josh made a careful point never to lord it over them.

In fact, Josh did not attempt to get around Cum Posey's inviolate rule against drinking at the ballpark. On the bus, however, the same regulation was, well, fudged a bit when a weary Josh would climb aboard and topple into his seat needing something to ease the aches and pains. And as usual, Sammy Bankhead would be there to pass it to him.

"We didn't allow no beer to be brought in the bus," Buck Leonard recalled, "but you know the good players are privileged a little more than some of the other guys, and those two would bring bottles of beer on the bus. Well, I don't remember Josh *bringing* them on, but I remember Bankhead bringing them on and Josh would help him empty them. Vic [Harris] let them get by with it, and the other players didn't resent it."

There were many reasons for this latitude, the foremost

being that Josh was Josh, a man with a sunny disposition who would not allow himself to be a sloppy drunk. He was of course also Josh the Basher, the big gun. And the first few weeks of the season, he carried the team through an early slump that had seen the Grays drop three straight games to Newark by the embarrassing scores of 9–0, 13–8, and 9–4.

Those jarring defeats had made Cum Posey livid, and his ire could be gauged by the tone of the *Courier's* summation of the games. "Not at all pleased with the showing their baseball investment made [against] the youthful Newark Eagles," read a blind item on May 2,

> co-owners Rufus Jackson and Cum Posey expect to do some housecleaning . . . if the guilty ones fail to revitalize their sluggish manner of ball playing before . . . the middle of May.
>
> Early this year, [Jackson and Posey] dickered and compromised with a few holdouts. They raised salaries here and there to make sure that the Negro National League pennant would again return to Homestead. . . . With Josh and Buck Leonard doing most of the extra base hitting, the Grays would have the edge on every team in the loop, so they figured. Then came the unprecedented, ridiculous showing against the Eagles.

When the two teams met again on May 4, Josh lit a flame under his teammates. As the *Afro* reported the match, coming off the earlier wipeouts, the Eagles

> got cocky, told it all over the circuit that the Negro National League champs were easy pickin's.
>
> But [now] in Newark, where the Eagles do their playing— and bragging—they were jolted, and beaten with one punch. Newark was leading 2–0 in the ninth, when Whatley and Carlisle got on. Josh Gibson came to bat. Judging from what had gone on before, Gibson was just another easy out. But Leon Day pitched the wrong ball to Josh and he jolted it over the centerfield wall—to win the ball game 3–2.

Even though the Grays had done nothing but win with Josh gone, his return was heralded in the black papers. Hailing him, Butts Brown in the *Newark Herald* opined,

> The Grays [in the mid-thirties] were a rough and cocky team and were dubbed by this scribe as the "Gas House Gang." They lived up to this reputation. . . . [But] when Gibson left the club for better pickings in Mexico, the boys lost some of their zest and took on more of the Sunday School attitude.

Josh, for his part, took the theme of his rebirth and redemption seriously. When he came back to Pittsburgh he and Hattie made a stab at reconciliation; in July 1942—according to information supplied to the Hall of Fame in the early seventies by Josh's sister, Annie Gibson Mahaffey—they were married in Alabama during a Grays road trip, though no marriage certificate seems to exist and Josh Gibson Jr. doesn't believe it ever happened.

"Nah, he didn't wanna get married no more," Josh Jr. said. "He was just a player."

Still, in wedlock or not, in bliss or not, Josh and Hattie were again cohabiting under the same roof at 2157 Webster Avenue. But nowhere was it evident that his personal life was in order or that he was going to be chained down.

From the start of the 1942 season, one of its main story lines was the individual rivalry between Josh and Satchel Paige. And both men seemed to know how important this showdown was in the minds of Negro league fans during this boom of black ball popularity.

But before the Paige-Gibson main event, the latest integration moves had to be played out. The new buzz in black ball began when the antediluvian major league commissioner, Kenesaw Mountain Landis, made himself heard on the issue, announcing with dubious sincerity that "there is no rule, formal or informal, no understanding, subterranean or otherwise, against hiring Negro players." Consequently, rumors were afoot all year about impending big league tryouts for Negro-leaguers, and Josh's name was often involved.

During the season, a report came across the Associated Negro Press wire that Pirate president William Benswanger had authorized Wendell Smith, now the sports editor of the *Courier,* to select Negro league players who would be given Pirate tryouts, which "will not take place until after the close of the season as Bob Rice, Pirate farm director, who will supervise them, is busy with the farm teams." Smith's chosen candidates were Josh, Sam Bankhead, Willie Wells, and Leon Day, all of whom heard nothing more about the alleged tryouts during and after the season.

But Josh did hear from Benswanger in July, when he and Buck Leonard were summoned to Benswanger's office for what they assumed would be a skull session with the man who was about to sign them, an assumption made plausible by Benswanger's recent comment that "colored players are American citizens with American rights." Benswanger had implied he would be willing to give blacks a shot, since, as he said, "somebody has to make the first move."

But when Benswanger had his meeting with Gibson and Leonard, he told them what he told the press later, that signing them would trigger a rush of signings that would decimate the Grays, and that Cum Posey had personally made a plea for him not to do it. This may have been the case, since Posey had in mind a more gradual phasing in of integration, one that would hold back the big Negro league stars until they would command a higher price and force baseball to recognize black ball owners' proprietary rights.

But out of Benswanger's mouth, such an explanation sounded more like an alibi to get him off the hook than an exercise in good conscience about black ball. Years later, Benswanger was still using the same canard, insisting that "I tried more than once to buy Josh Gibson" but that Posey had ordered him to "lay off."

This contention seemed preposterous, given that few within the big league power ring cared whether the Negro leagues lived or died. Nor would the major league brass defer to what Posey was proposing, that Negro league players were tied to the Negro league power elite; if integration was to come, the big league owners wanted absolutely no part of the black ball owners, and would surely bypass them to sign Negro league talent. Still, the "destruction of the black game" bromide would become a common apologia as the battle intensified.

But now a new phenomenon entered the integration conversation: black *ambivalence*. Suddenly, in the midst of the noise generated by the black papers, players began to openly question if the time was right for such a momentous shift of tide after all. Satchel Paige, as was his wont, created a ruckus when he issued his thoughts on the matter and seemed to turn thumbs down on integration just before the East-West Game that August.

Interviewed by the Associated Press, Paige—who had been led to believe that he was about to be signed up by the majors many times, only to be let down—brought up the reasonable concern of "unharmonious problems" that might occur when blacks would travel with white clubs in spring training in the South. Said Paige: "All the nice statements in the world from both sides aren't gonna knock out Jim Crow."

The furor over these comments, which were like manna to big league obstructionists, forced him to make a public retraction of sorts on the field, with microphone in hand, between innings of the East-West Game. But Satch was not alone in expressing lukewarm sentiments about the cause. Josh, in his only known remark for attribution on the subject, harbored no such cynicism. When a reporter asked him about the validity of the spree of big league signing rumors, he replied hopefully, "I don't think they'd kid about a serious thing like that."

However, among those Negro-leaguers who voiced their doubts in the press, some players were genuinely concerned that the black game would in fact collapse, leaving the vast majority of players not promoted to the majors but out of work. Others candidly worried that certain undeserving players would blow it for everyone. One, Baltimore Elite Giant player-manager Felton Snow, without naming names, made the harshest comments.

"I don't know that it would be a good thing, we've got so many guys who just wouldn't act right," Snow told the *Courier.*

Some of these fellows who are pretty good out there on the diamond would give you a heartache elsewhere. You see, there are so many that get three or four dollars in their pockets and right away want to tell "the man" where he can go. . . .

We have some good players, yes. And some of them would certainly qualify, but it is quite a task finding the right combination. Many of the good players are bad actors and many of the ordinary players are fine characters.

The players were also loath to be used as political pawns, as they saw it, for pressure groups such as the Communist Workers Party, whose newspaper, *The Daily Worker,* had embraced their cause.

"I wasn't in favor of too much agitatin'," Buck Leonard recalled, "because if the owners were forced to take black players before the owners were ready, we would have had a hard job stayin' up there."

Far from being prepared to jump right into the big league pond, then, a good many Negro-leaguers found reason to justify their existence in baseball's netherworld. For men like Josh Gibson, however, the yearning for the call was there, but never would he let it show. To pitch himself for promotion would be considered a breach of Negro league honor.

"Of course Josh wanted to go to the big leagues; we all did," Gene Benson said. "But we were satisfied with what we were doin'. We weren't just pining away for the call to come.

We had full lives and, you know, we didn't do too bad financially. We were playin' winter and summer, getting a lot of acclaim. But the thing with Josh was this, I don't think he accepted this greatness like a lot of other great ballplayers who set their ambitions real high. Because he really did play for the love of the game."

And so Josh, and the Negro leagues, carried on, comforting themselves with their private assumptions of equality even if the calls never did come. In June 1942, for example, a game was arranged at Wrigley Field for the benefit of the Navy Relief Fund, pitting the Kansas City Monarchs against a white team fronted by a washed-up Dizzy Dean and composed of minor-leaguers and *former* big-leaguers. This was the first time blacks had been allowed to play in this ivy-walled baseball yard, and as the Monarchs' 3–1 win demonstrated, the price of admission for the black players was to face second-rate competition.

The financial success of that game, which outdrew a White Sox game across town on the same day, led to a second match, with the Dean All-Stars meeting the Grays a week later in Griffith Stadium. For this contest, Satchel Paige was permitted to pitch for Cum Posey's team, reuniting the Paige-Gibson battery for one day. Satch went five innings, striking out seven, and Josh collected a run-scoring double in the Grays' 8–1 win before a large and boisterous crowd.

Reveling in this rough treatment of such a lame excuse for big-leaguers, the *Courier* still laid it on thick in its game story: "The 22,000 wild-eyed fans saw sepia baseball's greatest battery, Josh Gibson and Satchel Paige, supported by one of the greatest all-around clubs in baseball, outplay and outclass the All-Stars from the first through the ninth."

The reteaming of Josh and Satch was a cause célèbre, since with the depleted state of the big leagues, there were no *white* equivalents. Now a spate of profiles retelling the familiar legends of Paige and Gibson popped up in the black papers. And while Josh could not yet boast of having Paige's éclat in the white press, he did win another crossover notice in July 1942 in a magazine called *Spot;* in this piece, writer Haskell Cohen, linking Josh with some fast company, used him as a prod for integration. He wrote:

> After 12 years in colored baseball, and at the age of 30, Gibson has compiled so many records with his hickory stick that it is doubtful if the great Babe himself did any better. Josh [has] hit homers in all 11 major league parks he played in. He has hit prodigious drives against the best hurlers in the big leagues and in colored baseball.
>
> Why then isn't he in the National or American League, catching for the World Champion Yankees, the Dodgers or one of the other pennant contenders? An unwritten law of the majors bars from its field all colored [players]—a prissy prohibition that is out of line with big time baseball's reputation for sportsmanship. Thousands of fans, both famous and humble, have strenuously objected to Jim Crowism on the diamond, pointing out that it is ironical to find discrimination in America's national game, that the big leagues deprive themselves of much valuable talent, and that it's not logical for a sport that had a Black Sox scandal to exclude representatives of a race that boasts such outstanding sportsmen as Joe Louis, Henry Armstrong and Jesse Owens. Be that as it may Josh and many another colored star can't play with white boys.

The renewed emphasis on black ball's top-billed attractions naturally heightened coverage when the Grays and Monarchs met in interleague competition. In fact, casting an eye on the clubs' meeting on June 18 in Griffith Stadium, Paige began priming the classic confrontation in the afterglow of the victories over the Dizzy Dean team.

"Josh can hit anything you throw him, and I mean hit it hard," he said. "He really lays that wood into the ball. . . . I got a catcher [on the Monarchs], Pig Greene. . . . They're calling him a second Josh Gibson out west. He smashes [the] hell out of a ball but don't let them tell you he's a Gibson. There is just one Josh Gibson—he's terrible."

Between these onetime friends and companions, though, the rivalry was becoming less cordial and the game of dare less jovial. Sometime later, Paige recalled that their ragging had taken on a gruffer edge. "[When] he and I was playing in Porta Rico, he said, 'One of these days I'm gonna be up against you,' and he says, 'And shame on you. I'm gonna have my family there,' and blab-blab-blab. And that went on for two years."

Josh, trying to forget how Satch dominated him on the island, was getting mouthier about Paige. Interviewed on the radio early in the season, he was asked about how he'd done against Satch over his career. "I hit him about like every other pitcher," he lied, "four hundred—and seven hundred in the pinches."

Informed of that, Satch dryly reiterated that Josh was great but he had one weakness. Said Paige: "He can't hit what he can't see."

On Thursday, June 18, in the first Negro league game to be played at night in a big league ballpark, twenty-eight thousand people streamed through the turnstiles at Griffith Stadium, which was considered a record crowd for a regular-season black ball game. Paige started against Roy Partlow and was scheduled to pitch five innings, which in his advancing years had become his norm. But Josh—coming off a 410-foot homer in Yankee Stadium a few days before against Philadelphia—made the first statement, though not with his bat but with a neat decoy.

The first Monarch up, William Simms, tripled. Then, as the *Courier* reported,

Art Allen, a cagey veteran, lifted a long fly to Benjamin in center field. The sacrifice effort seemed good as Josh Gibson stood near home plate with both hands at his sides. Simms, certain that no play would be made from that distance in center, jogged homeward. But as he neared the plate, Gibson tagged him out standing up. Benjamin had made one of the greatest and most perfect throws ever seen in a ball game.

The long-awaited Paige-Gibson confrontation at last was at hand in the bottom of the second. Josh, first up, dug his cleats in, wiggled his bat, stared out at Paige, and with high voltage crackling in the air, Satch reached back and delivered heat right into Josh's kitchen. He got ahead 1–2, then threw another beebee. Josh leaned in to meet the pitch—and swung through it as it rose through the strike zone.

This was the opening shot in black ball's greatest show-down, and for Josh it did little to relieve his angst about Paige. Worse, Satch was on his game this night. Breezing through one Gray after another, he had yielded only two scratch singles, and only one ball had made it to the outfield when Josh came up for his next turn, in the fifth. Again, he went down swinging hard at fastballs that were nearly invisible in the dim light.

As it turned out, this splendid game contained much more drama than that of Paige versus Gibson, which was truncated when Satch left after his five prescribed innings. After nine scoreless innings, the Monarchs pushed one across in the tenth, but a pinch hit by the aging Boojum Wilson tied it in the bottom of the frame. Wilson then scored on Partlow's triple to win it, whereupon, according to the *Courier* story, "The fans surged onto the field and carried Partlow off. Excitement reigned for a full half hour."

And yet Paige grabbed most of the press attention for his seven-strikeout half-game performance. Satch "put on a great show, unapproached by any other hurler anywhere and anytime," said the *Courier,* though fortunately for Josh the game within the game between him and Satch was buried in the overall hubbub.

Still, it was an embarrassment Josh could not soon forget, and Satch had made sure he wouldn't. After Hilton Smith also fanned Josh, later in the game, Paige jumped from the bench and yelled across the field into the Grays dugout, loudly enough for reporters to hear upstairs, "Say, you guys, don't let me ever hear you ranting about Josh Gibson. Against the Monarchs, he is just another batter who takes his three and then sits down!"

When the teams met again, on July 21 at Forbes Field, Paige was riding the crest of his PR wave, having drawn crowds as large as thirty thousand people to Monarch games at Yankee Stadium and Detroit's Briggs Stadium, shattering the short-lived record set at Griffith Stadium. Before this clash, the *Courier*, which had remained at least as loyal to Paige as it was to Josh, wrote that "when Satch comes shuffling home Tuesday, he will be cock of the walk. He has proved this year that together with Josh Gibson . . . he is still the super showman of Negro baseball and one of the greatest individual drawing cards in all baseball history."

The Paige-Gibson rematch, which was billed as Satch's homecoming, brought in 11,500 fans, which the *Courier* said was the largest crowd ever to attend a black ball game in Pittsburgh. And it was practically a replay of the last game. Again Paige went against Roy Partlow and again his fastball was steaming. And this time, he decided to go the distance rather than five innings. Starting out on fire, he struck out the first Gray hitter on three pitches, and drove in the game's first run with a base hit. He also gave Gibson another hosing, as Josh's only triumph was to make contact, flying out to center twice and popping out weakly to the infield. But he struck out twice as well, making it four whiffs in seven at bats over the two games against Paige.

Satch, who by now had to know he had Josh's number, even took the ostensibly suicidal step of walking the number two hitter, Howard Easterling, with first base open to pitch to Josh, setting up a pressure-packed moment—which he climaxed by striking Josh out.

Judging by the press coverage, few would have known

Paige *lost* the game, 5–4, in the eleventh inning, when Jerry Benjamin singled in Ray Brown. "SATCHELL" STRUTS HIS WARES HERE AGAIN AS THOUSANDS CHEER was the *Courier* headline, and in his column Chester Washington waxed ecstatic:

Many highly publicized stars have come here and not lived up to advance notices. Like shooting comets, they have blazed streaks of glory across Sportsdom's skies. . . . But with sepia baseball's superman "Satch," he came, he saw and he conquered. . . . And to top the evening off, he held the mighty jolter, Joshua Gibson, hitless, fanning him one particular time when the chips were really down.

In view of his failure against Paige, Josh could be relieved that his reputation remained intact. Indeed, J. L. Wilkinson took advantage of the publicity surrounding the last game to "nominate" both Paige and Gibson as the top two among twenty-five Negro league candidates for big league citizenship. According to the Associated Negro Press, "Wilkinson regards Josh as the Negro Babe Ruth, a fence-busting champion who clouts on an average of 40 circuit blows a year. He has a lifetime batting average of .349, possesses a good arm and is one of the fastest men in sepia baseball."

The August 1 *Courier,* running with this news, published a large photo of Gibson in catching gear, over a caption reporting that Josh "is the No. 1 candidate for major league baseball. The Courier has agreed to pay Gibson's expenses to any major league city if he should be granted a trial. Star of Homestead Grays, Gibson has been rated by baseball experts as a $200,000 catcher."

Moreover, Gibson's next crack at Paige produced more-satisfying results, at least to a point. This came at the East-West Game, the one Paige held up before the seventh inning to announce over the P.A. system he hadn't really come out against major league integration. Because Satch did not start the game, his and Josh's personal encounter was not a major subplot in the coverage, though this latest chapter of that story did demonstrate that Paige had a healthy fear of the big man still.

When Paige got in to start the seventh—after his race per-oration had guaranteed that all eyes in Comiskey Park would be riveted to him—Josh had already gone 2-for-3, with singles in the first and fifth, the second of which drove home Boojum Wilson to put the East up, 2–1. In between, in the third, he had slammed one off Hilton Smith that was caught at the wall in dead center field.

Now, with the game tied at 2–2, Newark's Lenny Pearson led off with a fly ball that was misplayed into a double. Boojum Wilson then dragged a perfect bunt to put runners on first and third. Sammy Bankhead delivered the go-ahead run with a sacrifice fly. Willie Wells then singled, and he and Wilson pulled off a double steal. That brought up Josh with first base open.

And now, with 48,400 people watching and all that drama waiting for release, Satch went soft. He walked Josh intentionally.

This itself was a kind of victory for Josh, but even now Satch won out, because the next guy up, Wild Bill Wright, hit into a double play to kill the inning. Still, Paige didn't have it today, giving up another score in the seventh. And when sloppy fielding put men on second and third with one away in the ninth, once more Paige took the safe way out versus Josh—another intentional walk. But this time the strategy backfired on Satch, when Wright singled in the last two runs in the East's 5–2 win.

No amount of favoritism in the black papers could turn Paige into a hero in this game—that role went to Newark's Leon Day, the winning pitcher in relief. And no one knew better than Satch that he couldn't sidestep Josh again and continue to claim supremacy in this clash of supermen.

What's more, all those maddeningly close losses to Josh's team were driving Paige nuts. When the Monarchs faced the

Grays again in Griffith Stadium on August 20, Satch was luminescent, retiring the first nine hitters in a row. And the Grays seemed cursed when, in the first inning, the Monarchs cleanup hitter, Willard Brown, singled up the middle with two outs and a man on first. When Brown tried to steal second, Josh's throw struck him on the shin, the ball caromed into left field, and a run scored.

But the Grays' Roy Welmaker also turned in a gritty performance on the mound, and by the sixth it was 2–1, Kansas City, when the Grays put two runners on with one out. Now Josh stepped in and Paige challenged him with heat. Unable to get good wood, Josh got under the ball and lifted an easy fly ball to left. Satch then got Buck Leonard to end the threat.

The next time Satch got around to facing Josh, it was the bottom of the ninth, the score still 2–1. Paige gave up a leadoff single to Jerry Benjamin, who quickly swiped second. Howard Easterling moved him to third with a long flyout, and next it was Josh's turn. Ric Roberts's story in the *Afro* described the moment this way:

> After long deliberation by the entire club, Paige went to work on Josh Gibson. It was a tense moment while the fans waited with baited breath. Gibson exploded a long one to left field, a 450-footer that was foul by several feet and later, getting nothing good to hit, walked. Buck Leonard stepped in and singled to right to tie up the ball game, 2 to 2, as Benjamin charged into the dugout.

For Paige, then, the strategy against Josh seemed to be to act according to whether he sensed Josh could be pitched to during any given at bat. Scared off by the long foul blast, he again begged off—only to be punished by Leonard. Deprived of the win, Paige was determined not to leave the hill until he had one. He mowed down the Grays for two more innings to notch twelve strikeouts in all, and disposed of Josh once more on a ground out. But in the twelfth inning, Vic Harris singled and went to second on an infield out, and Dave Whatley once more did Paige in with a single to score the gamer.

With two losses and one no-decision against the Grays, Paige must have seriously wondered what he would have to do to beat them, considering that Josh was still looking for his first hit against him. Providentially, he would get another chance, several of them, in fact, when the Monarchs and Grays won their respective league pennants and agreed to compete in the reinaugural of the Negro World Series, which hadn't been played since 1927 because of a lack of fan interest.

Now, with black ball booming and the Paige-Gibson showdown a natural drawing card, more than twenty thousand fans turned out on a cold Tuesday night when the series commenced on September 8 at Griffith Stadium. For Josh and Satch, the mind games began even before the first pitch; making the scene at the Crawford Grille on the eve of the series, they had kept the place hopping by taking turns at promising to beat each other on the field. This was not a comfortable game for Josh, but his nerve was aided by the drinks set up for him and Satch as they ragged each other.

Satch kept the game going during Josh's first at bat the next night. As Josh came to the plate, Satch twitted him by yelling, "C'mon up here and see how you can hit my fast one."

Even now, after having hit against Paige a number of times, Josh could not be sure how to read his verbal salvos, whether to take the bait and respond or just treat the whole dare as a joke. In fact, Josh was probably thinking too much about these verbal taunts and too little about the simple act of hitting what was pitched, because—having convinced himself that Satch would try to cross him up and throw a breaking ball—he let a fat fastball go right by him for strike one.

"Look at you! You ain't ready up there. You ain't gonna hit with yo' bat on yo' shoulda!" Paige clattered, and a tensed-up Josh could only foul-tip the next fastball. Still looking curve, he eventually took strike three.

All through the game and the rest of the series, recalled Paige's catcher, James "Pig" Greene, Satch's woofing came nonstop, and each time Josh looked as if he was lost in the woods. "Satchel would say, 'Get ready, I'm gonna throw you one at the belt line, so don't get up on the plate,' or, 'Look out, here's one low and outside on the corner.' And Josh would be turned inside out. He'd step away, step closer. He didn't know what to do.

"Even I wanted him to get himself straightened out, 'cause that's what the series was about; the people wanted to see them two tangle up. Josh'd move his left foot closer to the plate to hit the outside pitch Satchel say he was gonna throw him, and I'd tell him, 'You don't hit like that, Josh. Move your foot back.' But he thought I was messin' with him too, and it made him more fouled up."

Josh did have a shot to turn it all around, in his second at bat that night. The game was scoreless in the fourth when Paige, who had retired the first ten Grays in order, gave up singles to Bankhead and Easterling. Now it was Josh's turn, and with the chance to be the game's hero before him, the *Philadelphia Tribune* reported, "the big catcher whaled Paige's second offering 420 feet to left center, where Willard Brown made the catch as both runners [tagged up and] advanced."

As the soaring drive climbed high into the night and then fell and was caught, Paige knew he had dodged a bullet. The Grays failed to score, and Satch had little trouble from them and came out leading 1–0 after five innings; Jack Matchett then pitched no-hit ball the rest of the way as the Monarchs cracked it open in the late innings, benefiting from seven Gray errors, and won, 8–0.

Now the feeling all around was that Josh's chance to shut Paige's mouth with a cannon blast was gone. Indeed, though the series turned into a cakewalk for the Monarchs, the real margin of victory may have been only a couple of feet, or the distance between Willard Brown's back and the other side of the left field wall at Griffith Stadium. If that's so, and if Josh knew it, then that at bat was at least as critical as the one regarded by historians as the zenith of the black game.

The latter, the topic of more after-dinner stories at Negro league reunions than any other, took place during Josh's third time up in game two, which was played on a dank Thursday night, September 10, at Forbes Field before a small crowd of 5,219. The Monarchs had staked Hilton Smith to a 2–0 lead when Paige relieved him in the sixth. Now, an inning later, Satch got two quick outs before Benjamin singled.

It was then that Paige was inspired to create some unforgettable history. Inverting the usual black ball custom, he intentionally walked Vic Harris *and* Howard Easterling—so that he could pitch *to* Josh Gibson with no place to put him and everything on the line in this high-stakes side game.

In actuality, this noontide of apparently excruciating pressure was almost too easy for Satch, given Josh's muddled state of mind when he hit against him. But there were other considerations that further lowered the risk, as was shown when Satch walked Easterling to get to Josh in the earlier Forbes Field game. Though Josh in any condition could murder a baseball, in recent weeks people had begun to notice he was wearing down. After a dozen years of Josh's nearly ceaseless squatting and rising behind the plate, every joint, ligament, and muscle seemed to be inflamed and pleading for a rest. He was also beset with intensifying headaches and fatigue.

Rest was a solution Josh always brushed aside, but now he had already determined to pass up winter ball to try to recuperate. As it was, he could get no lower while catching than a semicrouch, and at times he stood nearly straight up awaiting the pitch. Worse still, his physical deterioration—which, of course, had only been accelerated by alcohol consumption—was affecting his hitting, though he may have been denying it. The first sign was a swing that had become just a bit slower.

Josh had hit, by some accounts, a league-high eleven homers in 1942, to go with a .344 batting average. All the same, even if he was in denial about his laggard bat, he had given cogent oral testimony about his decline only weeks before, following a game against Baltimore. After pounding one ball to deep center for another 400-foot out, he told the *Afro,* "I just can't pull them to left this year. I'm hitting more balls to center than ever before. Gosh, I should hit some of them to right center, or even right field."

Josh had never before had to think about going to the opposite field; by instinct, he merely hit the ball where it entered his wheelhouse. Now, to overcompensate for slower reflexes, he was attempting to pull everything, which left him vulnerable to pitches that tailed away from him—which was precisely what Paige dished up to right-handed hitters with his cross-fire pitch, a wicked sidearm fastball that broke like a crisp slider diagonally across the plate.

Satch surely was aware of the change in Josh's swing, and while anything less than a perfect pitch would meet Josh's heavy bat, the slight slowdown in his bat velocity would likely send the ball on a ride to center, as had happened in the East-West Game, as well as game one of the Negro World Series.

Many years later, Paige revealed the epiphany he had had about Josh. "I had learned that he couldn't hit a sidearm pitch," he said. "I never did tell anybody that, until I pitched to him [in game two]." Of his melodramatic maneuver to walk the bases drunk to pitch to a hitter he called peerless, he explained with simple and impeccable logic, "I guess the fans thought I was crazy, but I knew Josh better than I knew Easterling."

Some of Paige's own teammates thought he was deranged as well, but everyone on the field and in the stands that night seemed to understand that this was one time when deviation from the norm was required and expected—that this watershed had been presaged by two decades of Negro league baseball and might not come again. So here it was, Satch and Josh, alone on the summit.

Again Satch did his talking, reminding Josh about the Puerto Rican challenge, how Josh had said it would be "shame on you" when the big moment came, telling him he was getting nothing but fastballs and where they would be. The Monarch first baseman, Buck O'Neil, who would make a career on the banquet circuit delivering his own embroidered account of the event, said it unfolded like this: "First Satch says, 'All right, Josh, I'm gonna throw you some fastballs'—and Josh says, 'Show me what you got.' But now right before he winds up he says, 'Now listen, I'm gonna throw you a fastball letter high'—and *boom,* it's strike one; Josh didn't move the bat.

"Satch gets the ball back and says, 'And now I'm gonna throw you one a little faster and belt high'—and *boom,* strike two. Josh didn't move the bat."

O'Neil's wonderfully entertaining yarn slightly skews the facts. In truth, Josh fouled off the first two pitches. O'Neil then finishes his account the way Satch did, with a flourish.

"Now everybody's standin' and goin' crazy. And Satch looks in at Josh and says, 'Okay, now I got you oh-and-two, and in this league I'm supposed to knock you down. But I'm not gonna throw smoke at yo' yolk—I'm gonna throw a pea at yo' knee'—and *boom,* strike three; Josh didn't move the bat. And Satch walks off the mound and the crowd is yellin' and screamin' and he walks by me and he says real slow, 'You know what, Buck? Nobody hits Satchel's fastball.'"

Again, a slight correction and expansion is in order for verity's sake. On the third pitch, knee-high on the outside corner, Josh, looking fastball, inched a bit deeper in the batter's box. Uncoiling, he got a good look at the pitch, timed his swing to the quick break, took his cut . . . and missed, his huge swing whooshing under the ball.

According to various colorings of the legend, Gibson at that moment either *(a)* laughed; *(b)* slammed his bat into the dirt; or *(c)* slammed his bat into the water fountain in the dugout, though it is possible he merely went and put on his catching gear for the next inning. Paige, in his memoirs, had an oddly fuzzy recall of the pitching sequence but wrote that after the job was done, "Josh threw that bat of his four hundred feet and stomped off the field. . . . It was just something to strike out Josh like that after I'd told him I would."

But, curiously—or maybe not so, considering the regular omissions in the black press—the mother of all strikeouts, and of all black ball moments, passed with mention of it made in only one newspaper, the *Afro*. Once again, this was because the game was played in the warp of lead time preceding the next two series games, which were more timely when the papers hit the street the following week.

The only concrete record was the *Afro*'s brief description, in the meat of the game story, that the fans had "thrilled to the 'storybook' duel . . . between two of baseball's greatest stars," as well as a subheadline reading, "Satch Paige Fans Josh Gibson with Three on Bases." And yet, this modest etching is today a black ball liturgy.

Back then, it also marked the denouement of the series and Josh's active role in it. It also, for a time, seemed to bode ill for Paige, who was cuffed for four runs only an inning later and gave way to Hilton Smith, who snuffed the Grays to get the victory when the Monarchs roughed up Roy Welmaker and won, 8–4.

Satch also had a rough time in game three, when the series—in another sign that black ball cared less about local team identities than broad-based mercenary interests—switched to Yankee Stadium. In the first inning, Easterling took him out of the park. Josh then walked, stole second, and came home on Buck Leonard's hit. Paige got through the fifth, but his arm was tired and he came out, replaced by Jack Matchett, who pitched superbly to preserve a 9–3 win for Paige.

Despite his travails, Paige went on to stamp the series in his image. In game four, played in Philadelphia's Shibe Park, he relieved Matchett in the fourth inning with the Grays ahead, 5–4. For the rest of the game, he allowed only two runners to reach base, both on walks, and struck out seven. When the Monarchs rallied late and won, 9–5, Satch got the series-clinching win. (This game stood in place of a 4–1 victory against Paige that was invalidated after J. L. Wilkinson protested Cum Posey's signing of four other Negro league players for the duration of the series, including Leon Day, the winning pitcher.)

As for Josh, he shrunk from sight, literally. Still unable to hit Paige, the worn-out and hobbled Gibson—who had gone 2-for-16 in the series, 2-for-20 including the voided game— had to bench himself after two innings of the final game, with the Grays leading, 3–1. Paige, however, still had one more dance on his card. After being unexpectedly detained to pay a speeding ticket in a Pennsylvania traffic court, he entered the contest in the fifth inning, with two outs and two on and the score now 5–4. His first hitter would have been Josh, but instead, he struck out backup catcher Robert Gaston to begin his roll toward victory.

The epic confrontation of the ages over and done with, the Negro leagues could celebrate with pride their first twenty years of survival and, now, prosperity. But black ball would soon have to confront a new reality, one that would see both Josh and Satch in decline. While both of these magnificent icons would go on to more days of grace and headlines, and Satch to a whole new baseball life later in the majors, they were nearing the end of their meaningful days within black ball. And Josh needed every one of them desperately.

15

Tomorrow May Not Come

Gibson has been repeatedly threatened with disciplinary action during the past several weeks, it was authoritatively disclosed. The big catcher is said to have been warned about his habit of breaking training and, shortly after leaving Washington following the opening day double-header, was given what was supposed to be his "final" admonition.

Notwithstanding, he is reported to have again disregarded the warnings and was unfit for use last Saturday when the Grays played an exhibition game at Orange, N.J.
—AFRO-AMERICAN, MAY 27, 1944

If one were to judge by the public record, the 1943 season was Josh's year of annunciation, when word of his legend crested in the black press and spilled over into the mainstream of the white press. Gibson more than deserved the attention. But the truth was that, even as he seemed to be peeling back time, he knew his time had begun to run out.

This became horribly apparent just as the year began.

Though Josh had rested his battered body for two months, his lethargy and his headaches continued. But because his drinking had also continued, he assumed these problems were more symptomatic of hangovers than physical decline.

What's more, he and Hattie were bickering again, another side effect of his boozing, and the strain of this troubled union made it no easier to rest, but easier still to take a drink. But even if Josh disregarded serious physical warnings, he could not drink away the pain and fatigue in his body. On New Year's Day 1943, after an all-nighter at the Crawford Grille, a monster of a hangover did not let up, and early that morning, he had a seizure and lost consciousness.

In a panic, Hattie called Josh's physician, Dr. Earl Simms, who summoned an ambulance to meet him at 2157 Webster Avenue. Half an hour later, Josh was in a room in St. Francis Hospital. Had he not gotten to the hospital, it is probable he would have died that morning. Even now, as he lapsed into a coma, the doctors weren't sure he was going to pull through.

According to what Annie Gibson Mahaffey has said through the years, her brother was diagnosed with a brain tumor. The doctors wanted to go in immediately and remove it but Josh, when he awakened later that evening, refused to allow the procedure. As Annie has told it, Josh rejected the surgery for fear that, if he survived it, he would wind up living his life as a "vegetable."

Josh never spoke about his condition or the path he took, which isn't surprising. In his life as a ballplayer, such an admission would have created pity, and on the fields of black ball, where strength was a primal trait, pity was worse than a bases-loaded strikeout. Rather than have someone in the press find out about his hospitalization, which lasted ten days, Josh apparently asked the doctors to cover for him, both with the press and with Cum Posey and Sonnyman Jackson.

When the Courier, having been fed the news by St. Francis, broke the story on January 9 under the headline FAMOUS

CATCHER SENT TO HOSPITAL, the facts came out looking like this:

> The Pittsburgh Courier learned this week that Josh Gibson, $200,000 catcher of the Homestead Grays, has been confined to the St. Francis Hospital following a nervous breakdown. Gibson entered the hospital Friday morning and will probably be confined for at least two more weeks.
>
> According to reliable sources, the giant catcher has been ailing since the middle of the 1942 baseball season. Although his condition is not regarded as critical, it is serious enough to keep him in the hospital for a thorough examination and long needed rest. . . . Rufus Jackson, co-owner of the Grays, said this week that his prize ball player has been ailing since last August. . . .
>
> Meantime Grays' officials are deeply concerned over the condition of the brilliant catcher, who, with the possible exception of Satchel Paige . . . is the most famous Negro baseball player in the country.
>
> Gibson's failure to play his usual game last year was one of the main reasons the Homestead Grays succumbed to the Kansas City Monarchs in the world series.

A week later, the paper, keeping on top of the stunning story, reported that Gibson was "considerably improved," and that

> although no visitors have been permitted to see Gibson it was learned that the ruling was made by doctors as a precautionary measure. "Gibson is doing fine," the Courier was informed, "and should be able to leave the hospital by no later than next Monday. He is now up and around and feeling all right again."

If Josh did have a serious and potentially life-threatening condition, he and his doctors did a splendid job of news management to conceal it. In fact, not even Sammy Bankhead ever knew of it. Neither is it certain that Dr. Earl Simms was trusted with the information; when Josh's medical charts in Simms's office were examined years later, there was no citation of a brain tumor, only of nervous exhaustion and hypertension, though it is also possible Simms complied with Josh's wishes and expurgated this data. It is possible as well, given the unreliability of other information from Annie Mahaffey, that he did not have a tumor at all.

Whatever the truth, Cum Posey didn't question the plausibility of the nervous-breakdown explanation, and, in truth, such a breakdown could have easily contributed to Josh's collapse. Now Posey found himself again having to reassure black ball fans about his big man's condition.

"Josh Gibson, who was confined for ten days at the St. Francis hospital, was a visitor at Homestead Grays' headquarters Saturday," Posey wrote in his January 23 column.

> Josh was ailing during the past baseball season but attempted to catch every day. He was worried about his batting and overworked himself in an effort to hit his usual playing stride. He was ordered to take a long rest by his physician at the close of the season, but did not follow the doctor's orders until he was completely run down. He is now the same Josh who never knew the candle had two ends.

Cum was right about that last part—Josh had no intention of slowing down, nor was he even willing to sit out the second game of doubleheaders, and Posey had no intention of forcing him to do so; Josh's only concession would be to play left field in selected nightcaps. Most of all, he wanted nothing more said of the hospital stay. Pledging he was fully healed and feeling like a colt again, he dutifully went to Hot Springs on his own in early March to work himself into playing shape and then reported to spring training on time two weeks later. Then, when the season began, he immediately made his hospitalization seem irrelevant. In the Grays' opener against Baltimore in Griffith Stadium, Josh—pointedly reinstated in the cleanup spot in the order, with Buck Leonard hitting third—came up for his first at bat. He walked, sprinted to second on a Sam Bankhead bunt, and tore around third and home on Vic Harris's base hit. His second time up, he cracked a double and scored on Howard Easterling's hit. The Grays won, 2–1. In game two, a 7–0 blowout, he went 3-for-4 with two doubles.

GIBSON BIG GUN AS ELITES BOW TO GRAYS, the hometown *Afro* bannered its game story, sounding Josh's unquestioned return to form. For the rest of the season, stories of the "new" Josh, dried out for now and with a quicker bat, ringing up one humongous game after another, were stitched into a running story in the black papers, in the kind of prose that to black baseball fans must have read like a valentine:

WASHINGTON, May 27 (*Courier*)—The Homestead Grays twice defeated the Philadelphia Stars, 9–3 and 8–2, to maintain an unbeaten record in the Negro National league race Sunday, before 6,500 fans at Griffith Stadium. . . . Josh Gibson scored four times and drove home a total of seven runs. He hit for a total of 12 bases, including a 440-foot, two-run home run to left field in the sixth inning of the second game. Buck Leonard, who had walked, scored in front of Big Josh.

WASHINGTON, June 4 (*Afro*)—John Wright tossed a one-hitter at the Baltimore Elite Giants here at Griffith Stadium on Monday night but what set the 10,000 fans shouting was the thunder of Josh Gibson's big bat. Gibson led the way with two tremendous homers, two singles and a double to drive home seven runs as his mates added 19 other savage base blows to gain a lopsided 17 to 0 victory for the Homestead Grays. . . . The feature of the evening was Gibson's line drive homer into the centerfield stands, 422 feet away in the seventh. He had previously raked Glover with a 440-footer to the middle of the bleachers in left center.

WASHINGTON, July 8 (*Afro*)—With Josh Gibson walloping the ball for three hits in four trips to the plate, including a double and a two-run homer, the Washington Homestead Grays took a doubleheader from the Newark Eagles before 6,000 fans at Griffith Stadium Sunday. . . . [With] the Eagles ahead 5–4 [in the second game] the climax [came] when Josh Gibson banged a 430-foot home run into the centerfield bleachers after Leonard had walked.

CLEVELAND, July 21 (*Afro*)—The Washington Homestead Grays took both ends of a double-header from the Cleveland Buckeyes here Sunday, winning 14–10 and 9–5 before 7,500 fans. . . . Josh Gibson banged a home run over the wall in the second inning with one mate aboard [in game one]. The ball cleared a 30-foot screen, 290 feet away from home plate.

Within this renaissance season there was also retribution paid to his nemesis, Satchel Paige, albeit belatedly and with the stakes not nearly as high as in 1942. On June 22, the Monarchs came to Griffith Stadium for a three-game set with the Grays. They won the first game, 2–1, then Satch took the ball two days later before twenty thousand fans in the opener of a Sunday doubleheader—and walked into an inferno.

Cool Papa Bell led off the Grays' half of the first inning with a walk, then, an out later, Buck Leonard doubled him in. Josh then ripped a hard single to center to post another run. Before the inning was done, the Grays batted around and put up five runs. His next time up, Josh lined a double, scoring another. In what was surely one of the worst shellackings of his seemingly endless career, Paige was gone after three innings, having surrendered six hits and seven runs. And when the Grays had completed the sweep, by scores of 10–2 and 7–6, the *Kansas City Call* went with the theme of the day:

None other than the celebrated Satchel Paige was pounded to cover in the first game as the Grays, rising in wrathful rage on a team that had pinned their Homestead ears back five consecutive times, jammed home five runs in the first inning.

Paced by the great Josh Gibson, whose big bat accounted for six runs on four doubles and two singles in nine attempts, the champions from Kansas City saw the winners explode 26 base hits in a wild afternoon of revenge.

Josh, in fact, got back at Satch more than once this season, and even though Satch put in an airtight five innings at the August 1 East-West Game, getting the decision in the 2–1 West victory, he could not dress down Josh. When he led off the second inning, Paige would not challenge him this time and walked him on five pitches. Josh then took second on a passed ball, before Satch busted the rally by striking out Sammy Bankhead and Cool Papa Bell to end the frame. Later, Satch retired Josh on a fly ball, but Gibson had a satisfying 1-for-3 game in defeat.

When the Monarchs next returned to Griffith Stadium, on September 9, for another twin bill, it was even uglier for Paige than the last time he was on that D.C. mound. For Josh, though, it was a lovely afternoon. In game one he led off the ninth inning of a 6–6 game with a single up the middle. He was bunted to second, and when Bankhead grounded to short, Josh took off for third, normally a bonehead play. But he beat the throw to the bag and two hitters later he trotted home when Vic Harris was walked with the bases loaded.

Then, in game two, Paige was again taken apart in the first inning, giving up four. This time he lasted four innings and went out, down 6–0. While no box score of the game was printed, only a line score, Gibson likely had a hand in the carnage, since Paige yielded ten hits in the eventual 8–1 Grays walkover.

Cum Posey tried to further help Josh upstage Satch. When a Satchel Paige Appreciation Day was held in Wrigley Field on July 8, Posey scheduled Josh Gibson Night for September 9 at Griffith Stadium—an obvious site, Posey noted in a press release, since "fully half of the top thrills at the stadium have centered on the tremendous drives from the bat of this great diamond star. His long line drives have thudded off the far reaches of all the stadium's fences, and he has hit more homers there than hundreds of white American Leaguers of the first rank."

On that damp Thursday evening, when the Grays suffered a rare loss, 4–2, to Philadelphia, some five thousand people witnessed black baseball's lone tribute to its home run god. In ceremonies held between the sixth and seventh innings, according to the *Courier,* "the fans gave him a gigantic bat, a horseshoe floral wreath and on behalf of the management, Cum Posey presented him with a handsome set of traveling bags. [Sonnyman] Jackson introduced the fans' representative, Russell Bowser, who made the presentations. Cum Posey, Edward Ross, Elks' head in D.C., made short speeches."

The next week, black newspapers across the land carried a photograph of Gibson clutching the oversized bat, which was inscribed "Josh the Basher," with one hand and the two suitcases with the other, surrounded by bouquets of flowers, which perfectly emblemized a season spent in clover.

The heat of summer brought even more recognition for Josh. When the July 19 issue of *Time* magazine hit the stands, most of white America learned for the first time that there was a black version of Babe Ruth. Until this time, these pages had previously been liberated only by Joe Louis and then Satchel Paige, who had been given his due in June 1941. Now, with Paige becoming a stale icon, Gibson was presented in sober contrast to Paige's clownish and self-centered ways.

Using the increasingly catchy parlance of "Josh the Basher" as its title, the unbylined piece, avoiding for the most part the mock aggrandizement so common in white reportage of black sports heroes in the past, described him as "a hulking 215-pounder with features vaguely suggestive of a very dark Babe Ruth," whose only excesses were mere quirks.

"At bat, Josh Gibson has a peculiar habit: he rolls up his tongue and sandwiches it like a hot dog between his lips," it read. "Thus fortified, he can swat a ball a country mile."

Indeed, while the familiar litany of Gibson's longer-than-long home runs was faithfully recited, as well as the fictional "international incident" allegedly propagated by his defection to Mexico, as much space was given to the still-extant image of him as a straight arrow off the field. Unlike Paige, said *Time* approvingly, Gibson "is no gaudy eccentric. He drives no cerise roadster, makes no startling statements about a strict diet of fried food, and receives no $40,000 a year salary. Josh's salary is $750 a month plus bonuses."

Actually, Gibson's bonuses had lifted him above $1,200 a month by now, which was more than some white big-leaguers' income. But as with Haskell Cohen's plaint about Josh being enjoined from playing with white boys, the exemplary and humble image of Josh Gibson provided an opportunity for *Time* to make its own pitch for baseball integration. Unfortunately, it was marred by the magazine's need to fall back on condescension, such as by referring to Effa Manley as a "hula-hipped Harlem beauty" and by tiptoeing around the race issue without a flat-out call for inclusion:

> Though U.S. newspapers probably give more space to baseball than any other sport, little of it goes to Josh Gibson, the Homestead Grays, or Negro baseball in general. Yet colored baseball could have been good copy at any time since 1885. . . . The Negro teams rent white clubs' ball parks [and] have a large following of white fans who like their fancy windups, their swift and daring baserunning [and] their flashy one-handed catchups.

The black press too was kneading the Gibson legend once again into fresh copy. In the July 24 *Afro*, Art Carter com-

posed a four-column ode under the headline JOLTIN' JOSH
HELPS GRAYS HIT THE JACKPOT. Gibson, wrote Carter, "hits
more homers than any player in baseball annually, and has
hit for distances unequalled by the great Babe Ruth and
Jimmy Foxx of the big-time majors."

For Cum Posey, this pyramid of publicity was a godsend,
confirming the wisdom of his decision to lure Josh back from
Mexico. In fact, one could almost hear the sound of Posey
chortling when, war or no, Jorge Pasquel made another sor-
tie on black ball in 1943. Pasquel had limited success this
time, luring the likes of Roy Campanella, Wild Bill Wright,
Pee Wee Butts, and Henry McHenry, and reupping past Mexican jumpers Willie Wells and Ray Dandridge. But aside from
signing Roy Partlow again, Pasquel had no luck with the Grays'
big guns, as Posey happily reported in his July 24 column.

"Josh Gibson refused to talk with the Mexican promoters
at Forbes Field on July 5," Posey wrote. "Sam Bankhead told
the Grays' owners that the Mexican promoters had been after
him throughout the season, but he had no intention of going
to Mexico." Posey added with sarcasm: "It is too bad the
Mexicans are spending so much money attempting to get
[black] players to jump their contracts. . . . Do they think the
Negroes of America don't wish to see first class baseball?"

Posey had more reason to brag than he may have known;
when black ball finally rid itself of the Mexican threat, it removed the last impediment to the black game's wartime
boom, as well as its right to petition the big leagues for inclusion. (Josh, however, was not above using the Mexicans to
score a higher salary for himself and Buck Leonard; when the
two threatened in tandem to jump to the Mexican League in
1944, Posey raised them both, Josh to $1,300 per month in-
cluding bonuses, Buck to $1,100.)

For the Grays, who battled all season for first place with
Newark and Philadelphia, the jump-off point came in mid-
August, when they played the Eagles in two doubleheaders
within twenty-four hours. First the Grays rousted them in a

Saturday game at Forbes Field by scores of 7–5 and 11–7; then on Sunday the teams met at Griffith Stadium for two more. In game one, Cool Papa Bell walked to lead off the home first, and two outs later, Josh put one into the center field seats to jump-start Homestead toward a 9–5 win.

And though the ageless Mule Suttles secured the nightcap with a missile of his own over the wall, the Grays had moved into first place and stayed there. They then dispatched the NAL champion Birmingham Black Barons in seven games in the Negro World Series as Josh went 3-for-5 in the final game, played in Montgomery, Alabama.

Cum Posey's stat men, who didn't need to stretch much, wrote the closing sentence of the season. Gibson, according to league figures, hit no less than .526 with fourteen homers and thirty-two doubles, all league highs. Posey, selecting his annual Negro league All-Star team, wrote, "Gibson still gets the nod [at catcher] because of his tremendous hitting power and ability to play day in and day out at top speed."

This, however, was a stretch. In a near carbon copy of 1942, by the end of the season Josh had again run down and couldn't play in every game against Birmingham. Far from playing at top speed, which had always been mentioned as a quality right up there with his slugging, he now almost never stole a base or even tried to, as he generally took a lead off first of no more than a few steps. What's worse, the Grays had watched with mounting concern as Josh began to display unstable behavior no one had ever seen in him before.

This behavior usually followed drinking binges, in which he consumed thick red wine and hard stuff such as bourbon or scotch, which he downed straight, one shot after another. Jim Canada, who played first base for the Black Barons that season, could not help but notice what this routine did to Josh on the field. Canada told John B. Holway, "I've seen him when he [was] drinking all that wine and got kind of doped up on it—I've seen him come up there and tell the manager that he wanted to pinch-hit. He pushed his cap bill up and hit the ball over the fence and ran around the bases the third base way. That's when they knew he'd been drinking."

It is possible Josh knew exactly what the parasitic effects of alcohol were doing to his mind and his body, but that being numbed from head to toe was as important as hitting a home run now. If tomorrow might not come, what did it matter anyway?

Buck Leonard, one of the very few Grays who have spoken on the record about this side of Gibson, recalled an incident during a Grays road trip to Norfolk, Virginia, when Josh again had trouble keeping his clothes on. "He got started drinking and there were six of us staying at my wife's sister's house there. And he was walking around the house naked. We were on the second floor, but women were in the house, too, and the only bathroom was upstairs. And we told him, 'Don't be walking around naked. What's the matter with you?'"

But no one really did know what was wrong with him, certainly not the root cause of such dementia. Without an answer, the Grays could try only one solution. When Josh's drinking reached a point where he could not play without embarrassing or even hurting himself, Buck and a few other Grays would put him in a cab and take him to St. Francis Hospital, in order, as the ballplayers called it, to "boil him out."

This presumably meant sleeping it off under doctor's orders but in time entailed more serious treatment as his stays lengthened from one or two days to one or two weeks, depending on how sick he was. Although no one on the team knew the nature of the treatments or of other possible maladies, it was clear Josh was being kept under sedation. When he came back to the ballpark after the layoff, there would be needle prickings in the crook of his arm where the IV tubes had been run.

Cum Posey, of course, made certain no newspaper reports of these hospital visits saw the light of day. Gibson's absences were always explained as days of rest and sometimes weren't even noticed since Posey would send Josh to boil out when the Grays had barnstorming, nonleague games in the countryside; for the Saturday or Sunday league games, he would sometimes bring Josh directly from the hospital bed to the park, accompanied by attendants in white coats, then send him right back afterward.

Buck Leonard winced at this shamefaced practice, in which Josh, he said, looked as if he were being "led around like a drunken monkey." What it did to Gibson's pride must have hurt as much as the pain inside his head. And yet, as though he could squeeze every ounce of strength from his weary body into his bat, Josh would wobble up to the plate and hit one out of sight. And when he was relatively clean and sober and could watch those drives soar, Buck would swear it did for Josh more than anything the doctors tried.

"When he was batting," Leonard said, "he became a kid again, just like that, right before your eyes."

Those wonderful moments and the hope that Josh would somehow cork his self-destructive behavior—or at least hold it in check like other players—kept Cum Posey perpetuating the con of Gibson's "rest days" and kept him footing the bill for his extended vacations at St. Francis. But in the process, Posey may have alienated the finest manager his team ever had.

When Vic Harris opted to give up managing in 1943 so he could work in a defense plant and play ball part-time, Posey hired Candy Jim Taylor, a wily former third baseman who had been playing and managing in black ball since around the turn of the century and was one of four brothers who had excelled in the black game through the years. As Buck Leonard said, "the players responded to Candy Jim better than to Vic. Candy Jim knew what he was talking about," yet the Candy man was appalled when he had to make allowances for Josh when he overstepped the rules.

Although booze had always been forbidden by Candy Jim on the bus and in the clubhouse, he too had to get used to the smell of beer wafting from Gibson's seat and to keeping quiet about Josh's therapeutic visits to the hospital. But Taylor nearly imploded when he saw Josh sneak a brew in the bull pen before one game, and he benched Gibson several times when he was ready to play as a form of punishment, something Posey did not appreciate.

When the 1943 season ended, Taylor demanded more authority to discipline the big man. For Posey the 1944 season loomed as a test of how far he was willing to go to deal with the Gibson problem.

Candy Jim's task was made all the more difficult by new complications in Josh's life when the new season came around. Making a statement about his grit, Josh had gone back to playing ball in Puerto Rico over the winter. When he got home, he was in the mood neither for rigorous training nor to perpetuate a semblance of a home life.

Where he had been fat the last few years, now he was fat and lazy, and at times he showed up at the park glassy eyed and speaking in disconnected sentences. To the players, there was something different about him, something unrelated to his drinking; although he wasn't slurring or mumbling, he would run on at the mouth, with his eyes darting back and forth and his brow sweating heavily. When he ran down, he seemed much more tired than usual, not hung over as much as burned out.

Nevertheless, he was in the cleanup spot when the season began, by virtue of getting himself straight enough. In early May, in a Yankee Stadium doubleheader against the Black Yankees, he caught both Gray wins and went 4-for-6 in the opener, though all the hits were singles.

But clearly, Gibson was now pushing his privileged status with Candy Jim Taylor. With no explanation, he had refused to show up for spring training games, telling Sammy Bankhead that he needed no training "against those little country boys" who provided the competition. His late arrivals at the park and flagrant disregard of Taylor's authority were too much to keep out of the papers. On May 27, Sam Lacy broke the story in the *Afro* of Gibson disregarding a "final" admonition to accompany the Grays to an exhibition game versus Newark in Orange, New Jersey, and being declared "unfit" to play.

The following day, when the Grays played the Eagles in a league doubleheader at Ebbets Field, however, Josh was made available, which prompted Lacy to comment on this inconsistency. Without mentioning Taylor or Posey, Lacy drew a thinly veiled explication of the power struggle and Posey's apparent overriding of Taylor's disciplinary measures regarding Josh.

Lacy—who had been the first sportswriter to break ranks with the Gibson amen corner in the black press, pronouncing that Josh was no Bill Dickey—wrote that Gibson was on display for purely mercenary reasons, "due to the fact that the Gray management felt an obligation to the large number of fans who had made the trip to Ebbets Field from Newark. [His absence] from the Grays, it was held, would not be entirely fair to these customers."

Although Josh had gotten one hit, a single, in nine times up in the Ebbets Field twin bill, Lacy noted that "the crowd of 7,500 persons, most of them followers of the Newark Eagles . . . actually pleaded with him to give them a hit." Lacy went on:

To the naked eye this may not seem much, but to me it represented the height of admiration. In a situation where ordinary baseball fans such as these would call for "striking out the bum," the air of Ebbets Field was filled with a reverent chant, "We want a hit!"

Believe me, folks, a crowd loves a guy when it disregards entirely the feeling of their home town club to encourage him in his efforts to beat that same club. It's something that just isn't done, that's all. Baseball fans worship a hero, no matter which side he's on, but they save their cheering until after he's done his specialty—it doesn't come in front.

Being very careful with his words, Lacy then offered a gentle reproof of the hero:

Ironical, isn't it, that this should happen on the same day I learned Josh had run afoul of his bosses' wishes? I wonder whether it struck him the same way it did me. And whether he could appreciate the paradox which made him a hero in the eyes of those customers and something else entirely in the minds of his teammates, who had seen him thumb his nose at the team's training rules just the day before.

Of course, it isn't too late for Josh to turn around, and I'm hoping he will, but I feel a sort of responsibility to you and him to pass along this comment.

For even with his faults, he's a likeable, big lug—and a hell-firing good ball player, too, when he's in shape.

Josh did not take the advice. In fact, his increasingly brash manner got only worse. Still, some players had become so used to Josh's cutting remarks on the field that even when those remarks lost their lighthearted buoyance they considered themselves privileged to be ragged by the great Josh Gibson.

Intriguingly, much of Gibson's blather sounded a good deal like the psych-out bombs Satchel Paige had lobbed at him. Larry Doby, the Newark infielder who in 1947 became the second African American to make it to the majors and the first in the American League, recalled his first game against the Grays as a rookie in 1943. Doby got a hit and when he came up again, Gibson, through his mask, chattered, "Well, you hit that fastball pretty good, kid. Now let's see how you do with the curve." Doby said he got another hit, and the next time up Josh tried to distract him by asking him where he was from.

Doby, normally a meek man, said, "I was feeling pretty sure of myself by then and I said, 'None of your damn business! Just call for the pitches!'" Doby laughed. "That shut him up, but it was also the last time Josh told me what was coming."

Josh had better luck playing this head game with Josh Johnson, who went from the Grays to the NAL Cincinnati Tigers in 1942. "I was down two strikes and he said, 'Namesake'—that's what he called me, Namesake, 'cause of my first name—he said, 'Namesake, let's see how you hit this one, 'cause it's comin' straight down the middle.' And I didn't say nothin' but I figured he was kiddin', that it was a curveball.

"And sure enough, the pitcher threw a fastball right down the middle and I just looked at it, couldn't get the bat off my shoulder. And Josh, he smiled and said, 'I told you it was gonna come down the middle. I was just tryin' to help you out.'"

In time, Satchel Paige himself received some verbal payback for the old humiliations. In 1944, Josh hit a tremendous home run off Satch in Comiskey Park, which clanged off a large clock that used to be on the scoreboard in dead center field, about 435 feet away. As Josh waddled around the bases, he cupped his hands over his mouth and called to Paige, "I love ya, man. If you could cook, I'd marry ya!"

Oh, if only he could have uttered that line two years before.

Even an owner could get sliced to bits by Josh's wit and cherish the experience. Effa Manley, for example, once cheerfully told of the time in 1944 when Josh slammed a three-run homer to beat her Eagles before a sold-out house in Ruppert Stadium. Seeking out Gibson as the Grays left the locker room, the emotional Effa recalled telling him, only half in jest, "How could you do a thing like that, Josh? You broke everybody's heart."

"Miz Manley," he said without a pause, "I'm known to break hearts."

Others, though, simply arrived at the conclusion that the Gibson of the mid-forties was a bad actor. On June 15 of that 1944 season, the Grays swept Birmingham in a doubleheader at Griffith Stadium. In the seventh inning of the nightcap, with Homestead down, 3–2, Buck Leonard tripled home Cool Papa Bell to tie it. With Buck on third and two outs, Black Baron manager Winfield Welch ordered up an intentional walk for Gibson. As the fourth wide serve came in, Josh, after mugging and making menacing gestures with his bat at the first three wide pitches, nearly stepped across the plate to swing at the fourth—a move not in keeping with baseball etiquette—and just managed to hold himself back. But Welch jumped from the dugout and demanded that the home plate umpire call Gibson out for interference.

Then, the *Afro* reported, "When [the ump] refused, [first baseman] Slats Davis . . . pushed him in the face. Jerry Benjamin . . . pushed his way into the scuffle and attempted to quiet Davis. The latter swung at Benjamin, who immediately locked with him. Here was the signal for both teams to join in the scuffle and it took police several minutes to restore order."

Josh was getting weird, most players would come to admit, but he still engendered such loyalty that Wilmer Fields, even decades later, refused to admit he had ever seen Josh drunk, insisting, "There was not one bit of change in his behavior." This being the case, Fields grasps for an explanation of the obvious. "When I heard that he had passed away," he said, "I asked different people the reason why, and they told me about drugs and stuff. Well, that must've been what happened, but I never saw any of it."

This, the most serious complication in Josh's decline and fall, is territory no one can discuss with complete certainty. Josh Gibson Jr., who speaks frankly and at length about his father's other vices, admits to knowing little more than vague outlines about Josh's entanglement with drugs.

"I know he did a little reefer," he said, "and the story I got was that my father had got ahold of something, some hard stuff, in the Latin countries and he wasn't right after that, 'cause at times he wasn't the same guy. He'd be talkin' outta his head sometimes."

Gene Benson, from across Pennsylvania, also heard the stories that began making the rounds on Negro league ball fields and meeting places.

"I understand he run into somebody that might've been on drugs and he just went down. Most of this started happenin' to him when the Grays went to Washington to play most of their games. In Pittsburgh, he was okay. Then he ran into this woman in D.C. who wasn't any good for him who got him hooked on drugs."

In fact, it would be these last two obsessions—hard drugs and a shady woman—that brought Josh Gibson to the edge of his grave.

16

Last Call

In recent years Josh has had several physical breakdowns and has been forced to spend varying periods of time in [a] health sanitarium. There have been rumors that he had departed the straight and narrow path preceding each of these breakdowns. In his early thirties Josh has been one of the great stars of baseball and would have been a stand out in the majors. His clouting for distance has been one of the highlights of a great career which now seems definitely to have ended unless he mends his ways.
— W. ROLLO WILSON, *PHILADELPHIA TRIBUNE*, AUGUST 11, 1945

Sometimes a man don't wanna admit he's messing himself up. My father once told me, "A man ain't nothing unless he's got a good alibi." He had a whole lotta alibis.
— JOSH GIBSON JR.

By the summer of 1944, Josh was spending so few nights at home with Hattie at 2157 Webster Avenue that she almost never saw him. The Grays were now playing in Washington every Sunday the Senators were away—which prompted speculation that Clark Griffith was a silent partner of the Grays—and Josh stayed down there, bunking at several hotels with various women during the week. When he did come back to Pittsburgh for a game at Forbes Field, he'd hang out at the Crawford Grille long after closing hours, or else prowl around the red-light district of Homestead, where Sonnyman Jackson had his nightclubs and cathouses.

Josh Gibson Jr., who by now had grown old enough to witness his father's ballplaying and his more indelicate habits firsthand, was taken along for the ride on many of these trails, as Josh again made a stab at fathering. Half a century later, memories of these trips haven't dimmed.

"When I'd travel with him on the bus, I used to sit right next to Wilmer Fields; that was my dad's seat. The two big men, Wilmer and my dad, used to sit up front. But then my father would go and get in the backseat and ride the 'hump.' They used to gamble and stuff back there, play dirty hearts, and he'd keep me away from all that. In fact, the first thing he'd do when I'd get into town was, he would find a young guy for me to hang with. Somebody he knew would have a son my age and I'd hang out with him while my father did his thing.

"The first thing my father taught me was that after you'd get to D.C. you'd read the signs—colored and white. They played in Griffith Stadium but we stayed at the Dunbar Hotel on Fourteenth Street, or the Carver Hotel. These were black-only hotels. But it didn't matter to them guys none. They knew who they were—the Washington Homestead Grays. They wore that W on their uniforms and they were more popular there than the Senators. To black people, that W was like the NY the Yankees wore; they were our Yankees. They were big, tough men. I remember how big my father was but they all looked big, man.

"And us kids, we'd try and look like the Homestead Grays. We had a club, the Bobcats, and we'd do everything the Grays did. When we played ball, we dressed like 'em. We put on that green liniment, same as they did, so we wouldn't have no sore arms. It was never like I played catch with him in the backyard or anything, he didn't have time for that. The Negro ballplayers never dropped the ball. But if they played at Forbes Field, I always took my friends there so they could get in. I didn't wanna pull no rank so I'd wait with them at the gate, and one guy would carry Buck Leonard's bag in, somebody'd carry Luis Marquez's bag, or Sammy Bankhead's. And we'd all get in."

Away from the team bus and the ballpark, the scenes were just as impressionable, if less idealized.

"Oh yeah, like I'd go down to the Crawford Grille with him. I'd get some potato chips and sit up there and hear the players talk that bullshit. The Crawford Grille, that was the showplace. The vibe in there was suits and ties and plenty of money and Gus Greenlee at the head of the table. The Grille was the mecca. You'd get to see Nat King Cole and Duke Ellington. You could see all that great entertainment and wouldn't have to leave the black community for nothin'.

"And I'd go around to the whorehouses, too. See, they had fifteen whorehouses in Homestead. U.S. Steel was there, and they used to say Homestead had more money than any little town in the United States. And right across from the mill gate they had fifteen whorehouses on Sixth Avenue. I would come out there and I'd sit in the Skyrocket Cafe, Sonnyman's club. He had a beer garden and in the back he'd have gambling tables. But around the corner was the whorehouses; see, you didn't mix numbers and whorehouses, that's how you get busted. It's just like pimps and dope.

"So when I was there, Bankhead and my old man would be around the corner. When you went into a whorehouse, they played poker in the front, and in the back was the rooms. And I'd have to go find them guys, 'cause the bus would be ready to leave and I had to get my father and them outta there!"

For Josh, womanizing had long been a sporting activity, but lately it had become a more dangerous one. Now, he didn't trifle with the best-looking woman or even a white woman; rather, the prize was being able to pry a woman away from another man. This game was a common routine in the Negro leagues, where players paid respect to one another on the field but dissed one another off it by stealing the other guys' women. On the Grays, not even Cum Posey was safe, and when Jake Stephens once persuaded one of Posey's mistresses to go out with him, Cum raged at Jake and swore he'd trade his ass if it happened again.

Monte Irvin recalled that Josh, with his fame and money, was the master of cuckold making and even used it as one of his psych-out weapons. After picking up Eagle infielder Lenny Pearson's girlfriend at the bar of Newark's Grand Hotel, Irvin recalled, Josh let fly with some choice and very racy personal barbs during a doubleheader the next afternoon.

"Hey Monte, tell Lenny something for me," he woofed to Irvin in the on-deck circle one time when Pearson was at bat. "Tell him I screwed his lady last night! Tell him she was *gooood!*"

Said Irvin: "Lenny went oh-for-nine that day."

But Josh may have figured he had become all-world at this game when he took up with a black woman in D.C. Her name was Grace Fournier and she was tiny, comely, vibrant, and light skinned. With her dark, flickering eyes and easy smile, Grace was in every way the polar opposite of the stern and unadorned Hattie Jones. Not only was Grace a pip, she was also potentially hazardous, which in this stage of his life no doubt made her all the more desirable.

What was dangerous about her was that she was married to a serviceman who had shipped out to the South Pacific.

More dangerous was something Grace constantly reminded him about, that her husband was an insanely jealous man involved in D.C.'s gambling and drug trade.

Most perilous of all, though, was that Grace Fournier lived on the edge. Although none of the Grays ever got close enough to her—by conscious choice—to confirm it, they strongly suspected Grace hadn't met a drink or drug she didn't like, again and again. The oddest thing about Josh's liaison with her was that he apparently didn't seem to mind who thought what about her.

While he had seldom brought Hattie to the ballpark, and cautioned people not to try and banter with her, he presented Grace as his possession to his teammates and encouraged such repartee, which was part of Grace's giggly, effervescent manner. While Josh did not care to be photographed with Hattie, and no photographs of her seem to exist, he gladly posed with Grace in a loving embrace, looking happier than he had at most other times in his life.

Indeed, when the introductions to Grace were made, the players would sometimes feel as if they were intruding on Josh and Grace's private world. The two of them would make eyes at each other and laugh at their often incomprehensible dialogue, while everyone else would stand there and wonder what in hell was so funny. It wasn't hard to understand why they were so hysterical, however, since they both usually stank of booze.

They both also had the same hollow circles under their eyes and the same habit of sweating even when it wasn't overly warm. Grace would be seen in the stands, still sweating yet also shivering under a blanket, even on brutally hot days, her knees pulled up and tucked under her chin.

An inference that may have been drawn from this unrestrained cavorting was that Josh now feared just about nothing, neither public shame nor private depravity. If so, this may have been the earmark of a man who knew he wasn't long for the world. While other men might have carried on with a woman like Grace only in shadowy corners, Josh went as far as to buy a house in Pittsburgh where he could lodge her when she came there to see him. The digs were a two-story brick house at 614 Morgan Street, on the north side, and Josh Gibson Jr. saw enough of Grace in the house to know of his father's attachment to this woman, though he describes her brusquely as "just another of my father's girl-friends."

That Josh had still not tried to remove Hattie from 2157 Webster Avenue was a begrudging concession that, even if Hattie was not officially Mrs. Josh Gibson, she had earned her domain at that house after enduring his excesses for so long, and in time the deed would be placed in her name. But 614 Morgan Street was Josh's writ of independence.

Hattie apparently was mollified by the trade-off, accepting Grace as Josh's new woman. Still, if it came to it, she would again be there if Josh came home.

And so Josh pushed on through the war years, further punishing himself with the ravages of drink and probably narcotics, all done in the name of love and illicit adventure. In the coming months, his manic-depressive behavior would leave many wondering if some of those track marks in his arm were put there by a different kind of IV needle. Their suspicions were justified given that, years later, Sam Bankhead would become the first to come out and say to a reporter that Grace Fournier was a junkie and that "what she was taking, Josh was taking."

That was enough to convince Josh Gibson Jr. "If Sammy said it, it had to be, 'cause he knew more about my father than anyone else in the world," he said.

Evidently, though, Josh did not make heroin his drug of choice; as with booze, he was after any high he could find, in any variation. Josh Jr. recalled a seamy episode at Margaret Mason's home during one of his visits.

"I heard my grandmother arguing with him," he said, "and I think it was because of some marijuana she found that he must've stashed in the house. And she was fussin' with him about it."

In 1944, Mrs. Mason moved her family to a new location, a town house a half mile up on the Hill at 2712 Bedford Avenue in a complex called Griffin's Houses. Once there, she forbade Josh to have a key, as he had had in the past, and asked that he stay away until he could act like a proper father. And while he was in his Grace period, he did stop coming by, even to drop off the child support checks. When that happened, Margaret Mason would march to the ballpark, wait at the players' entrance, and demand that he pay up. Clearly embarrassed, and wishing not to rile this hornet of a woman, he'd dig into his wallet and peel off the necessary bills.

These sick scenes were as regular as his ongoing success on the ball field. Black fans, who had absolutely no reason to suspect anything was amiss with Gibson, went right on reading those resonant game stories featuring Josh's bashes. The July 22 *Courier,* for instance, looked to the heavens to find his only real rival:

> It took a terrific electric storm—one that ripped up trees and tore down building structures—here at the Polo Grounds Sunday afternoon to stop the great Josh Gibson from tearing down the ball park as the Homestead Grays and famous New York Cubans battled to a 5–5 deadlock before 14,000 cheering fans.
>
> Three tremendous blows, two home runs and a robust triple by Gibson, kept the Grays in the ball game as the fighting little Latins of Manhattan fought desperately to keep the league leaders in check for eight innings.

Josh's timing was impeccable, as well. When the Grays clinched the first-half title in 1944 with an 8–4 win over Newark in Ruppert Stadium, the *Afro* tooted, "The thrill of the evening came in the ninth when Josh Gibson . . . connected with one of McDuffie's fast balls to slam it over the left field bleachers for a home run to put the game on ice."

As late as mid-September, the *Courier*'s sports editor, Wendell Smith, wrote that Gibson had "come back fast after a slow start. [He] is hitting .339 and is the home run king of Negro baseball." Fortuitously, Josh also went 2-for-3, with a single and a double, in the August 13 East-West Game before 46,247 fans, which brought his composite average in seven East-West Games to .538 (14-for-26).

Nonetheless, it was becoming obvious to those who were in a position to see that, aside from the occasional power surge, Josh Gibson had become the highest-paid singles hitter in black ball. Because the Elias Sports Bureau had been commissioned to keep accurate Negro league statistics, Cum Posey's flacks could do nothing to pump up Josh's long ball numbers; though his average came in at a still-impressive .345 that season, his home run total fell from fourteen to eight, doubles from thirty-two to eight, triples from eight to five.

Candy Jim Taylor, seeing Josh in decline as a power man, couldn't afford to keep him in the cleanup slot on reputation alone. By the time the Grays again met Birmingham in the Negro World Series, black fans were probably stunned to see Gibson hitting *sixth* in the Grays order, with Buck Leonard fourth and right fielder Dave Hoskins fifth. But for many fans, the real shocker may have been a photo in the September 23 *Tribune* of a jelly-bellied Josh covered by yards of flannel uniform swinging at a pitch. This picture, which said what the sportswriters wouldn't about his degeneration, soon appeared in many other black papers.

And yet this was still not enough evidence to shuck Josh of his Ruthian aura; indeed, the photo originally ran as accompaniment to a game story focused on his homer in the Grays' 8–3 win in the series opener in Birmingham's Rickwood Field, a game in which he went 3-for-4. Thus, it was overlooked that while Gibson hit .400 for the series, which the Grays took in five, over the last four contests he notched only three singles.

Josh's standing was certainly unchanged as far as Cum Posey was concerned, and as a result Candy Jim Taylor had no chance to win a bitter war of nerves with Josh. While Josh had said nothing publicly about his demotion in the batting order, he was steaming about it the whole season. And when it was over, he and Buck Leonard, again in solidarity, refused to play in two exhibition games, a move that the sharp-eyed Sam Lacy wrote in the *Afro* "was being interpreted as general dissatisfaction with the conduct of the club."

This was a veiled slap at Taylor, and by late October, the scuttlebutt was that Gibson and Leonard had demanded Candy Jim's ouster or they'd walk. Though Lacy again didn't personalize the dispute, anyone familiar with the Grays could easily read between the lines of his October 28 story. Lacy reported that "rumor is rife that Taylor [is] about to be fired" and that the manager "has not been too well liked by the players and has come in for much open criticism from some of the more outspoken veterans of the team."

Confronted with the rumors, both Cum Posey and Sonnyman Jackson gave Candy Jim precious little support. While Posey ducked the issue by telling Lacy, "It's very hard to replace a man who has won two world championships in two years, isn't it?" Sonnyman all but wrote out Taylor's pink slip by saying, "Nothing has been decided in connection with the next year's manager."

Josh, who wanted to avoid being made into the heavy, said nothing about the matter. When Lacy cornered him and pressed the issue, Gibson's lighthearted attempt to sidestep the controversy gave Lacy a chance to frame the controversy in terms that were not altogether favorable to Josh. He wrote:

> Josh Gibson, catcher and cause celebre of many headaches for the Gray management during the early part of the season,

was questioned. Asked if he had heard that he might have a new manager next season, Gibson replied:

"How is everybody in D.C., Sam? Tell 'em I say hello and that I'm leaving Thursday for Santurce, Puerto Rico."

Only weeks later, Candy Jim was a memory, replaced by Vic Harris, who began his second tenure as Grays manager when the 1945 season arrived. Harris came back to the job with no delusions about cracking down on Gibson, though he chose to bat Josh fifth, thereby protecting Buck Leonard's scalding bat, which he left in the cleanup spot.

But if Josh believed Vic was going to be a pushover as in the past, the newer, higher levels of Gibson's misconduct incensed Harris as much as they did Taylor. In fact, it was Vic who demanded that Cum Posey hand down the harshest disciplinary measure ever taken against Gibson.

For Harris, the problems began to mount early in the 1945 season. For one thing, Josh seemed to have no use for training rules, for arrival and departure times on the bus, even for simple conditioning. Not only because of his weight and his knees but out of plain laziness, he went after pop flies only when the spirit moved him; by rote, Buck Leonard had to cover for him by running under virtually all pop-ups on the right side of the infield from the mound to the backstop.

As usual, Josh's name was at or near the top of the list of the league's hitting leaders all year, and by the week of the July 29 East-West Game, he carried a .383 average, third to Buck Leonard's .396 and Gene Benson's .389. His selection as the game's starting catcher was foregone, as the two Negro leagues had taken the selection process away from the fans after twelve years in order to keep individual players—especially Satchel Paige—from gaining too much leverage in their salary demands. (As a concession, the chosen players were now paid $200 and traveling expenses—in no small part because of Josh, who had made himself vocal on the issue.)

That week, the *Defender*, playing up the game, billboarded

the starting lineup with a photo of Gibson. But on the after- . noon of the game, Josh was not behind the plate nor even in Chicago—this time not by his own misdeed but by order of the man who had shielded him for years, Cum Posey. Whereas Posey had defended Josh in the Candy Jim Taylor affair, he was so turned off by Josh's failure to make an effort to behave for Vic Harris that he took the drastic step of sending Josh home only hours before the contest.

W. Rollo Wilson, covering the story in that week's *Tribune,* came down harder on Gibson than Sam Lacy had, and depicted Posey and Harris as men at wit's end in dealing with Josh:

> Josh Gibson has played his last ball game for the Homestead Grays, according to Cum Posey. Since Cum is one of the owners of the club his declaration should carry some weight. . . .
>
> Following a steady infraction of training rules by the big catcher he was suspended by Manager Vic Harris and ordered to turn in his uniform; even easy-going Vic could no longer tolerate the antics of the temperamental home-run hitter. This action made Josh ineligible for the East-West Game and Roy Campanella had to work the entire battle for the seaboard nine. In the Grand Hotel that Sunday Posey offered to sell or trade Gibson to any club-owner but nobody was willing to take him up. His offer to trade Gibson for Campanella was laughed at by Tom Wilson, league president and owner of the Baltimore Elite Giants.

This take—plus Rollo Wilson's follow-up revelations detailing Josh's "several physical breakdowns" and "varying periods of time in [a] health sanitarium," as well as the need for him to "mend his ways"—was clearly overcharged, and likely designed by Posey to scare Josh straight. And while Josh no doubt laughed it off, as he had done with similar newspaper reproofs in the past, these harsh public condemnations—which never would have been published when Gibson was whole—represent a point of departure in Gibson's fall from grace and from serious consideration as a potential major-leaguer.

Fittingly, Josh was joined in Pandemonium by Satchel Paige, who had been excluded from the 1944 East-West Game after making outrageous demands for a cut of the gate and, upon being rejected, attempting to get other players to boycott the game with him. Like Josh's misconduct, this was a last gamble that failed; Paige, resolving to give little of himself to black ball, petulantly held himself out of all future East-West Games.

Where the absence of the two great icons would have been deemed unacceptable in the past, now it hardly caused a squawk; the East-West Game, which had grown much bigger than individual players, pulled in over forty-six thousand people in 1944, and over thirty-one thousand in 1945. Widely known around baseball as a showcase of glittering talent, it was a regular stop for big league scouts interested in checking out black ball's best. In fact, the East-West Game had outdrawn the major league All-Star Game in 1938, 1942, and 1943 and would do so again in 1946 and 1947. Meanwhile, Josh Gibson and Satchel Paige, having lost much of their power base, began to take on the look of dinosaurs. In the black game, their excesses were now seen as relics of an era best forgotten, now that younger, more relevant players were surfacing.

One manifestation of this transition occurred on June 28 when the Grays and Monarchs met for a doubleheader at Griffith Stadium. Around twenty thousand fans attended, drawn mainly by the residual lure of yet another Paige-Gibson face-off in game one. But when the day was done, it was only of minor interest that the Grays blasted Satch from the game, strafing him for ten runs in six innings in the 12–3 win, or that Josh tripled in five at bats, or that the Grays smacked the Monarchs' Lefty LeMarque around in game two and won, 10–6.

Instead, the two black ball veterans were overshadowed by one of those new names on the black ball horizon—the Monarchs' twenty-six-year-old rookie shortstop Jack Roosevelt Robinson, the former UCLA football All-American, who went 7-for-7 in the twin bill, establishing a putative Negro league record.

Ever since the death of Kenesaw Mountain Landis in December 1944, big league people were taking a closer look at men like Jackie Robinson. Minus the forbidding presence of the prunish Landis, behind whom recalcitrant white owners had hid for decades to escape the heat of the race issue, and given the favorable stance taken by the new commissioner, former Kentucky governor A. E. "Happy" Chandler, big league scouts fanned out across the breadth of black ball. As of yet, people in the black game didn't know that the majors would refuse to recognize either the Negro leagues or black players too closely associated with those leagues; looting black teams of their best players would be the plan of attack, one that would lead to the systematic destruction of black ball.

But by 1945, the feeling was palpable that when—there was no "if" about it anymore—African Americans finally got to breathe big league air, the old standbys—Josh; Satch; Cool Papa; the two Bucks, Leonard and O'Neil; and others— would not be among them.

Jackie Robinson, on the other hand, carried the scent of a man about to change the world. Certainly the hints were there. The September 15 *Courier* ran a piece about Robinson in which, in a throwaway line, the paper reported, "Recently, he was called to Brooklyn by Branch Rickey, [chief executive, general manager, and quarter-owner] of the Brooklyn Dodgers, where he held a 'closed door' conference with the Dodgers' boss."

What few outside that Dodger office knew, because those who did were sworn to secrecy until the time was deemed right, was that Branch Rickey had signed Robinson that day to a Dodger contract for the following season. Robinson was given a salary of $600 per month, $200 more than he was making in Kansas City, and a $3,500 signing bonus. According to a clause in the contract, the Dodgers would owe no "written or moral obligation" to any other club. Rickey thus indemnified himself from ever having to compensate the Monarchs, and this was the precedent that would allow major league baseball to decimate the Negro leagues. The blueprint was that Robinson would play with the Dodgers' International League farm team in Montreal in 1946.

Like Gibson, Paige, and a host of others, Jackie Robinson had gone through the charade of a bogus big league tryout, most recently with the Boston Red Sox before the 1945 season. But Robinson differed from most Negro-leaguers in many significant respects. For one, he had already excelled in a white man's world, having lettered in four sports at UCLA, and served as an officer in the U.S. Army. Whip smart and cocksure, the stocky but fleet Robinson harbored a good deal of moral resentment about racism and the good sense to know he had to contain it in public. (Robinson had been court-martialed while in the army for refusing to ride in the back of a bus on his base, but he pleaded his case with eloquence and the charges were dropped.)

As an added bonus, he detested the Negro leagues as a servile life-form. A nonsmoker and nondrinker, Robinson made few friends in the rough-and-tumble black game and had no doubt that he was above men he considered both uncouth and too willing to accept baseball peonage.

But because the Robinson signing was still secret, the sound and fury that would surround this act did not begin until after the 1945 season, leaving Josh contented that he was still getting his share of newsprint, though the stories about his 400-whatever-foot homers seemed to be rather less zealous. When league stats showed Josh atop the pack with a .393 average for the 1945 season, the *Afro* accommodated him by running a huge photo of him under the words "The Champ." But the hometown *Courier* merely noted it with the small column heading "Josh Gibson Wins NNL Batting Title," a tepidness that may have reflected the fact that Gibson, according to the same figures, had hit only four homers in league competition.

The entire Grays picture, in fact, had gotten a little musty by now. Wendell Smith, in his September 22 column, cast a pall over the team by reprising an old charge. "Right now," he wrote, "the Grays are 'gloom-stricken.' They don't seem to have the old fire and dash they once had," though Smith could not bring himself to indict the big man, adding, "Josh Gibson, Buck Leonard, Dave Hoskins and Jerry Benjamin seem to have plenty of spirit, but the rest of the club seems to be in a rut."

The Grays did eventually win their eighth NNL flag in nine years but ran into a buzz saw when they played the underdog Cleveland Buckeyes in the Negro League World Series. In the first two games, played in Cleveland's cavernous Municipal Stadium, the Buckeyes, led by center fielder and future big-leaguer Sam Jethroe and the longtime black ball catcher-manager Quincy Trouppe, won two tense pitching duels, 2–1 and 3–2.

For the Grays, all life seemed to drain away in the ninth inning of game one. With Homestead down, 2–0, and one out, Dave Hoskins singled, Buck Leonard walked, and Josh singled to left to make it 2–1. But then Buckeye hurler Willie Jefferson got Sam Bankhead to ground into a double play to end it.

Wendell Smith, as if he had struck a mother lode of fresh copy, called the victors the "Battling Bucks" and "baseball's Cinderella team" in his game stories and wrote that "the scent of a world championship [was] tickling in their nostrils. . . . As they head for the Smoky City with two victories under their belts, the inspired, confident Buckeyes are sizzling hot and as they put it, 'It's going to take more than a bunch of squirts like the Homestead Grays to put 'em out!'"

The Buckeyes made the vow Smith put in their mouths stand up, blanking the lifeless Grays in the next two games by scores of 4–0 and 5–0 to terminate the series and the Grays' dynasty; going down seemingly without protest, the legendary team from Homestead would now face its extinction in much the same manner.

For black America, arguably the most consequential date of the century was October 23, 1945. On that day, acting as proxy for Branch Rickey, the Montreal Royals president Hector Racine announced the signing of Jackie Robinson by the Brooklyn Dodgers before introducing a confident, smiling Robinson to reporters.

This epochal moment crested a yearlong series of delicate maneuvers by Rickey that were designed to make big league integration as natural and painless as possible—most of all for Robinson and Rickey, both of whom knew that days of fire lay ahead.

Both before and after these two chief protagonists had come to terms back on August 28, Rickey's motives and plans regarding integration were unknown, even in the incestuous baseball world. What was known was that Rickey, the inscrutable "Mahatma," who with his corpulent ego and prissy sense of moral virtue was at once the most astute and most unpredictable of baseball men, had committed the Dodgers name and a portion of the team's capital to a third Negro league, the United States League, which began play with eight teams, including the Rickey-backed Brooklyn Brown Dodgers, in May 1945.

Even this minor move made Rickey the target of criticism in both black and white quarters. Many blacks believed Rickey was yet another white man bidding to exploit black ball. Big league caretakers, on the other hand—New York Yankee president Larry MacPhail in particular—suggested that Rickey's adventurism would only stir up the integration issue or, worse, that he was pandering to black fans or, worse still, that he was trying to get a jump on the rest of the league by lining up the best black players.

During the months when it seemed Rickey was foursquare behind the United States League, the most contented man alive must have been Gus Greenlee.

The exiled Big Red, who had been stripped of his crown jewels, the Pittsburgh Crawfords and the Negro National League, in 1938, had in the early forties become restless and hungry for baseball power again. At league meetings before each season during the war years, Gus petitioned for reentry into the league, offering up numerous propositions to revive the Crawfords, only to be politely declined by Cum Posey, who wanted nothing to do with the man he had vanquished.

When these entreaties failed, Gus worked as a provocateur behind the scenes at the East-West Game, trying to foment player dissension about the game and expense money. By doing this, he hoped to wreck the two established Negro leagues and siphon off players for the United States League, of which Gus was vice president and the new Crawfords a member. While few players took the bait, some did jump to the new circuit, and for a few heady months Gus was able to bask in the credibility of a league in which he was partnered with Branch Rickey.

But for Gus, this hallucination lasted only until the Jackie Robinson announcement, which exposed the fact that Rickey's involvement in the United States League was merely a diversion, and hastened the Mahatma's withdrawal from the league altogether. Greenlee held on to the remnants of his shriveling second kingdom into the 1946 season, by which time lack of interest and the decline in quality play made the league little more than a rumor in the months before its official death after the season. Then, Gus Greenlee was back in the black ball wilderness, soon to be sharing space there with the rest of black ball.

Before that happened, there would be a final season of grace and glory for the Negro leagues—a year which with pungent irony would be Josh Gibson's last.

·   ·   ·

For both Gibson and black ball, the 1946 season would play out as a last gasp of rarefied air. Fed by the postwar economic boom that had created an instant black middle class, black fans pushed Negro league profits over the $2 million mark for the first time. And yet a massive portent of what was to come took place on the eve of the season, when Cum Posey died at age fifty-five in his home on East Thirteenth Street.

For Posey, who had been suffering from lung cancer for months, these last couple of years had been filled with a deep melancholy about black ball's impending doom. In yet another demonstration that black ball allegiances were ephemeral and largely a sham, the latest power shift in the black game, in 1945, had cut Posey out as NNL czar. He was replaced by Eddie Gottlieb—the very man who had helped him unseat Gus Greenlee but who later sensed that Cum was finally out to eliminate the longtime influence of black ball's white promoters.

With that prospect now dashed, the black game lost its last chance to demonstrate that it was not, as Branch Rickey construed it to be, a booking agent's paradise, a mere exhibition show rather than a legitimate business concern with proprietary rights. Because Rickey had taken this stance, among the black owners Jackie Robinson's ascension represented not only a pinnacle for their game but a crisis as well, since their tight little world of gentlemen's agreements was about to change forever. And still some of them held to the chimera that the Negro leagues would somehow endure in symbiosis with the majors.

Others, like Cum Posey, knew the truth, that the looting was about to begin. Not even Posey, had he lived on, could have found a way to save black ball from the abyss. But without him, there was simply no hope of dealing with the crisis and nothing close to a united front.

As for Posey's legacy, the haughty Washington Homestead Grays, their decline was precipitous. Even so, Josh Gibson's fans persisted, clinging to his decreasing number of headlines in the black press, even as the impending age of integration made Gibson a relic.

The *Afro*, for example, wrote up an early May Grays–Elite Giants doubleheader at Baltimore's Bugle Field, which the teams split, by rhapsodizing upon Josh's first-inning grand slam in the opener. The blow, the paper said, was "a smash that cleared the area roped off for the overflow crowd." Later that month, the *Tribune* told of a 440-foot shot against the Black Yankees in Griffith Stadium, "Gibson's second long homer in four days . . . having hit a 457-foot homer in Forbes Field Wednesday night [against the Black Yankees]."

In early June, the *Tribune*'s Alvin Moses, noting two intentional walks given Gibson by the New York Cubans, brought to mind an era when such a tactic was normal procedure:

> Virtually everyone came to see mighty Josh Gibson knock the ball out of the park and he might have at that except for one concrete reason . . . the opposing moundsmen (Lefty Tiant and Scantleberry) wouldn't pitch to him. Tiant walked the "great man" twice while the crowd booed him to Ireland and back. Scantleberry did throw one pitch in there (with his heart-in-his-mouth after it) that Josh hammered back at a waiting fielder.

There was as well a kindhearted paean offered by Cleveland's Sam Jethroe, who would soon receive a big league call. In late September, Jethroe said in an interview that he played so deep for Gibson that "if Josh hits one over my head, we're gonna play the rest of the game with a softball."

Indeed, outfielders still had much reason to play Gibson with their backs to the wall. There is a yellowing scorecard in the archives at the Hall of Fame of a game between the Grays and Buckeyes played in Sportsman's Park on July 9, 1946. On this card, left by the official scorer, is scratched the notation "Josh Gibson hit one of the longest homeruns (over 600 feet) at old Sportsman's Park."

Going by Negro league statistics, in fact, Josh Gibson left the game like an aging heavyweight calling up one last hay-maker, and landing with it. He was credited with a league-high eighteen homers in 1946, even though the talk among Negro league pitchers was that the post-Mexico Gibson was not nearly as scary a hitter as he was in his prime. As Hilton Smith, the Monarchs' great curveball pitcher, maintained years later, "Up until '42, I had more trouble with Josh than I did any other ballplayer. Gibson had those great big old muscle arms, weighed about two hundred five. He would swing flat-footed, wouldn't stride. The first time I faced him, he hit a home run off me. But in '42 I didn't have any trouble with him at all. No, from then on I really began to get him out."

In the end, this proud, troubled, and desperately ill man strapped on the catching gear, hitched his belt over his bloated belly, and took his place behind the plate in nearly every league game on the schedule. There would be one final East-West Game, an 0-for-3 performance before 45,474 wit-nesses, who may have thought they knew something about Josh Gibson but were about to discover that they in fact knew tragically little. When that last season was over, he walked away with a .361 average. Like a champ, and one helluva beautiful dinosaur.

As the countdown began for Jackie Robinson's major league debut in Brooklyn, Negro league evergreens like Josh Gibson were quickly becoming an afterthought. In the black papers, there were more urgent matters at hand, such as the subse-quent, if quieter, signings of Roy Campanella, Homestead's John Wright, and Newark pitcher Don Newcombe by Branch Rickey to the Dodger chain in 1946.

From the moment that Robinson ambled up the dugout

steps and went out to play first base when the Dodgers played the Boston Braves on April 15, 1947, at Ebbets Field, the top story—the *only* story—in the black press was set: actual big league steps taken by Robinson. He was soon followed, although much less successfully, by erstwhile Monarchs Willard Brown and Hank Thompson with the St. Louis Browns; in 1948, Campanella would be catching in Brooklyn and Larry Doby would be playing in the Cleveland Indians' outfield. And old Satchel Paige himself would be reborn as a cause célèbre, taking those long-awaited big league steps in Cleveland at age forty-two.

The Negro leagues, so recently in vogue but suddenly so gauche, were practically abandoned by the black press, ignored by the same people who had doted on them for decades. Within two seasons, the Negro National League would waste away, leaving the Negro American League to carry on as a pale shadow of its former self until the mid-fifties.

Foreseeing the impending disaster, a few isolated voices in the black ball elite, most noisily Effa Manley, objected to the shameless desertion by the black cognoscenti, who knew full well that black fans would follow. And in the unkindest cut, these career nativists, who had helped build and preserve a tradition that was nothing less than the centerpiece of African American culture, were branded in the papers as traitors to the cause.

This was the new reality of black baseball. But for Josh, his final days in the Negro leagues remained comfortably familiar. In fact, his behavior had become so predictably odd that people became anesthetized to it and seemed to stop worrying about him since his batting average remained uneroded. Despite hearing stories that he had needed to be restrained by straitjackets during stays at St. Francis Hospital, many continued to believe his incoherent speech and unexplained absences were the result of booze, drugs, and nervous breakdowns, all of which they believed he could handle.

Sammy Bankhead, for one, became accustomed to getting phone calls in the dead of night and being told that Josh was lying in a gutter or on a bar floor and to come and take him home. One night, it was that Josh was six flights up on the ledge of some hotel on the Hill, threatening to jump. Sam, who knew how to play on Josh's anxieties in order to defuse them, went down there, leaned out the window, and told him, "Go ahead and jump, then. See if I care." Josh, slapped back to his senses, crawled back inside.

Of all the men of the Negro leagues, Buck O'Neil was one of the few who saw clearly what he knew was the slow death of the big man. O'Neil once told John B. Holway that the Josh of these days was "just a shell of a man. . . . He couldn't remember things. . . . The last time I saw him he was calling me Buck, but he was thinking [I was] Buck Leonard. We said, 'Josh is going crazy.' Actually, he probably was . . . from a tumor on the brain."

He may have even gotten too weird for Grace Fournier, though for a time she seemed only to indulge and encourage his bizarre doings. The Grays were agog one day when Josh and Grace came to the ballpark dressed in matching trench coats and navy blue pinstriped suits. Josh became so obsessed with Grace that when they were in a restaurant and Grace had to go to the rest room, he would escort her and wait outside the door, as though standing guard, until she came out.

He even demanded that unless Cum Posey allowed Grace to travel on the train with the team to Brimingham during the 1945 Negro World Series, he wouldn't play in it. Posey, gritting his teeth, went against all team rules and gave in to the demand.

But by early 1946, when her husband had returned home, Grace went back to her man, for fear, she said, that he would kill both of them if she didn't. This was something she had always told Josh would happen, and Josh was prepared for it. He didn't try to convince Grace to stay, which indicated that he may have had more important things on his mind than sexual conquest. As Hattie Jones had anticipated, Josh eventually returned to her door, and they lived together on and off while he rented out his other house, on Morgan Street.

During this time, Josh Gibson was, quite plainly, preparing to die and trying to put his life in order before the big sleep came. Ravaged and tired as he was, he decided not to play in Puerto Rico. He also passed on the last great spectacle of black-versus-white competition, the monthlong barnstorming series in October 1946 between the Satchel Paige All-Stars and the Bob Feller All-Stars, which as an immediate if anomalous preface to baseball biracialism earned a truckload of cash for both the white and black players on the tour.

Instead, he stayed at home, attempting to make his peace with the family he had mostly shunned for baseball and the high life. His first priority was sixteen-year-old Josh Jr., who had grown big and strong, just like his old man, and was playing amateur ball around town just as Josh had. Frequently, Josh came to Margaret Mason's new home at 2712 Bedford Avenue with a touching request.

"He said to my mother, 'Let me stay with the children,'" recalled Rebecca Mason. "So my mother said, 'I don't have that much room, Josh,' and he said, 'Well, I'll sleep with little Josh.' And Josh was kinda big then, he wasn't a baby no more. But she let him stay there, and he did until he stopped comin' 'round when he got so nervous from the headaches or whatever it was."

For Josh Jr., whose aging memories of his father are still strong and sentient, those winter nights when he shared his bed with him was his first introduction to the man separate from the uniform and press clippings.

"I was just beginning to know my father then," he said, "and know his weaknesses and all. And lying next to him, that's also when I found out how much beer stank."

By early January 1947, though, it was Josh Sr. who needed the comfort of a long-absent parent. Once more, he was suffering from nervous exhaustion. His immune system disarmed by drink and severe hypertension, he had fallen prey to kidney and liver dysfunction and bronchitis. This once-hard rock of a man had shriveled to around 180 pounds, eaten away by various illnesses and poor nutrition. When it got so bad that he was unable to care for himself, he moved back into his mother's house on Strauss Street, the place where he had grown to manhood but that he had consciously avoided as an adult.

That too was probably a source of guilt; even after Mark Gibson had died in 1943, Josh had never sought rapprochement with Nancy Gibson, possibly to evade the remorseless truth that, just as he had feared from the start, he had indeed become a copy of the woman whose habits had once repulsed him.

For Nancy, and for Jerry and Annie Gibson, the sadness that hung over these days was unbearable, since they all knew Josh, who was sleeping in his old room, might well die there. Accordingly, all three of them kept a vigil in the house.

And yet, on some days, a chipper Josh would get out of that old cedar bed feeling like a new man. Then he would saunter over to the Crawford Grille or another neighborhood tavern on the north side and drink himself out of his mind, something he could do even though he had by now blown nearly all of his money on his shameless lifestyle. As his one-time teammate Josh Johnson noted, "As famous and as popular as he was, there was always someone waiting to buy him a drink." Indeed, if Josh ever had any reason to ruminate on why he was in the condition he was in, he may have concluded that this was part of the problem all along.

But by now Josh knew any one of these rounds might be his last call. On one such afternoon when he was up and about, Ted Page, his old Crawford teammate, stepped into a north side bar and came upon a bizarre scene that was like something out of a bad movie. Seeing a gaunt, sickly man making a ruckus, Ted had to look twice before he realized it was Josh.

"He was drinking heavy," Page recalled, "and he had a hold of some stranger's collar and he was shaking him. When he saw me, he said, 'Hey, Teddy, tell this guy who hit the longest ball anyplace!' Because, by then, what with Jackie Robinson and everything, there were people who didn't know him like everybody used to know him."

Other witnesses privy to his last days told of Josh carrying on imaginary conversations with Babe Ruth and Joe DiMaggio, men of rank and honor with whom he believed he shared an eternal bond. In those twisted moments, there was order for him, just as there always had been on the field. Whenever he needed solace, he could turn to baseball to insulate himself. But now not even baseball could do that.

On Sunday, January 19, again feeling well, he toddled to the Crawford Grille. As it happened, Harold Tinker this time crossed paths with him, and the old Crawfords manager, who had given Josh his first break, may have been the last of his black ball buddies to see him alive.

"He came out of the beer garden, which I thought was unusual for him, or at least I thought so because I had no idea he had turned to alcohol the way he did," Tinker said. "And he saw me and took me in and he was tellin' these guys, 'This here is the greatest center fielder that's ever lived.' That made me feel good, but it's a tough thing to remember, 'cause that's the last time I saw Josh alive."

Later that day, in the early evening, Josh, his headaches becoming more and more severe, decided to go to a movie at the Garden Theater, hoping the darkness would ease the pain. When the lights came up, he was found slumped in his seat. Unable to awaken him, patrons looked in his wallet for identification, found a card with Dr. Earl Simms's name on it, and called him to the theater. Dr. Simms, who again may not have known the extent of Josh's illnesses, had him taken to his mother's home. He injected him with a sedative and left him in a deep sleep, apparently believing Josh would come out of it.

Nancy, Jerry, and Annie, fearing the worst, did not leave

his room as he slept. Annie, years later, told author Robert Peterson that Josh did awaken late that night, and when he did he said he was about to die, and that Nancy Gibson gently told him to hush up and not talk foolish. Josh, she said, then had Jerry bring all his baseball trophies into the room and assemble them at his bedside.

At 1:30 A.M., according to Annie's narrative, Josh was again awake and sitting up, laughing and having a good time. Then, she went on, he "raised up in the bed and went to talk, but you couldn't understand what he was saying. Then he lay back down and died right off."

However it happened—it is entirely possible Josh never regained consciousness after blacking out at the Garden Theater—at one-thirty in the morning on January 20, 1947, Josh Gibson's noble heart cracked. For black ball's onetime boy king, as for black ball itself, daylight would not come again.

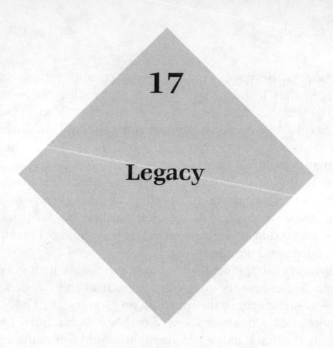

17

Legacy

*Every man is as Heaven made him, and sometimes a great
deal worse.*

—MIGUEL DE CERVANTES, *DON QUIXOTE
DE LA MANCHA*

The coroner fixed the cause of death as a brain hemorrhage, with hypertension as a contributing factor. But even
before Josh was buried, some in the black press had already
begun to put a revisionist spin on the man's life and his
legacy.

Although the January 25 *Courier* took a somewhat flip-
pant approach by captioning a large photo of Gibson HE'S
BEEN CALLED "OUT," the paper's crusty sports editor, Wendell
Smith, authored a dramatic account of Gibson's life and career that set the tone for how he would be remembered thereafter. Smith's obituary-eulogy, which ran under a subheadline
reading in part, "He Was a Big Leaguer But Color Kept Him

Out," began with one of the most famous lines to ever appear in the black press:

They're laying Josh Gibson in the cold cold ground this week!

But his brilliant, unequalled deeds as a baseball player will live on forever!

For he was a mighty man—Josh Gibson was. He was the answer to a manager's prayer, the slugger supreme, the home run hitter extra-ordinary, the dinosaur of the diamond!

He was the "King of Sock" and he ruled with a majestic splendor.

Pitchers quivered in his quake, infielders trembled at his power, and outfielders scurried to the hinterlands at his very sight.

He was the personification of destruction and devastation, and though he lies motionless in death, the baseball skies still vibrate and resound from his thunderous wallops, and the smashing crescendo echoes across baseball parks in this country and into the foreign lands of Canada, Mexico, Cuba, Porto Rico [sic] and Venezuela. . . .

Had his color been of another hue, Josh Gibson would have been a major leaguer, swinging at the slants of such greats as Dizzy Dean, Bob Feller, Carl Hubbell and the other "million dollar gems" of the big leagues. But he had the unfortunate experience of being born a Negro and he paid a penalty for that carelessness throughout his baseball life. . . .

Perhaps if Josh Gibson hadn't been a victim of the vicious color line in the majors; if he had been given the chance to make the big league he so justly deserved; if he could have swung his big bat against the type of competition for which he was born, he might be living today.

For he was a big leaguer, and he knew it. He was a thoroughbred and he should have been with them. But they slammed the door in his face, his kindly black face, and left him standing on the outer fringes of the glistening world to which he belonged.

That treatment, more than anything else, sent the "king" to his grave. It made him morose and synical [*sic*], down-hearted and resentful. It sent him to the "land of drink" and into the pitfall of human errors. Finally, his health went and he slipped away into eternal darkness. . . .

I know the real reason Josh Gibson died. I don't need a doctor's report for confirmation, either.

He was "murdered" by Big League Baseball!

From a vantage point half a century removed in time, Smith's screed reeks of hypocrisy—not just because of the way it shamelessly manipulated Gibson's flaws, but because Smith himself did much to turn black ball into a corpse by murdering it for black readers.

The year before, when Jackie Robinson was proving his mettle in Montreal, Smith had been put on the Dodgers payroll to fill the *Courier* with puffy and picaresque copy about Jackie's minor league travels. Smith continued in this public relations role when Robinson came to Brooklyn only three months after Gibson's death, turning his attention back to Negro league matters only to help sink the game further into the cold, cold ground.

When the commissioners of the two Negro leagues meekly petitioned Happy Chandler for entry into the white ball structure as official minor leagues, only to be dismissed until they could demonstrate that they could "clean up" the black game, Smith blistered the black ball czars for "whimpering before Chandler," even though Smith concluded that "all they cared about was the perpetuation of the slave trade they had developed."

Added Smith, who never admitted to these sentiments before the coming of Robinson: "[They] will shout to the high heavens that racial progress comes first and baseball next.

But actually the preservation of their shaky, littered, infested, segregated baseball domicile comes first, last, and always."

By Smith's edict, the *Courier*'s coverage of black ball was reduced to filler items throughout 1947 and 1948, and by the time of the 1948 Negro World Series, when the Grays recaptured a facsimile of their old mystique and took out Birmingham in five games, the poorly attended series drew only a couple of paragraphs; not by coincidence, it would be the last Negro World Series ever played.

Still, during that mournful January week in 1947, Smith's interpretation of Gibson's career was embraced as fact by almost everyone. To this day, his premise is echoed by many a Negro league survivor.

"I knew he took it awful hard when they didn't take him into the white majors," said Gene Benson. "I think he really started goin' down more after they started takin' blacks in the minors."

Similarly, Ted Page felt that the weird bar scene he had witnessed days before Josh's death, when Gibson was trying to tell the world, or at least the bar, who had hit the longest home runs in history, could be traced to Josh's exclusion from the majors.

"I think the Jackie Robinson thing broke his heart," Page once said. "He didn't think he would get the recognition he deserved."

This is not a portrait of Josh that others can recognize, though. Wilmer Fields, who had ridden the hump with Gibson along black ball's backroads for endless hours, had a different slant.

"Sure, Josh wanted to go, all of 'em wanted to, Buck and all of 'em—'cept me. I turned down the Yankees, 'cause the minimum salary was fourteen hundred dollars. Hell, I made that much in two months in the Latin countries. This was my goal, to play in black baseball. That's what I done for twenty-five years. And to an extent, I think Josh had the same attitude about it. He enjoyed hisself. He just wanted to be out there and play baseball, and when he did he gave it a hundred and ten percent.

"Josh coulda played in the majors; he coulda contributed. But that's not what killed him. He had nothin' to feel short-changed about."

Josh Gibson Jr. agrees. "When I hear all that stuff about how my father died of a broken heart, that [pisses me off]. 'Cause that wasn't my father. He was the last guy to brood about something he couldn't do nothin' about."

Surely, the timing of his death was ironic and made for easy inductive reasoning. What's more, Wendell Smith's hypothesis is not entirely off base. Being betrayed by the white structure of the game he indeed seemed to be born to play really might have sapped some of the life from Gibson.

But if Josh Gibson had gone where Jackie Robinson went, would he have gone there straight? If he had thought it was possible, would he have lived his life differently? Would a big league Gibson have possessed big league common sense? No one can safely answer these questions, but it is hard to suppose that, somewhere along the way, Gibson hadn't become aware that he was killing his chances for a big league career. If so, his reply was, so be it.

In a tangible sense, then, Josh Gibson was murdered by baseball, since he made baseball his whole life and baseball spited him. But in the end, like Achilles, he had no defense against his own mortal flaw: himself.

Upon the news of Josh's passing, Nancy Gibson reacted with a strange diffidence, or so Rebecca Mason thought.

"She said her home wasn't fixed up nice, so she asked if we would keep the body over at our house. And while my mother said it wasn't right, that his mother should've provided the space, she said, well, for the children's sake, she would let the body stay at our house."

For the first three days after his death, Josh lay in state at the Crunkleton Funeral Home on the north side, then for three more days in Margaret Mason's home in an open casket. "Right in the middle of the living room, in a suit and tie and lookin' like a man at peace with himself" was how Josh Gibson Jr. remembered his father during those days, as he watched a long line of people filing through the house paying their respects.

But the biggest crowds gathered outside the Macedonia Baptist Church when the funeral service was held in the same sanctuary where Josh and Helen Mason had been married and where Helen's funeral had taken place. On that day, Josh Jr. said, "There were folks lined up half a mile down Bedford Avenue. They say it was one of the largest funerals ever in Pittsburgh."

Among those invited inside the church were Gus Greenlee, John L. Clark, Cool Papa Bell, Buck Leonard, Chet Brewer, and other Negro-leaguers who could make it in from across the country; Satchel Paige was not there, and Sammy Bankhead was unable to return from Latin America, where he was playing winter ball as usual. Harold Tinker, who wasn't invited, is still miffed about it to this day.

All the proceedings were managed by Hattie Jones, who took charge of the details as if she were every bit Mrs. Josh Gibson. According to plan, the body was taken by limousine to Allegheny Cemetery on the outskirts of town and buried in section 50, plot 33. Through the years, some Gibson histories reported that Gibson had died too poor for his family to afford a gravestone. Josh Jr. says that's not quite the whole story.

"Nah, he provided for us. He didn't leave a will or nothin' but he had some type of insurance. He wasn't broke when he died. He wasn't a man that saved his money but at least he bought two houses out of his baseball money, and he was makin' like seventeen hundred dollars a season at the end. He was doin' all right.

"After he died, there was fifteen hundred dollars given to

me and my sister, and the house on Morgan Street. Hattie got the house on Webster Avenue, which is still standing even though Hattie is dead. We got title to the other one. For years I would go and collect rent on it; it was forty dollars a month, and that helped support us—hell, a loaf of bread wasn't but a nickel back then. We continued renting out the house until the city ended up comin' in with the bulldozer and put up one of them goddamn glass buildings.

"It's true we didn't have money to give my father a headstone. But it wasn't just that nobody came forward with any money. Over there where he's buried, you can't make a big deal. You can't even put no flowers around there; they don't allow that for black people. It's a racial thing. Even in death, he got caught in a black-and-white thing."

As it happened, it fell to Josh Jr. to try and keep his father's name alive, by following him onto the baseball diamond. In 1948, at age eighteen, he stood six-foot-one and 185 pounds and had hit some tape-measure homers of his own playing for Schenley High, one of which wound up on Center Street outside the field, a 425-foot drive. With the built-in advantage of his name, Josh eventually went where his father had not—to the white minors.

That summer he was signed to play second base by the Cleveland Indians' Youngstown, Ohio, farm team in the Class A Middle Atlantic League, becoming the first black player in that circuit. That story made the *Pittsburgh Post-Gazette,* but in his first few at bats it became apparent that Josh Gibson Jr. was no Josh Gibson.

As introverted and shy as his father was gregarious, Josh Jr. didn't share Josh Sr.'s maniacally focused concentration, and struck out seven of his first eight times up. Then he was hit on the head by a pitch, sustained a concussion, and missed most of the rest of the year. After hitting .130 in eight games, with three singles in thirty-three at bats, he was released.

His white ball adventure over, Josh Jr. found a more comfortable home in the Negro leagues, or what was left of them in 1949. The Grays, who were now operating as an independent team after the collapse of the Negro National League, signed him. In Homestead, the kid played sparingly over the course of two seasons, though he did get to hit against Satchel Paige in a game out in the sticks. And he was there when the legendary team made famous by his father finally expired.

Over the 1949 and 1950 seasons the Grays lost $30,000, and See Posey, who had been running the team after Sonnyman Jackson's death in 1949, dissolved the club before he too died in 1951. By coincidence, Gus Greenlee also died that summer, taking the black Pittsburgh baseball tradition with him. At the time, bad luck had caught up with Big Red, in the form of the IRS, which came looking for thousands of dollars in back taxes. Then, days before he died, a fire razed the Crawford Grille; soon after, a parking lot marked where the epicenter of high-toned black society had once stood.

Josh Jr., meanwhile, had one last chance to carry on his father's legacy, thanks to the graces of Sammy Bankhead. When Margaret Mason died in 1951, Josh moved in with Sam and Helen, who had become his surrogate parents. Once there, Sammy, feeling some kind of filial responsibility to Josh Jr., made Josh his protégé but never once spoke candidly of his father's vices.

"He would start to, sometimes, but he'd cut it short, because there were things he didn't want me to know about. He gave me that respect. Sam would be talkin' about my father with other guys and he'd say, 'If little Josh wasn't here, I'd really tell y'all something.' Same with Buck Leonard. Buck never said anything about the bad stuff. Wilmer Fields never said anything. All them guys were protecting me. All I heard, until much later, was how good a guy my father was and how he never got mad at nobody."

It was in 1951 that Sammy, whose younger brother Dan pitched briefly for the Brooklyn Dodgers in 1947, and again in 1950 and 1951, made some history as well. He was hired as a player-manager of the Pittsburgh Pirates Class A Provincial League team in Farnham, Quebec—which made Sammy Bankhead the first black manager in organized baseball. At age forty-six, he would hit .274 in his last season in the game.

On Sammy's recommendation, Josh Jr. was imported to Farnham to play third base. But rather than being blessed by his legacy, he seemed cursed by it. He was hitting .230 with two homers, twenty RBIs, and twenty stolen bases when he broke his foot sliding, and never again stepped onto a ball field. Both he and Bankhead returned home, working elbow to elbow collecting garbage for Pittsburgh's sanitation department for the next twenty years.

During this stretch, Josh Gibson's name began to fade for most baseball fans, though a waning generation of blacks never forgot what he had meant. When baseball historians began to revisit the Negro leagues in the early seventies, the Gibson fables reemerged.

Satchel Paige, who had only recently finished living out the last of his many baseball lives, making his final appearance in organized ball in 1966 with Greensboro in the Carolina League at age sixty (in a final big league stint, for the Kansas City Athletics in 1965, he hurled three shutout innings at the Boston Red Sox), was now called upon to embellish Josh's herculean home run hitting, and he did it in typical Paige high style.

Forgotten now were his successes against Josh and the conquests of 1942. In Satch's memory "Josh was the greatest hitter I ever pitched to, and I pitched to everybody. I used to get [Ted] Williams out with my screwball on the outside. Musial, the same thing. DiMaggio, with my sidearm stuff. Mays, he's no Josh, I got him with a fastball on his letters. Mantle had to bunt on me. But Josh, I had to throw sidearm curves, break it on the outside corner, and pray."

Paige then spawned what would become one of the most repeated of Gibson fables. When they had been Crawford teammates, Satch swore, Josh hit a ball in Pittsburgh so far that it vanished from sight. The next day, when the Craws played in Philly, a ball happened to fall from the heavens and landed in an outfielder's glove. The call, according to Satch, was that "the umpire says to Josh, 'You're out, boy—yesterday, in Pittsburgh!'"

But once Wendell Smith's version of Gibson's life and death reemerged and was combined with black ball folklore and white guilt, Josh Gibson couldn't avoid becoming the official martyr of black ball.

About this time, baseball began its effort to rectify its ugly, racist past. In 1971, prodded by baseball writers clamoring that the game should provide an apt if postdated tribute to all the Negro league martyrs, commissioner Bowie Kuhn worked toward lifting baseball's final race barrier—permitting lifetime Negro league players into the Hall of Fame, something that had been resisted for years.

While Kuhn gently twisted arms among the Hall's rigidly conservative caretakers, he impaneled a ten-man committee to nominate appropriate names for entry. The committee was a perfect microcosm of black ball society. The players were proxied by, among others, Roy Campanella and Monte Irvin (both of whom had made the Hall for their big league contributions) and Judy Johnson. Eddie Gottlieb sat for the owner–booking agent faction, Wendell Smith and Sam Lacy for the tribunes of the game.

When the committee reported in February 1971, Satchel Paige was the unanimous choice to go in first, though not before Kuhn created a furor by hedging the honor just a bit. Paige's plaque, he said, would not hang in the main hall at Cooperstown, along with the white Hall of Famers, but in a separate wing. Trying to explain what he called the "special" nature of this honor, Kuhn admitted that "technically, you'd have to say he's not in the Hall of Fame. But I've often said the Hall of Fame isn't a building but a state of mind."

This explanation, however, did not go over well among both black and white critics, who saw nothing special about a side-room treatment that seemed only to extend segregation. Kuhn, to his credit, removed the hedge and decreed that all Negro league inductees were to receive full membership privileges. On August 1, 1971, Paige was enshrined under the same roof as men like Ruth, Cobb, Gehrig, and DiMaggio.

This set the stage for the much less frenetic induction of Josh Gibson the following year, when Gibson was elected by unanimous vote as well, along with Buck Leonard, who received near-unanimous support. They were inducted into the Hall in the class that included Yogi Berra, Sandy Koufax, Early Wynn, and Lefty Gomez.

On August 7, 1972, Josh's surviving family members— Josh Gibson Jr., his sister, Helen Gibson Dixon, and Annie Gibson Mahaffey—journeyed to Cooperstown for the ceremonies. (Jerry Gibson had died at age thirty-three in 1952, as had Mark Gibson from pneumonia; Nancy Gibson had died at age seventy-one in 1963.)

Josh Jr., who was chosen to speak on behalf of his father, rose to accept the plaque from Bowie Kuhn. A little nervous, but with his voice booming, he thanked baseball for "recognizing such a great talent" and said that "the whole Gibson family and the city of Pittsburgh is very proud of this award."

Then: "Before I leave here I would like to say something personal to my father. Wake up, Dad, you just made it in."

For Josh Jr., the trip to Cooperstown was only a temporary diversion from the realities of his life. Years before he had learned his blood did not carry his father's on-field greatness. But in the late sixties, living now on Haverhill Street in downtown Pittsburgh, he learned of a sadder inheritance when he was stricken with hypertension and life-threatening kidney failure, the condition that had killed his mother when he was born.

In the wake of Josh's induction into the Hall of Fame, news of his son's plight drew attention in the press. As a result, $20,000 was raised, which financed a kidney transplant operation in 1972; twenty years later, another transplant was performed.

Looking back, Josh Jr. said, "I got money from people all over, because so many people seen my father play and it didn't cost them nothin'. And I'm tellin' you, man, that's the only reason I'm alive now, is on account of him. The fact I'm here is his legacy."

In the seventies it also came time to finally mark Josh's inconspicuous burial plot in Allegheny Cemetery with a headstone. Through the years, the gravesite had become nearly impossible to find, since it was marked not by name but by number and had not been tended to in years, during which time grass and weeds had obscured it. When this too became news as an epilogue to the Gibson theme of exclusion and heartbreak, Bowie Kuhn's office once more came through with money for the family to clean up the grave and attach a silver marker on it.

Coupled with the Hall of Fame, this far less ostentatious reward for a life spent in the baseball shadows finally relieved the sins and guilts of the game. Now, there was a new Gibson epilogue: that this lost son of major league baseball had at last been given a name.

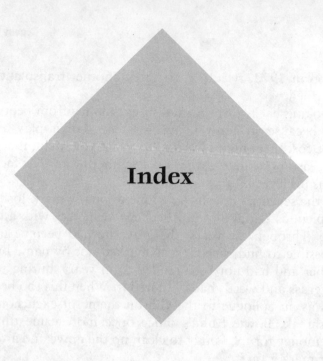

Index

About the Author

MARK RIBOWSKY is a freelance writer based in New York. His articles have appeared in numerous publications, including *Sport, Inside Sports, People,* and *TV Guide.* He is the author of four previous books, most recently *The Complete History of the Negro Leagues, 1884–1955* and *Don't Look Back: Satchel Paige in the Shadows of Baseball.*